D1606609

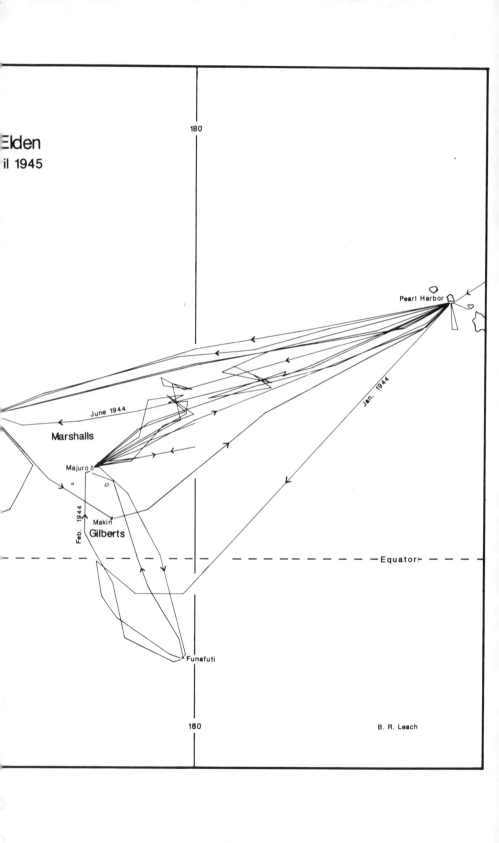

Elden
il 1945

180

Pearl Harbor

Jan. 1944

June 1944

Marshalls

Majuro o

Feb. 1944

Makin

Gilberts

Equator

Funafuti

180

B. R. Leach

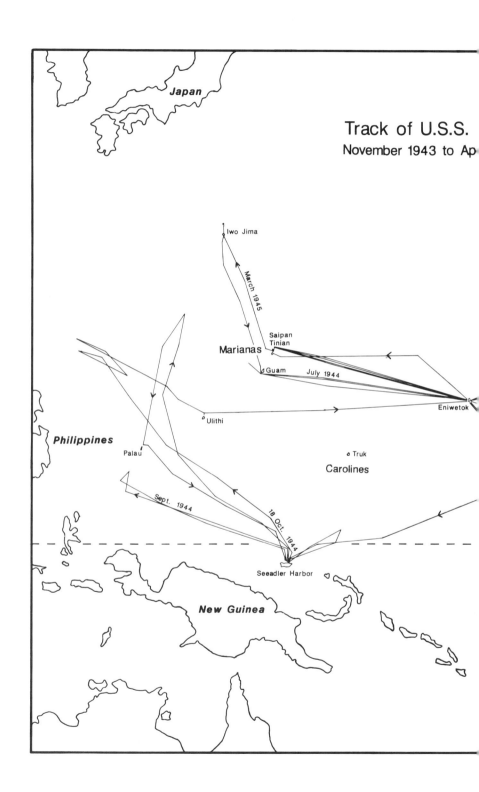

Japan

Track of U.S.S.
November 1943 to Ap

Iwo Jima

March 1945

Saipan
Tinian
Marianas

Guam   July 1944

Ulithi

Eniwetok

Philippines

Palau   Truk

Carolines

Sept. 1944

18 Oct. 1944

Seeadler Harbor

New Guinea

NOW HEAR THIS

The Amiable Warrior. Ensign Douglas E. Leach in December 1942.

NOW HEAR THIS

The Memoir of a Junior Naval Officer in the Great Pacific War

Douglas Edward Leach

WITHDRAWN

THE KENT STATE UNIVERSITY PRESS

Kent, Ohio and London, England

The paper in this book meets the guidelines for permanence and durability of the
Committee on Production Guidelines for Book Longevity of the Council on Library
Resources.

Library of Congress Cataloging-in-Publication Data
Leach, Douglas Edward, 1920-
  Now hear this.
  Includes index.
  1. Leach, Douglas Edward, 1920-
2. World War, 1939–1945—Naval operations, American.
3. World War, 1939–1945—Campaigns—Pacific Area.
4. World War, 1939–1945—Personal narratives,
American.   5. United States.   Navy—Biography.
6. Seamen—United States—Biography.   I. Title.
D773.L43   1987   940.54'5973'0924   87-3905
ISBN 0-87338-344-3 (alk. paper)

British Cataloguing in Publication data are available.

309729

REMEMBRANCE—GRATITUDE—FAITH

The old Y.P.F. at Calvary, including "Uncle George" Jones.
All shipmates, especially Russ Morrow.
And Tom Buffum.

CONTENTS

ILLUSTRATIONS

PREFACE

I have in my possession a small framed photograph of a ship at anchor, identified as "U.S.S. ELDEN." The view is side-on—bow to the right, stern to the left. Anyone familiar with the design of modern warships would recognize that trim, flush-deck, single-stack sliver of gray steel as an antisubmarine vessel, in fact, a destroyer escort. Clearly visible on the ship's forecastle, lounging almost casually, is a lone American sailor in blue denim work uniform, the sole representative of the several hundred young men who at one time or another served in the *Elden* during the climactic years of the Second World War. I have no idea who the lone seaman may have been, or whether he is still alive today. What I do know is that I myself spent some eighty-nine weeks on board that ship, passing through a seemingly interminable round of routine watches, hoping impatiently for victory and a return home. So, for me she stands as a symbol of a most important segment of my life, markedly different from all that had gone before and all that was to come later.

I am writing these words in 1985 while approaching the end of my career as a professor of history at Vanderbilt University. Sitting now in my office, gazing thoughtfully across the lush green campus, I have no difficulty harking back to the ominous autumn of 1941, my senior year at Brown University, when I was wondering whether my draft board would permit me to complete my studies and take my degree, or require me to leave college and report for duty in the

U.S.S. *Elden* (DE 264).

army. Then, on the unforgettable 7th of December came the surprise Japanese attack on Pearl Harbor which, at one deadly stroke, crippled American sea power in the Pacific. President Roosevelt's angry call for a declaration of war against Japan was speedily answered by an equally aroused Congress. Three days later Germany and Italy, the other major aggressor powers, declared war against the United States. Thereafter, we were fully engaged with Great Britain and the other Allied nations in a life-or-death struggle against the Berlin-Rome-Tokyo Axis.

My students today have some difficulty envisioning the virtually unprecedented degree of national unity displayed by the United States at that time. Once our government had proclaimed that a state of war existed, most able-bodied young men regarded induction into the rapidly burgeoning armed forces as a normal and logical next step in their lives. From 1940 to 1945 the United States inducted more than fifteen million men and women of all classes, races, and religions in order to gain victory in the most devastating of all wars. At the climax of that tremendous effort at least one out of every ten living Americans was in uniform; each had a unique personal experience. There was enormous variation, and no two experiences were identical even within the same military unit. If only, at some later date, each participant could record his or her individual experience, a highly personal memoir of what the war really was like, we would have an incomparably rich supply of authentic sources for later generations to ponder. This book is my effort to provide one such account. You must not expect to find here a constant diet of daring and derring-do—as a matter of fact, most of my voyaging, although always potentially hazardous, was what I would have to call routine. The *Elden* did see some action and did have one or two close calls with disaster, but she was a remarkably lucky ship and never was hit by enemy fire. So, if flying steel and blood are what you crave, this is not the book for you. On the other hand, if you'd like to find out what prolonged service in a destroyer escort really was all about, I'll be glad to show you, as fully as I can.

I remember it all very well, but fortunately I have also been able to check and reinforce my memory with excellent sources. For one thing, I have a personal diary which I kept faithfully during my college years and on into the training phase of my naval experience. After receiving orders for sea duty, I gave up that habit for reasons of security, and did not resume until victory had been won. Shortly after the war, however, when my memory was still very fresh, I composed a month-by-month summary of my experiences and impressions for the period when the diary was laid aside, as a practical way of bridging the gap. In addition, I have the complete file of my wartime letters home to my family, together with their letters to me. Beyond that, I have consulted both the log and the captain's official diary of my ship. All these sources have enabled me not only to check and clarify my own vivid recollections of people, places, and events, but even to plot the *Elden*'s track from day to day throughout her extensive voyaging. Finally, too, I have had occasional recourse to certain reliable secondary accounts of the war, most notably the masterpiece of my old Harvard mentor Admiral Samuel Eliot Morison, *History of United States Naval Operations in World War II* (fourteen volumes, 1947-60). Morison "tells it like it was" and, on a much smaller scale, I have tried to do the same.

Fast-paced, authentic-sounding dialogue may enhance the excitement and verisimilitude of a military memoir, but in general I have avoided the technique of trying to recreate conversations that, after so many years, I simply don't remember. With more than two hundred men on board there was plenty of chatter, you may be sure, but you'll just have to imagine the actual words for yourself. The opening scene of the book is an artificial composite but true to life. So is the later description of the *Elden* and the introduction of her officers. Except in two cases, I have used the actual names of the men who served with me. Thus, in general, everything you will find here is true, narrated just as it happened, or at least as it appeared to me.

A number of individuals and institutions have contributed to the authenticity of my work, and to them I express my sincere gratitude. These include Peter Steele, curator at the Boston National Historical Park, Charlestown Navy Yard; H. A. Vadnais, Jr., head of the curator branch, Naval Historical Center,

Washington Navy Yard; and the staff of the National Archives. At Seawolf Park in Galveston is the U.S.S. *Stewart* (DE 238), long since decommissioned, the only World War II destroyer escort available for public inspection. The manager of the park, Chuck Fulmer, was most helpful in enabling me to explore that ship topside and belowdecks, as a means of refreshing my memory of the shipboard environment.

The staff of the Kent State University Press, including Director John T. Hubbell, Editor Jeanne West, and Managing Editor Flo Cunningham, have functioned like a well-drilled gun crew at every stage of production, offering sound advice while also understanding the author's personal preferences and whims. In addition, Dr. Laura Nagy was constructively critical and always helpful in the final polishing of the text. If this book is a pleasure to hold and read, at least part of the credit belongs to such as these. Finally, I am proudly grateful to my son Brad who drafted the map showing the *Elden*'s track across the Central Pacific, and to my wife Brenda who has heard so much of the story long since and knows its meaning in my life.

Also, I must tell you at the outset that I have not composed this narrative in order to glorify combat or celebrate American military prowess. Rather, I have tried to approach the war, as I did at the time, from a Christian perspective. Indeed, for many committed Christians even a so-called "just war" poses a serious moral dilemma; I understand and respect sincere religious pacifism, and for anyone now contemplating this problem I recommend Richard V. Pierard's chapter in *The Wars of America: Christian Views* (ed. Ronald A. Wells. Grand Rapids, Mich.: Eerdmans, 1981). But in the tragic circumstances of 1939-45 most American Christians, myself included, became convinced that to fight in defense of our nation while also defending weaker countries and liberating captive peoples was a righteous endeavor. In other words, a military response to brutal aggression might not be the worst of all possible evils. My own resolve, as I went into the war, was to eschew personal hatred; all I could hate were the enemy's philosophy, program, and manifest cruelty. Under the circumstances in which I served, that pious resolution proved relatively easy to keep; it was not so easy for many other Americans having quite different experiences. Now, more than forty years and two wars later, I remain convinced that the peacemakers must prevail, in accordance with God's will, for the sake of all humanity.

And now, if you wish, come back with me into those memorable days of the Second World War. What we experience together will not be the soldier's war, or the marine's war, or the airman's war, or even the sailor's war, but only *my* war, my little fragment of the bigger whole, which was all I could really know. My safe return from that terrible conflict is a blessing for which I shall ever be thankful. More than three hundred thousand of my generation of young

Americans, to say nothing of the youth of other lands, did not return. Them I remember and honor, for they, too, loved life and looked forward to a hopeful future that for them was not to be.

PROLOGUE

The gray steel deck on which I am standing is twice alive. It throbs with the surging power of the twin General Motors diesel-electric engines belowdecks; it heaves and dips as the slender but mean-looking destroyer escort rolls and pitches in the ever-restless sea. I am at the lee rail on the open main deck amidships, arms resting on the flat top of the breakwater rail, feet braced against the motion. I watch the relentless march of successive green combers sweeping toward the gray hull, hear them smashing and hissing past the ship's side ten feet below me. I say ten feet but in reality, with the ship rolling so, that's only an average. One moment it's more like fifteen feet, another only five. I am carried up and down, up and down, until the tomato juice, toast, scrambled eggs, and strong navy coffee inside my own hull all seem to be plotting a mutiny—a sudden uprising. I fight them down, and turn to climb the nearby ladder leading up toward the flying bridge. As I do so, the ship's public address system suddenly clicks alive and from loudspeakers belowdecks and topside all over the vessel comes the shrill wavering trill of a boatswain's pipe followed by a raucous voice: "Now hear this! Sweepers man your brooms. There'll be a clean sweep-down fore and aft. Sweep down all decks, compartments, and passageways. Sweepers man your brooms!"

I climb to the flying bridge, meet the rush of saltysea air whipping across it, toss a word of greeting to my two fellow officers conning the ship, and duck into the shelter of the sonar hut. There my two sonarmen on watch are operating the ship's underwater search equipment, directing the precisely spaced PINGs along a defined arc of search ahead of us, constantly listening for any faint echo that might betray the presence of a lurking submarine. I have a friendly word for them, too. Then I squat down on the heaving deck to listen for a few minutes. No echoes; the search goes on.

I leave the flying bridge, climb back down to the main deck, and walk aft, my stride somewhat erratic as I try to conform to the ship's almost rhythmic motion, walking uphill one moment and downhill the next. Hot exhaust from the stack streams off across the starboard quarter. On the superstructure deck above me two of the rapid-firing 20-millimeter Oerlikon guns are manned and ready for any occurrence. A sudden dash of salt spray moistens my khaki shirt. Approaching the curved fantail I greet the three men on watch at the depth charge stations—one by the four starboard K-guns, another at the four port K-guns, and the third by the stern racks. Each has a set of sound-powered phones clamped on his head, a line of immediate communication with the flying bridge. Unlike the two young specialists in the sonar hut, these men are ordinary seamen, but they have been trained in setting a depth charge to explode at any specified depth within its designed range, and to do so quickly. Producing a blindfold, I bind it on one of the watchstanders and commence a drill. "Set a thirteen-charge pattern—Shallow!" The sailor grasps his setting wrench and begins applying it to the depth-setting mechanism on his charges, finding the various settings by counting the clicks as he turns. My stopwatch indicates that he has accomplished the assignment in less than sixty seconds. Each of the other two seamen does as well. This team could perform their duties in the enveloping darkness of a stormy night. Concluding the drill, the men set all charges on "Safe" and resume their monotonous vigil.

I take a moment to contemplate the long wake of churning white water streaming from the ship's stern toward the distant horizon. Suddenly the wake begins to bend as the fantail on which we are standing sweeps sideways and the ship heels underfoot. The officer of the deck up on the flying bridge has ordered a change of course, a new leg in our designated zig-zag pattern. In another five or six minutes the course will again be changed, and so on throughout the day, watch succeeding watch. Again the loudspeakers: "Now hear this! Relieve the watch. Relieve the watch." I must climb back up to the flying bridge to begin a four-hour stint as junior officer of the deck, even though I would much prefer to stretch out on my bunk for a much-needed snooze, with greater hope of keeping my breakfast where it belongs.

What had brought me to this dangerous, demanding, disciplined little world of gray steel, pervasive noise, and ceaseless motion; of orders, shared peril, and male companionship; of wetness, fatigue, and longing? Of course it was Pearl Harbor and the war that we had to win if there was to be any decency, any security left on this deeply troubled planet. So, as much as possible, I was glad to be where I was, engaged in such a noble effort. But I remembered well, and missed very deeply, the better times now gone.

In 1920 I had been born in Providence, Rhode Island. I grew up in a modest but comfortable gray-shingled bungalow in the section of Cranston known as Edgewood. Ours was a fairly typical middle-class family consisting of my parents, my younger sister Marilyn, and myself. Dad was a manufacturing jeweler in a city noted for the industry. Those who knew him best remember two qualities above all others—a wonderfully puckish sense of humor that made him the life of any social gathering, and a natural talent in art. He could draw ludicrous cartoons in the old-fashioned style of an earlier day; his scenic pastels, watercolors, and oils brightened the walls of our home. Mother was a perfect helpmate and foil for Dad. A pleasant, fun-loving person who thoroughly relished parties, outings, and other group activities, she was at the same time deeply religious, civic-minded, interested in building bridges to all kinds of people. In the main, despite the Great Depression, our life together as a family was notably harmonious and happy.

After graduating from Cranston High School in 1938 I entered Brown University as a member of the Class of 1942, along with many of my Cranston friends. Some of us were "townies," living at home and commuting daily to conserve our limited financial resources. The next four years were to be one of the happiest and most satisfying periods of my young life. Daily I rode into downtown Providence with Dad or hitch-hiked along Narragansett Boulevard and then climbed from Market Square up the steep slope of College Hill to Van Wickle Gates, where I entered the tranquil, tree-shaded campus. I worked hard at being a good student, but also played trombone in the marching band and sang in the Gilbert and Sullivan productions. Late in the afternoon, or sometimes the evening, I retraced my steps down the hill and took the Broad Street trolley home. It was a program guaranteed to develop not only a mind but also a set of leg muscles. I remember a magic evening in the spring of 1940 when, in celebration of its complete renovation, venerable University Hall, a quietly dignified Georgian brick edifice dating from the era of the American Revolution, was beautifully illuminated with four candles in each of its many serried windows. On another occasion I noted that walking toward University Hall was like moving right into an old-fashioned watercolor—the quaint bell tower stood outlined before a pale blue sky decked with fleecy clouds. I was enjoying my years at Brown.

One day I made the acquaintance of a townie classmate named Tom Buffum.

His parents and mine had been good friends for many years, but Tom and I had traveled completely separate paths until this intersection at Brown. Somehow he and I now hit it off together in a very special way, like Rhode Island johnnycakes and maple syrup, so to speak. It was more than just a common interest in such pleasures as hiking and camping, music, good jokes, and fun-loving girls (not necessarily in that order). Tom's irrepressible cheerfulness, friendly manner, obvious sincerity, and delighted grin, all were warmly attractive. We found that we enjoyed each other's homes and families. We shared the same basic ideals and commitments. We could laugh heartily together, and also disagree without rancor. We came to confide in each other, as close friends will do. Ours was to be a flourishing, enduring friendship.

In general, though, my closest friendships were developing not at college but within the fellowship of Calvary Baptist Church, whose yellow-brick edifice still stands on the corner of Broad and Stanwood Streets in Providence. There I contributed my tenor voice, such as it was, to one of the choirs. There, too, I became actively involved in the Young People's Fellowship, a remarkably cohesive group of young men and women just getting started on their careers, aided by the friendly, mature counselling of "Uncle George" Jones, a very gentle man who loved and understood young people. In this bunch, no paraded piety or somber self-righteousness. We were a gang of friends discovering together a valid pattern for our lives, and in that process having a lot of good, clean fun. Soon I found myself eagerly anticipating every coming event, whether an Easter sunrise service and breakfast, a Halloween party, a square dance, a skating party on a country pond, or a Gilbert and Sullivan comic opera performed for an admiring audience of church folk. Tom Buffum also came to Calvary and joined the Y.P.F., as did his lanky younger brother Tim. And so the friendships grew and broadened. As for dating, we did plenty of that both within and outside the circles of Brown and Calvary, but in those relatively carefree days many of us weren't much interested in "going steady," at least not until we were more sure of our future and until "just the right one" happened along. So it was that we dated virtually (and, I think, virtuously) without consistent pattern, or in a variety of patterns, simply sharing our friendship and enjoying each other's company. Unquestionably, far more than I realized at the time, I was extremely fortunate in being part of such a great gang, all good friends together.

For all the fun and happiness, however, my four years at Brown rolled by under the shadow of international war, a very grim threat indeed. "England, France, Germany, Italy, Japan, and many other nations either are heavily armed or are furiously building up their armed forces," I wrote on 1 December 1938. "I am afraid that war must come eventually. It is my fervent hope that the

United States will be able to stay out of it this time." Already the Japanese Army was deep in China, and only nine months later Hitler's massive military machine precipitated the Second World War in Europe by invading Poland.

Our own country, too, was beginning to arm. In the spring of 1939 the students at Brown had designated a "Peace Week," inviting the well-known socialist and pacifist Norman Thomas to deliver an address on Faunce House terrace. Scarcely had he begun his impassioned speech when we began hearing a distant roar rapidly approaching, and almost before we could know what was happening a formation of ten "flying fortresses," the nation's newest, most awesome bombers, thundered across the sky above our heads at low altitude, drowning out the speaker. The contrast was overwhelming, almost as though the voice of History were saying, "All right, young people. Take your choice!"

On 16 October 1940 more than sixteen million American males twenty-one years of age and older registered for the first draft, among them over three hundred Brown men who enrolled in Lyman Gymnasium. Already, one of my friends, Roger Hard, had left college to begin training for a commission in the navy. Completing his rapid training, he appeared at Calvary in his ensign's blues on 10 November, en route to the battleship *New Mexico.* The first batch of Rhode Island men to be inducted as a result of the draft, twenty-two of them, reported for duty on 18 November as similar groups began assembling all over the country. Training camps and military bases were expanding rapidly to accommodate the influx. On campus I watched a gang of workmen gingerly easing a 4-inch naval gun into Lyman Gymnasium for the training of our Navy R.O.T.C. unit. With deep concern we listened daily to the ominous reports pouring in from around the world.

The National Guard had been called to active service, to be integrated into the armed forces. From Rhode Island went first the 243d Regiment of Coast Artillery, and then the local components of the 43d Infantry Division. With them went Prof. Robert W. Kenny of the English Department who, when he was helping me understand seventeenth-century English literature, seemed hardly the soldier. By March 1941 the U.S. Army numbered a million men and the Navy over 200,000. In Providence, on weekends, we saw more and more soldiers, sailors, and marines.

To a greater or lesser degree all of us in the student body were wrestling with the perplexing problem of deepening American involvement in the European conflict. Most of us favored continued neutrality, I believe, but few wished to see Britain go down before the German juggernaut. On 24 April 1941 President Henry M. Wriston, a tough-minded intellectual, standing in the same place where Norman Thomas had stood, applauded the worldwide commitments the United States was undertaking. Some time later a history class of which I was a member took a vote and discovered that a majority was in favor of American convoys to the British Isles, despite the German threat. At about that same time I was reading Walter Millis's study of how our country became involved in the First World War, an account I found "a little bit terrifying in view of present circumstances." Even Dan Braude's hilarious Class Day spoof of the draft could not obscure the seriousness of our situation.

On my twenty-first birthday, apparently quite unaware of that momentous occasion, President Roosevelt proclaimed a state of extreme national emergency. My age now made it compulsory for me to register for the draft on the next designated date, which was 1 July 1941. I duly signed in. Subsequently, when numbers were drawn in the draft lottery, mine came up seventy-fifth out of more than six hundred, which meant an early call. Naturally, I began wondering whether I even could return to college for my senior year. The summer passed, more thousands were inducted into the rapidly growing army, but in September when the bell in the tower of University Hall began ringing for classes, I was there among my classmates. On 11 October, shortly before kickoff time in the annual football encounter between Brown and Rhode Island State, a swarm of about forty fast fighter planes roared across the sky directly above the stadium, an unmistakable reminder of changing priorities.

As I write I am holding in my hand a slightly faded photograph showing the Calvary Y.P.F. grouped before a large fieldstone fireplace in a recreation hall near Chepachet, some miles from Providence. The photo is dated 15 November 1941, the occasion one of our super socials. I well remember most of the sixty-eight in the picture. There in the second row, wearing a dark suit, is "Uncle George." His son Leland, more serious than usual, is second row center. There are at least two married couples—our young choir director Harold Brown and his wife Isabel, and Herb and Virginia Tucker. I see also my good friend Roger Brown; the effervescent twins Clara and Ethel Miller; deep-dimpled Mary Noyes, who lived just up the street from me; our fun-loving, ever-loyal church secretary Trudy Kraus; Bob Greene in a plaid lumberjack shirt; Dick Johnson clowning in the back row; and at dead center, lanky Lambert Lindquist, grinning broadly, pipe in hand. On that memorable evening the group enjoyed a hearty buffet supper followed by dancing, singing, and a good time all round. Who of us in those carefree hours could have predicted that just three weeks and a day later swarming Japanese aircraft, appearing suddenly from nowhere, would savage the United States Pacific Fleet in Pearl Harbor and transform our lives?

Almost any American old enough to remember the event can describe with amazing precision where he was and what he was doing when struck by the news of Pearl Harbor. So great was the shock, with the sudden awareness of what it meant to our lives, that the moment became indelibly etched upon the memory. Tom Buffum and I were driving up to Brown for a Sunday afternoon rehearsal of *Patience* when the startling announcement burst from the car radio. Soon we were discussing the crisis with our fellow actors and agreeing that "the show must go on," as indeed it did a few evenings later, to great local acclaim. But the members of Gilbert and Sullivan's Forty-Second Dragoon Guards, resplendent in red and yellow ("primary colours"), knew that before long they would be donning other, more practical uniforms and marching to other music. Somehow, it seemed, a dark, heavy curtain had dropped suddenly between the good life of former days and the unpredictable, even frightening future. Instinctively we began to realize that our lives would never again be the same. That good past, with all its joys, was gone forever.

On the day after Pearl Harbor many of the classes at Brown were cancelled. Some of us from our history class trooped into Prof. Robert H. George's office, where we listened somberly to President Roosevelt's angry call for a declaration of war. Other groups clustered around the radio in Faunce House listening to the latest reports. In general, there was little evidence of unusual excitement; most of us seemed to be absorbing the news calmly and soberly. We simply knew that now we were into it, completely and to the end, whatever that might mean. And we were certain that some of us would have to die.

Rapid expansion of the United States Navy would require thousands of new junior line officers to help man the aircraft carriers, battleships, cruisers, destroyers, and other vessels of the fleet. In peacetime such officers came mostly from the United States Naval Academy at Annapolis. Now a more rapid form of training was needed to meet the navy's urgent requirement. The preferred model was, of course, the Naval Academy and its traditional program of officer education, but how could that be drastically condensed and still produce competent "officers and gentlemen"? The answer was the so-called V-7 program.

The navy, assuming that graduates of American colleges and universities would already be reasonably well grounded in such basic subjects as English and mathematics, had decided to superimpose on the usual college education an intensive three-month period of specialized training in naval customs and etiquette, navigation, seamanship, communications, damage control, gunnery, and other related subjects, together with a strong dose of drill and discipline. Upon successful completion of that program, the V-7 midshipman would be commissioned an ensign in the United States Naval Reserve and given an active-duty assignment. A fundamental requirement for admission to the program, obviously, was a college degree; accordingly, the navy was prepared to enlist currently enrolled college seniors in the V-7 program with a guarantee that they would be exempt from the draft and not called up to begin their training until after graduation. As Tom and I were now in our senior year at Brown, the V-7 program captured our interest—mine especially, since the draft board already was hard upon my heels. What never crossed our minds at the time was the fact that two circumstances in our lives made this option available to us—our parents had enough money to send us to college, and we were white. Today I understand how unfairly discriminatory that was.

Four days after Christmas Tom and I drove up Route 1 from Providence to Boston and made our way to Headquarters, First Naval District, located in an office building at 150 Causeway Street adjacent to the North Station. We found the recruiting section much like a department store on the opening day of a sale, with hordes of anxious young men crowding the corridors and offices, trying to work their way through the successive stages of the enlistment process. Accomplishing little on this first visit, I returned the following day and managed at least to have my credentials checked.

By this time I knew that I was slightly underweight. For the next few days I waged an intensive campaign to add the needed pounds, taking prescribed pills, spooning down bowlfuls of corn meal gruel, and drinking large quantities of milk. At last, on a bitter cold 7 January I presented myself for the decisive physical examination. With me I had brought a bag of bananas and a metal cup that would hold exactly a half pint of water, for I knew rather precisely how many quarts of water, supplemented with bananas, I would have to ingest in order to raise my weight to the required level. Accordingly, before going in to the examining room I secluded myself in a nearby men's room and did what was necessary. It worked like a charm, and I passed the examination with flying colors—that is, almost. As I was getting dressed and preparing to leave, a pharmacist's mate appeared from the inner sanctum to inform me that I had passed everything except the urinalysis. "What you gave us for that we couldn't analyze," he stated in a matter-of-fact tone. "It was virtually pure water!" Fortunately, the navy was understanding, permitting me to return on a later occasion and make that last required donation.

So it was that on 24 January 1942, again at Headquarters, First Naval District, I raised my right hand and was sworn in as an apprentice seaman, Class V-7. That was a decisive act, a major watershed in my life, for in wartime an enlistment in one of the armed forces is not for a term of years, it's for come what may, good or ill, victory or disaster—it's for the duration plus. Now I was into it foursquare, and no longer a free individual. I went home feeling different—and good. As for Tom, he had fallen somewhat behind me in the process, but about two months later, when his papers were complete, I accompanied him to Boston and stood by his side as he enlisted in the same program.

In the meantime, all during those months of desperately urgent American military expansion, our classmates and friends were choosing their own routes into the Second World War, some preferring the army, others the marines or flight training. Many simply waited to be caught up in the draft, which was feeding men into the army at a faster and faster rate. Whatever the choice, one by one our friends began going off to the camps and other training centers established all over the country. Successive issues of the Y.P.F.'s monthly newsletter *The Odyssey* included the service addresses of more and more of Calvary's young men, also publishing brief excerpts from their letters home. As a church, as a gang of friends, we were determined to maintain contact with each other no matter what happened. *The Odyssey* was to serve as our world-girdling trunk line.

During that extraordinary spring the news pouring in daily from abroad was deeply ominous. We could only guess at the actual condition of the Pacific Fleet, but the damage seemed serious. The Philippine Islands along with Malaya and important areas of the Central and South Pacific were being overrun by the Japanese, often with shocking brutality. One of my close boyhood friends, Dave Westcott, was missing in the Philippines after the fall of Bataan. German U-boats were prowling just off our East Coast, sinking merchantmen with apparent nonchalance; our government ordered a dim-out all along the coast to make these U-boats' depredations more difficult.

Periodically the local civil defense organization in Providence ordered a test blackout. Upon the eerie, prolonged wailing of the air raid sirens all lights were extinguished, the normal bright glow of the city giving way to inky blackness. Public buildings, including many at Brown, had pails of sand placed at convenient locations for smothering incendiary bombs. We were trying to learn from London's bitter experience. More and more women were taking up jobs outside the home, many in war production; the era of Rosie the Riveter was beginning. So, too, was the era of rationing, starting with gasoline and sugar.

Almost before we knew it the college year and our years in college were drawing to a close. The Class Night Dance, to which Tom took Ethel and I took Clara, was followed on Sunday by a baccalaureate service in the old First Baptist Meeting House at the foot of College Hill. Then, on a gray 18 May came Commencement, with a number of the graduating seniors already in uniform. Tom and I were graduated together, along with Leland Jones, my distant cousin Charlie Leach, and all the others in the Class of 1942. Our unofficial motto: "In with the hurricane, out with the war." Graduation, of course, made both Tom and me immediately subject to the navy's call. But the navy had its own plans, and somehow seemed able to carry on the war, at least for a few more weeks, without our assistance.

We filled those weeks of late spring and early summer with a delectable banquet of choice activities, relishing the last, lingering taste of all that was most precious—family, home, church, friends, good times together. A partial list will give the flavor: an informal reunion of my old high school crowd; sailing on Narragansett Bay in the Browns' catboat; a choir festival followed by a long walk home with Clara, Trudy, and Tom; dancing at Rhodes-on-the-Pawtuxet; a Y.P.F. party at the shore; tennis with Ethel at Roger Williams Park; bowling with Roger and Tom; bicycling with Trudy; an evening on the midway at Crescent Park; a circus with Mother and Dad; suppers in the back yard at home; a lengthy mountain-climbing excursion in New Hampshire with Tom. Tramping up the north end of Mt. Webster, we proceeded eastward along the venerable Crawford Path crossing summit after summit, just the two of us drinking in the hoary grandeur of these ancient mountains. After spending a night in one of the snug bunkrooms of the Lakes-of-the-Clouds Hut, Tom and I continued on up to the rocky summit of Mt. Washington, and then along the spectacular Gulfside Trail to the Madison Hut, where we passed a second night before finally completing the Presidential Range by climbing to the top of Mt. Madison. Descending at last to a world at war, we knew that we had had a high experience to remember throughout whatever the future might hold for each of us. I was moved to write in my diary, with clear foreboding, that "one of my greatest fears in going away is that I shall return to find my world as I knew it greatly changed—friends gone away, married, no longer holding common interests, etc. I find it hard to face the fact that the Choir and Y.P.F. will never be the same after the war." That concern, self-centered though it sounds, was genuine and deeply felt. Somehow I yearned to hold back the march of time, and there was no way to do that.

It was in July that my new master finally deigned to speak, first through a preliminary notice and then through official orders arriving by mail. I was instructed to report for basic training at the University of Notre Dame on 11 August. That was it, and it was incontrovertible. Tom was scheduled to begin similar training at Columbia University a few days later.

Now the pace of our preparations for departure began to quicken. On the first Sunday in August, Mother, Dad, and I took Communion together at Calvary; one can readily imagine the thoughts going through my parents' minds as we sat there side by side in the very sanctuary where they had been married twenty-three years earlier. Later that week Tom's parents hosted a farewell dinner party, with the phonograph blaring out "Anchors Aweigh" as Roger, Tim, Tom, and I escorted Clara, Ethel, Trudy, and Frances Weeden to the table. Then, to cap it all, on the evening before I was to leave Tom and I hosted a joint "open house" at my home attended by a multitude of relatives and friends, all showering us with good wishes for successful voyaging and a safe return. Seldom have such unheroic heroes been accorded such a farewell.

The navy had instructed me to travel by bus to Worcester, Massachusetts, where I was to board a train for South Bend, Indiana, on the afternoon of 10 August. Accordingly, suitcase in hand, I duly appeared at the bus terminal in Providence, accompanied by Mother, Dad, and Marilyn, all of us determined to keep the mood positive. Also there to see me off were Tom and his mother, and a number of other friends, including Trudy, Clara, Ethel, and Mary. There were cheerful hugs and kisses all round, and then a final wave as the bus started on its way. With me on the bus were at least two of my classmates, John Coakley and Fred Sherman, each of us glad not be going alone.

When the train coming out from Boston pulled into the station at Worcester, it was already teeming with V-7 recruits, whom we joined. All through that night the train roared westward, rapidly increasing the distance from home. For me, who had never been farther west than Washington, D.C., the ride itself was an adventure. The next morning, as we rolled through the countryside of northern Indiana, I made my way along swaying aisles to the dining car, but found that I had little appetite for breakfast. Were any of the others so nervous? At last the train slowed perceptibly and began pulling into the South Bend station. Peering through the windows as we gradually slowed to a full stop, I could see a string of navy men along the platform, all wearing the armband of the Shore Patrol, obviously waiting to receive us into their disciplined world. This was it. The process of transformation was about to begin.

1
NINETY-DAY WONDER

As our New England contingent poured out onto the platform of the South Bend railway station, the Shore Patrol herded us into the waiting room and, with impressive efficiency, got us lined up under the curious gaze of civilian bystanders. Then they led us out to the street, where a small fleet of open trucks was waiting to carry us and our luggage to the Notre Dame campus. Immediately upon arriving we were swept up in a wave of systematic, directed activity. Each new seaman recruit was handed a lengthy mimeographed list of instructions, the first dozen of which will serve to give a fairly clear impression of our first few hours at Notre Dame:

1. If you have luggage coming, leave the claim checks with the Company officer. Company officers will give a receipt with number of the check in return. A Navy truck will bring it to the campus.
2. Locate your room and take all your gear to it.
3. Fill out the questionnaires that have been handed to you and return them to the Company office.
4. Stow your locker.
5. Draw your bedding from the Storeroom, Morrissey Hall. Fill out and sign the small bedding card and take it with you.

6. Make up your bunk.
7. Report to the Chief Petty Officer on your deck that you have finished items 1 to 6.
8. Return to your room and remain there for further instructions.
9. When directed by the C.P.O., go to the Stadium and draw your uniforms.
10. Return to your room and shift into uniform.
11. When directed by the C.P.O., stow your civilian clothing in your suitcases.
12. When the word is passed for "Formation," go to the location pointed out by the C.P.O. and fall in at attention.

"Gear," "stow," "draw," "deck," "C.P.O.," "when directed," "when the word is passed," "fall in at attention"—left no room for doubt as to where we were and why we were there. At that point I was almost completely ready for the mold—eager to conform, willing to believe that the navy, a model of organizational efficiency, knew precisely the best way to accomplish every required task including the transformation of collegians into officers and gentlemen.

I found myself assigned to the Second Platoon, Fourth Company, with a bunk and locker in room 328 of Morrissey Hall, a dormitory room I was to share with Bryant Lassiter of Texas, Paul Lawrence of Indiana, and Warren Lawrence of California. The geographical diversity was significant. Recent college graduates from all parts of the country had converged upon Notre Dame as V-7 apprentice seamen to undergo a brief period of basic training and testing before passing along to Midshipmen's School.

As instructed, we drew our bedding and uniforms. Once in possession of the latter, again as instructed, we stripped off the college-boy clothing in which we had come, climbed into sailor whites, and packed our discarded garments for shipment home. That snapped the last tie with the free civilian world. From then on it was Uncle Sam's duds or none!

Nearly everything in our lives was new and different. Even sleep was not quite the same as before, being subject to interruption for night duty. In fact, my very first night in the navy I "drew a watch," and spent the hours from 0400 (4 a.m.) to reveille equipped with flashlight and nightstick, patrolling the corridors and grounds of Morrissey Hall. That night not a single enemy dared intrude!

For the next two weeks our time was crammed with a variety of activities designed to accomplish two things—weed out the incompetent and prepare the remainder for later rigorous training at Midshipmen's School, either at Columbia (where Tom Buffum was undergoing his basic training) or Northwestern

University. Early each morning, when the summer air was still fresh, we formed by platoons along the walkways outside our dormitories and were put through a vigorous sequence of calisthenics ("The next exercise will be the jumping jack. Ready. Begin! One-two, one-two, one-two, one-two!"). We learned that the proper response to a verbal command was not a cheery "Yessir!" but rather "Aye, aye, Sir!" (meaning "I have understood the command and will carry it out"). We learned how to stand at attention (interminably, if so required), stand at parade rest, stand at ease; how and when to salute; how to march in formation and perform the various evolutions of infantry drill. We were marched to meals and to the various activities for training, impeccably crisp in our white turned-up sailor caps properly squared on the head, white T-shirts, white bell-bottom trousers, black socks, and well-shined black shoes. Before long, with this kind of stimulus, we were beginning to feel quite navy.

Once in the service, with the whole nation committed to a good cause and hundreds of thousands of other young people flooding into the armed forces, one experienced an exhilarating sense of *belonging,* of being part of the national team. This sense of belonging was constantly reinforced by the uniform and the regulation haircut, as well as by certain almost ritualistic practices such as saluting. One took pride in knowing when and whom to salute, and precisely *how.* Traditional navy customs, ways of speaking and ways of doing, were an important part of the bond.

Much of our regular classroom time was devoted to mathematics, actually a brief program of review and testing. Then came our first experience with the navy practice known as the "bilge," the ruthless elimination of students found to be unqualified for further training as potential officers. We watched from a respectful distance as those unfortunates on the bilge list assembled outside Morrissey Hall with their luggage, a forlorn little band, awaiting transportation to the railway station. It was the Darwinian principle applied to the armed forces. All of us in the V-7 program hoped to remain among the fittest—and survive to receive our commissions.

On the Saturday before the end of the program at Notre Dame we underwent Captain's Inspection. The entire regiment, all in white, stood in precise formation facing the Rockne Memorial Building while our commanding officer passed along the rigid ranks of young men just twelve days removed from civilian life. Our quarters were to be inspected next, so as soon as we were "secured" from formation we repaired to our rooms in haste, there to flick away any lingering specks of dust before the captain arrived. Every personal item down to the last pair of socks was stowed in its assigned place; the corners of each tautly covered bunk had been painstakingly squared. Now the four of us were standing impatiently in line within our immaculate little *domicilium,* the lanky lad from California primed to sing out when the captain appeared, "Good morning, Captain. Seaman Lawrence in charge of room, Sir!" As we waited tensely, Warren suddenly wondered about the door. Was it standing open at just the prescribed angle? Seeing a chief petty officer passing by in the corridor, he impulsively thought to inquire, and called out "Chief!" At that very instant there strode into our room not the captain (thank goodness) but our battalion commander. Stifling a sudden urge to plunge through the window, the horrified Warren managed to warble, "Oh, good morning, Sir. Seaman Lawrence in charge of room, Sir!" whereupon the officer marched directly to the source of this message and grasped my roommate by the front of his spotless white jumper. Poor Warren's knees nearly buckled under him, but he was saved when the battalion commander explained, with a perfectly straight face, that he was there to "inspect jumpers." As for the captain, he never did arrive.

I was happy to find myself among those assigned to Midshipmen's School at Columbia University, for it meant that Tom and I would go through together, with perhaps even some opportunity for home leave. On 26 August that portion of our regiment destined for Columbia, having wished good luck to our friends ordered elsewhere, hiked from the Notre Dame campus to a nearby railway siding where two trains stood waiting. When all of us were aboard, the trains got underway for New York City. The next morning, arriving at a siding on the western edge of Manhattan, we detrained, formed up, and marched through the streets to the campus on Morningside Heights.

At Midshipmen's School we were to undergo a much more rigorous and exacting phase of training over a period of three months. Every few weeks at Columbia a class would complete the program and be commissioned, with a new class entering shortly thereafter to begin the process. Thus a sequence of classes was always moving through the pipeline, ours being the ninth to pass through. Those men who survived the program and received their ensign's commissions were known throughout the navy as "Ninety-Day Wonders," a term obviously tinged with ripe disdain on the part of the old-line regulars.

Most midshipmen at Columbia were housed in three large dormitories taken over by the navy—Furnald Hall (where Tom's battalion was quartered), John Jay Hall, and Johnson Hall (a former women's dormitory rising twelve stories above West 116th Street). In addition, there was the station ship *Prairie State,* actually the hulk of the ancient battlewagon *Illinois,* moored at the foot of 135th Street. Our contingent from Notre Dame was directed into Johnson Hall, where I found myself assigned to room 631 along with Randy Guyer, a midshipman from Oregon. Upon arrival we were issued new uniforms consisting of visor cap with changeable covers, khaki shirt and trousers, black necktie (worn tucked into the shirt), and web belt with shiny brass buckle. Earlier, at Notre Dame, we had been measured for our dress blues, including the traditional midshipman's double-breasted jacket with brass buttons, uniforms that arrived a little later. Now, at last, we began to look like midshipmen (and officers in embryo).

The regiment of midshipmen, some 2,700 strong, was subdivided into battalions, companies, platoons, and sections, which were led by selected midshipman officers under the close supervision of commissioned officers and chief petty officers of the staff. I found myself a member of Section Twenty, Sixty-First Company, Sixth Battalion. A quick roll-call of the section, as finally constituted, will reveal the geographical and academic diversity of our military community: Lassiter (Texas Tech '42), Lavender (Wofford '41), Lawrence (University of California '42), Leach (Brown '42), Leake (Tulane-Architecture '42), Leard (University of California '42), Leibowitz (CCNY '40), Levine (Bucknell '39), Levitt (Brooklyn '42), Levy (Wharton School '42), Lewis (University of Texas '41), Liebert (Creighton '42), Lienhard (University of Washington '42), Lindbeck (Marshall '42), Lindmark (Drake '41), Lippincott (Yale '40), Lockwood (Williams '41), Lorenz (Columbia '42). My roommate Randy Guyer, who was in the Fifty-Third Company, had graduated from Oregon State in 1942. The exuberant atmosphere of college days was far from dissipated, as yet.

At Midshipmen's School, however, our behavior during every moment was being rigidly molded by a multitude of regulations. Being placed on report for a violation usually brought a flock of demerits which had to be worked off by scrubbing corridor walls during weekends, when less careless midshipmen were on liberty. Anyone so feckless or unlucky as to accumulate more than fifty demerits was subject to expulsion. One of the men in my section, an extroverted comedian, ran up quite a score by neglecting an order to shave off his cherished mustache. This pervasive kind of discipline meant that we lived under constant tension, which probably was an important part of our conditioning for active service.

Tom and I had our first brief reunion on the second evening after my arrival, looking strange to each other in uniform. As we shook hands, exchanged news, and grinned over our new perceptions and problems, both of us knew how very drastic was the change in our lives. Providence and the old gang seemed a long way off. I suspect that each of us, subconsciously, was trying to demonstrate to the other that despite that change the old personality was still there, irrepressible, the same. And it was. Thereafter Tom and I saw each other only occasionally. Considering how close we had been during the preceding three years, our present separation despite proximity only served to emphasize the impact of discipline and the relentless demands of the service. We felt caught up in a huge, impersonal, inexorable machine that was systematically separating us from family, friends, and the free life we had known. Yet it was exciting and somehow satisfying, for we felt that we were doing our duty, and knew that more and more of our friends back home were entering the armed forces and undergoing a similar transformation.

At Notre Dame we had begun applying navy terminology to our quarters; we continued the practice at Columbia. Johnson Hall was our "ship." Its foyer, once graced by Columbia coeds and their boyfriends, was the "quarterdeck," where the officer of the deck held sway. Upon entering the ship a midshipman was expected to salute the "colors" aft, and then salute the officer of the deck, requesting "permission to come aboard, Sir." The stairs were "ladders," the elevators "hoists," the floors "decks," the walls "bulkheads," the corridors "passageways," the toilets "heads." On each deck having sleeping quarters was stationed a "mate of the deck" responsible for everything that transpired there, including prompt rising when reveille sounded at 0610. Because of the dim-out in the city we were required to keep the shades on our windows lowered after dark, even on the hottest nights, until lights out at 2200.

Meals were served in the basement cafeteria of Johnson Hall. On each long dining table stood several huge stainless steel navy-style coffee pots filled with a black brew so potent, it was said, that a knife blade passed through the pouring stream would be distorted beyond recognition. This hot and bracing beverage we sipped from thick, white navy mugs that had been born without handles. Generally speaking, the food was plentiful and reasonably good, although on one occasion my entire section, appraising the hash we were being served, began barking like dogs.

Also dished up to us in regular doses were infantry drill, with and without rifles, and six academic courses—communications, damage control, first aid, ordnance and gunnery, navigation, and seamanship. We attended these classes by sections. After entering the room the members stood at attention beside their desks while the section leader reported to the officer-instructor, "Section Twenty all present and accounted for, Sir!" "Very well, seat your section." "Section, seats!" Through hard, regular study we learned almost more than we really wanted to know about azimuth, breechblocks, cams, chain stoppers, collision mats, davits, nun buoys, righting arms, and trajectories, to name only a few of the bewildering mysteries. Quizzes were frequent, tests an ordeal to be dreaded. At the end of each week was posted the academic deficiency list known as the "tree," which nearly everyone consulted with alacrity, for inclusion meant curtailment of weekend liberty. Wrote one study-dazed midshipman:

Here lie interred my weekend plans,
    Nipped in the bud by harsh Fate's hands.
You ask me what has left them dead?
    My answer, sir, is quickly said:
Poems are made by fools like me,
But that ain't all. I made a Tree!

When the dreaded mid-term bilge occurred, Johnson Hall lost about 7 percent of its men, including one from my section. Most of us worked hard at our assigned tasks, whether physical or mental, and the time elapsing between taps and reveille seemed like five minutes.

Personal inspections, in formation out in the street, were exacting. The uniform had to be immaculate, with shoes buffed to black brilliance. Shortly before the time for one such scrutiny a friend in my section suddenly remembered that he needed a haircut, but by then it was too late to visit the barber. I very kindly offered the use of my electric razor, an offer which he accepted like a drowning man grasping at a floating timber. Three of us in succession did our very best to make him presentable, but the razor, alas, was not designed for such a task, and we were anything but deft. Each effort to mend errors only made things worse, and while our unhappy sectionmate peered into the mirror and moaned, we found it ever more difficult to suppress our mirth. At last, with the victim's ready consent, we gave the whole thing up as a bad job. By this time a stranger entering the room might have supposed that our unfortunate friend was wearing on his head an old, ill-tended theatrical wig. As he made his way back toward his own room, passing groups of immaculate midshipmen en route, we could follow his progress by the snickers and roars spreading in his wake. The outcome was not so funny. Our friend went to the inspection and stood heroically in the ranks, trying his best to look like the sharpest midshipman in the regiment, but there was no deficiency in the inspecting officer's vision, and condemnation was duly recorded, with appropriate demerits following. Fortunately, the victim bore no grudge—we had well and truly tried.

I myself took one deliberate risk, for the sake of a practical joke. As I have said, Johnson Hall had been a women's dormitory—hence no urinals in the heads. This meant that in every head immediately after reveille there was intense competition for the stalls, each of which was equipped with a partial door that could be bolted from inside. Sometime between taps and reveille on the night of 12 November I made a stealthy visit to the head nearest my room. Entering the first of the six stalls, I bolted the door, climbed up over the top and down into the next stall, again bolting the door, and so on until four of the six were effectively closed and apparently occupied. Then I returned to my bunk, where I awaited reveille with a sense of anticipation previously unknown. When the call sounded, I hurried with all the other sleepy-eyed midshipmen to the common goal, where we immediately discovered that four of the stalls had already been pre-empted. So we all stood waiting impatiently, shifting weight from one foot to the other, with much muttering and occasional cries of "Hurry up!" and "What's taking you so long?" At last one of the brightest (or most desperate) among us thought to peer *under* one of the doors, and when he saw no feet the game was up. Instantly, like a boarding party at sea, midshipmen were up and over and down, doors came unbolted, and all eventually returned to normal. I never dared reveal what I had done, and if any of my old companymates happen to read this, I hope they'll be forgiving. It was a bright spot in a long three months.

Every Saturday morning came the military high point of the week—a full-dress review of the entire regiment of midshipmen, held on South Field adjacent to the Butler Library. There in dress blues the battalions formed, seemingly endless rows of men at rigid attention, massive blocks of men at attention, awaiting the next word of command. It comes as a hoarse shout, echoing across the field—"Pass in review!" The band launches into the measured strains of "Anchors Aweigh," and the marching ranks pass by the reviewing stand, arms all swinging in unison, eyes to the right in customary salute. That was exciting and a cause for pride, especially when visiting parents or girlfriends were there observing. On such occasions Tom and I, in our separate units, might as well have been on opposite sides of the world.

On the weekend of 10 October, not being on the tree and having no demerits to work off, I enjoyed my first home leave, traveling by train from New York to Providence. Trains were crowded in wartime; often one had to stand for many miles, bracing against the sway, or else perch uncomfortably on a suitcase in the aisle. The conductor could make his way through only with considerable difficulty, but nearly everyone remained reasonably good-natured about it all. Periodically a pair of military police also threaded along the aisles, checking the leave papers of every person in uniform, another reminder of my new status. Of course, I felt elated at the prospect of being home again, and watched eagerly as the train approached Providence.

From the Union Station I took the trolley home, where Mother, Dad, Grandma Raybold, and my sister Marilyn greeted me enthusiastically. Later that evening welcome visitors arrived—"Uncle George" Jones, Tom's mother and father, Clara, Trudy, and Roger. When opportunity presented itself, toward the end of the evening, I went out for a night walk with the latter three, and it seemed almost like old times, though we all missed Tom.

That Sunday was an invigorating autumn day, one of New England's finest—

air crisp, leaves brown and rustling—perfect for hiking. After a good home-cooked breakfast, I got myself properly uniformed as though for inspection, and then made rendezvous with my three young friends of the previous evening. Our exuberant foursome strode along Broad Street to Calvary, a distance of several miles, passing houses and shops and the old "car barn" all familiar from many previous occasions. It seemed so good to be doing it again. At Sunday School I was heartily greeted by many surprised friends, as was every returning serviceman. Then, just before the morning service was to begin, I went down into the robing room for a brief visit with all my friends in the choir, and indeed, might even have donned a robe and joined them, just as though I had never been away, except that my train for New York was scheduled to leave the Union Station at noon. So I had to go, feeling again that strange, unwonted compulsion of service discipline that had taken such control of my life. Some hours later, at Johnson Hall, I saluted the officer of the deck and requested permission to come aboard. It was not denied.

Week followed week through the remainder of that fall, with the outside air becoming ever colder and the days ever shorter. Avidly I received and read all communications from family and friends—postcards, letters, successive issues of *The Odyssey*—which enabled me to keep track of what was going on at home and with increasing numbers of Y.P.F.'ers scattered throughout the armed forces around the world. Like all the midshipmen, too, I followed the news of the war on the various fighting fronts with something more than casual interest, especially the terrible destructiveness of Hitler's U-boats in the Atlantic and the impressive power of the Japanese surface fleet in the Pacific.

As the period of training drew toward its conclusion, one great personal concern for each midshipman was his post-graduation assignment. Where would he be sent? What would be the nature of his duty? Would he measure up? With many difficult amphibious landings presumably in the offing, the rumor spread that most of our class was destined for "amphib," which we assumed would have us driving very small and vulnerable assault craft onto hotly defended beaches. Eventually, the actual orders for individual midshipmen began arriving. Some of the men rejoiced in choice assignments to specific ships—a battleship, a carrier, a cruiser, a destroyer, a fleet auxiliary. Others of us were designated for specialized training or other duty at a variety of shore stations. Tom's orders directed him to Newport, Rhode Island, for duty in connection with coastal defense. I was assigned as an instructor at something called the Naval Training School (Indoctrination), Hollywood Beach, Florida. Florida!!! I had never been south of Virginia. To me, the assignment sounded great.

Tom's parents and mine, old friends together, came to New York for our

A pair of "ninety-day
wonders." Ensigns Tom
Buffum and Doug Leach,
December 1942, shortly after
graduation from
Midshipmen's School.

graduation and commissioning. On a cold, blustery 2 December 1942 all the
midshipmen who had completed the program marched to Riverside Church
where, in an impressive ceremony, we were commissioned as ensigns, United
States Naval Reserve, which meant that we now bore authority directly from
the president. After the ceremony was over, the Fifth and Sixth battalions
dispersed, never again to re-assemble. Every new ensign, flashing the shiny gold
stripe on his sleeve and the eagle on his cap, soon would be heading for his new
assignment afloat or ashore, wherever the navy was operating. We were awed
by the responsibility, a little apprehensive, perhaps, about the prospects, but also
prepared and very professional.

   The Buffum and Leach families returned to Rhode Island, anticipating a few
happy days when Tom and I could relax on leave and possibly stir up some
activity with the Y.P.F. gang. I had just five full days at home, days that I
crammed with experiences to remember. A visit to the Brown campus proved
revealing—there were few familiar faces, and the lower campus was being

turned into an obstacle course for the physical conditioning of service-bound students. As for the Y.P.F., it was becoming diminished on both sides of the gender line. I did enjoy a good chat with Mary, who soon would be leaving for basic training as a WAVE—the first of the Y.P.F. girls to enter the service. Somehow it was both gratifying and disheartening to think of all those lovely, very feminine companions departing from the old familiar home scene, dispersing to be stamped into the pattern of the military. But that was the way it had to be, and we all shared the exhilaration of being involved in a tremendous, terribly important endeavor.

On one memorable day Tom and I donned civilian clothing and took Clara and Trudy for a hike in the woods of southern Rhode Island, where we stopped to cook our lunch at a log shelter on the shore of a pond. We were surprised to find so much color and beauty in the woods that late in the year. It was lovely, and very peaceful. Returning to the city, we went dancing at Rhodes-on-the-Pawtuxet, our favorite dance hall, the party having been enlarged to include Ethel and Roger.

When Sunday came the Buffum and Leach families sat together in the sanctuary at Calvary, Tom and I feeling pleasantly conspicuous in our dress blues. That evening the two of us walked down to Y.P.F. with Clara, Ethel, Trudy, and Roger. Later Tom and I even ventured to sing with the choir at a special musical service. It seemed almost like old times, reminding me of what a firm attachment I had to home, family, and friends. But the very next day it all came to an end, like Cinderella's ball, at midnight when I boarded the southbound train for my new assignment in Florida.

By that December the United States had been at war for a year, a period during which our build-up of military strength had been gaining great momentum. During my time in Midshipmen's School, American forces had managed to turn back the Japanese tidal wave in the Solomon Islands, and, on the other side of the world, had begun a successful invasion of North Africa. As a consequence, the discouragement born of disaster at Pearl Harbor was gradually beginning to be replaced with cautious optimism. It seemed that we were advancing along a terribly difficult road—nobody really could say how long a road—to eventual victory.

The Naval Training School in which I taught navigation and ordnance for the next two months occupied all of a former luxury hotel situated on the most beautiful beach I had ever seen. In fact, I was quite enchanted by the whole scene—roaring surf on a sandy beach, sunny blue skies, soft air, graceful palms rustling in the sea breeze, exotic moonlit nights. My letters home were filled with accounts of my activities, which included swimming and sunbathing (in midwinter!). Yet even in such a paradise one could never escape reality, at least not for long. The whole of that beautiful sandy beach was off limits after sunset; anyone venturing there took the risk of being shot.

After the strict regimen of Midshipmen's School, I relished my newly acquired authority as a commissioned officer and especially the privileges that came with rank. There was a certain satisfaction in receiving as well as giving hand salutes, and being addressed as "Sir." Most if not all of the staff of the school, down to the most junior ensign, lived off station and enjoyed a large degree of freedom outside of working hours. I shared a small apartment with two other junior officers. Also, I was having my first experience of classroom teaching, and took satisfaction in discovering that I had some facility in that art.

Mail from family and friends always added to the sunshine of any day. Mother, Dad, and Marilyn were faithful correspondents, as were Clara and Trudy and a number of other good friends. I also managed to keep in touch with Tom. At fairly regular intervals came either *The Odyssey* or a more general mimeographed bulletin from Calvary, bringing news of our service people all around the world, keeping us remotely in touch with each other. Often, "Uncle George" would pen a brief personal message at the bottom. There was word from Aut Aker on the destroyer *Selfridge* in the Pacific; Floyd Brockway at Camp Livingston, Louisiana; Ted Elss at Fort Riley, Kansas; Stewart Hartley in England; Bob Noyes flying out of New York; Mary Noyes with the WAVES in Oklahoma.

A few miles south of Hollywood Beach, at Pier 2 on the Miami waterfront, was located a very different kind of navy school, the Sub Chaser Training Center, familiarly known as SCTC. Its principal function was to train officers and crewmen for the 110-foot wooden-hulled SCs (sub chasers) and 173-foot steel-hulled PCs (patrol craft), both types designed primarily to combat submarines. One of my superior officers at Hollywood Beach arranged for several of us to go down to SCTC for a day's experience at sea. And high time, too, for I had been wearing navy blue for nearly half a year without ever getting beyond sight of land. For this bracing excursion I found myself assigned to one of the PCs, a slender little craft reeking of hot diesel oil. Soon we were under way and heading out along the channel that lay parallel to the causeway road leading to Miami Beach. As I stood on deck with an air of professional nonchalance, I could see the people in cars moving along the nearby highway; they, no doubt, were observing our brisk sortie and wishing us godspeed as we plowed seaward! My euphoric feeling of elation and pride gradually began to evaporate, however, as the little ship emerged from the protected channel and started to breast the slow, incessant swells of the mighty Atlantic. To put it bluntly, my digestive system was giving unmistakable indications of mutiny while my efforts at suppression grew ever more desperate, gulp succeeding gulp.

One of the PC's drills that day was to simulate a breakdown and then be taken in tow by a sister ship. This meant that for eons of eternities we lay adrift, beam on to the endless parade of successive troughs and crests, rolling drunkenly from one side to the other and back again, up and down, up and down. Nearly half the men on board, it seemed, were miserably sick, lying here and there on deck or clinging groggily to the lee rail. Under those conditions it was well nigh impossible for a fresh young ensign in bright new shoulder boards to retain any degree of personal dignity. I retched and heaved repeatedly with the best (or worst) of them, and wondered why in the world I had ever been so mad as to join the sea service.

Fortunately, I did live to learn the inexpressible bliss of eventual return to the sheltered channel, where the water was mercifully placid and our agile little craft at last became stable in her passage. At the conclusion of our cruise I stepped thankfully onto the firm surface of the dock, not forgetting the ritual of saluting the officer of the deck and the colors aft. Soon I even began to consider a good meal within the realm of possibility, and so we dined and discussed our experience. Later, back at my apartment, a hot shower put the finishing touches to my restored sense of physical decency. But the memory of that day lingered. I had acquired a deep respect for the punishing power of the open sea.

After a little over two months of teaching at Hollywood Beach I received orders directing me to my next assignment—the deck officer course at SCTC for training in SCs and PCs! And so I moved down to Miami, where I was given quarters on the eighth deck of another navy-commandeered hotel, the Venetian, with a splendid view down Biscayne Bay. Although again living in relative luxury, I realized that I was advancing very definitely toward active duty at sea in the real war.

SCTC had gained a reputation as a realistic, no-nonsense finishing school where neophytes like myself were instructed and tested by officers experienced in the tough, dangerous fight against the German U-boats. Particular emphasis was given to the character of that struggle by an exhibit deliberately positioned close to where we would board our training vessels—a ship's lifeboat whose sides had been riddled by machine gun bullets. That was our first lesson, reinforced by the commanding officer's famous opening address to each new class. An intent, combative sea dog, he gave a memorable presentation, honed to perfection by much repetition. Laying special emphasis on the bestiality of the Germans, he regaled us with a graphic and lurid account of torpedoed merchant vessels and the machine-gunning of helpless survivors, and then summoned us to get out there and retaliate with a vengeance. Fight! Kill! The speech just hit me wrong. I never doubted the atrocities, but I knew in my heart that although I had accepted the obligation to fight, I was not free to hate. And so I silently demurred. I would have to do my fighting another way.

The class in which I was enrolled began the seven-week course on 8 March

1943. At once we found ourselves caught up in a demanding schedule of activity including eight hours of classes per day combined with occasional brief periods at sea on the SCs and PCs. In this way theory was quickly translated into practice. I became familiar with the measured PING-PING-PING-PING of the sonar searching the water ahead for any solid object below the surface. I was amazed to see how radar could reveal, even in the darkest night, the configuration of a shoreline or the location of another vessel. I saw the 3-inch gun fired, and peered toward the horizon for the sudden leaping of a white fountain. I spent my first night at sea, standing watch on the bridge of an SC and then going below to sleep, fully clothed, in a spare bunk.

On one occasion I was aboard an SC that had been authorized to drop one depth charge as a demonstration. The device consisted of a metal cylinder roughly two feet long and about fourteen inches in diameter packed with explosive powder. This potent antisubmarine weapon was positioned at the stern of our little ship, ready to be dropped overboard. When the captain was certain that the area was clear of other vessels, he gave the order to drop the depth charge. Over it went. Then, as the thing sank, we continued on our way, watching and waiting; I could not help but feel some concern about our seemingly turtle-like progress away from the drop point. Suddenly the little ship was jarred as though by the blow of a gigantic underwater hammer, a simultaneous shock wave flashed across the surface of the water with a thunderous BOOM, and then upward from the depths burst a huge geyser of white water that hung in the air while gradually turning into mist. After some seconds the mist settled back down into the sea, leaving only a smooth circular slick to mark the place. We were duly impressed.

At Pier 2 the numerous SCs often were moored in nests, that is, three or more of them abreast outward from the dock. A group of officer trainees assigned to an outer ship for a day's cruise thus had to cross the decks of several intervening ships in order to board. Always we were careful to observe the proprieties, saluting aft as we left one ship and stepped across to the next. One of my classmates was a large, beefy officer who, despite his flab, managed to wear his uniform with an air of resplendence and invariably saluted with true military eclat. One fine April day our group was proceeding to an outward SC in the manner described when this officer threw a smart salute aft, stepped out for the next ship, and plunged directly down between the two. The splash was enormous. Somebody sang out, "Man overboard!" and we all rushed to the side and looked down. There in the oily water below was our unlucky classmate calmly treading water while his visor cap floated nearby amidst scraps of garbage and other debris. Several seamen, barely concealing their delight, quickly reached down and, by dint of much straining and heaving, managed to

Depth charge exploding in the wake of a destroyer escort. U.S. Navy.

haul the dripping officer up to the deck. All of us, not excluding the victim himself, had a good laugh over this incredible accident, after which we proceeded with the day's business.

When my class began its training at SCTC each of us expected, after completing the seven-week program, to be assigned as one of the officers of an operating SC or PC. During that spring, however, a brand-new type of antisubmarine vessel known as a destroyer escort, considerably larger and more heavily armed than a PC, was beginning to come off the production lines of American shipyards. Eventually nearly four hundred such ships would be built, each one requiring a specialist in antisubmarine warfare to serve as the captain's adviser whenever an enemy submarine was encountered. Accordingly, some of the trainees at SCTC, I among them, were selected for further advanced training, first at Miami and then, for five weeks, at the Fleet Sound (Sonar) School, Key West, a program that would qualify each of us to serve as ASW officer on a destroyer escort. So it was that on 2 May I traveled by bus to the southernmost navy base in the continental United States.

Key West was my first real operating navy base. Located on one of the outermost of the Florida keys a hundred miles north of Cuba, it was crammed between the azure sea and the old town, where it lay broiling in the tropical sun. Although fairly small as naval bases go, Key West included a docking area sheltered by a long breakwater, repair and storage buildings, training facilities, barracks, mess halls, ball fields, a chapel, a library, a brig, and a contingent of marine guards. It served a small, miscellaneous fleet consisting mostly of training craft—an old four-piper destroyer, World War I "eagle boats," PCs and SCs, a few ancient submarines. My group of officer trainees was housed in a barracks.

Soon after settling in I received from Dad a letter in which, with words and sketches, he advanced several original suggestions for overcoming the U-boat menace. One of these, I remember, involved a special antisubmarine torpedo to be launched from our ships. This torpedo, as he graphically indicated, would have on its nose a large, powerful magnet so that, when launched in the general direction of an enemy submarine, it would be drawn toward the metal hull, thereby chasing the submarine relentlessly all the way to Berlin, as Dad put it. I thought it unnecessary to share this interesting scheme with the commanding officer of the Fleet Sound School, but was thankful for Dad's ability to see the funny side of a grim situation.

Even the official navy censor had a "censor" humor. In a letter to one of the girls back home I drew a most unflattering cartoon of that functionary, at the same time warning my fair friend that in consequence she had only a fifty-fifty chance of receiving the letter. She did receive it. Right beside my cartoon the censor had stamped his official circular mark of approval, and in the place where he normally would insert his initials had written simply "Hmm."

At Key West, in brilliant sunshine and sometimes oppressive heat, we concentrated heavily on the sonar technique employed in seeking and attacking enemy submarines. Operating what was called a "sonar stack" located in a special compartment near the bridge of an antisubmarine vessel, a sonarman was able to send out a sound wave from an electronic device just below the keel, and by turning a small wheel on the stack could direct that emission along any chosen bearing. The sound emitted was heard at the sonar stack as a distinct "PING" repeated automatically about every four seconds. Whenever such a PING struck a solid object beneath the surface of the sea within a range of about 3,000 yards, an audible echo (heard at the stack as a sort of "Bung") returned.

Now let's assume that we are at sea searching for U-boats, and the sonarman has been ordered to search continuously through an arc of 180 degrees extending from the port beam of our ship across the bow to the starboard beam. He directs the first ping out on the port beam, then immediately trains the mechanism 5 degrees toward the bow, and listens for an echo. Hearing none, as soon as the next ping goes out, he trains forward another 5 degrees and again listens. (This technique was reduced to the verbal formula: *Ping, train, listen*). Advancing thus in 5-degree steps, the sonarman soon is sending his signal directly forward. Still hearing no echo, he rapidly swings his mechanism to the starboard beam, and advancing in 5-degree steps as before, completes the 180-degree search to the bow. He follows this procedure continuously until a new order is given, or until relieved by the sonarman of the succeeding watch, which means that in the sonar compartment about all one hears, hour after hour, is PING-PING-PING-PING-PING. Thus the common nickname for sonarmen—"ping jockeys." Other sailors sometimes claimed that the sonarmen were "ping happy."

As soon as a solid echo (Bung) is heard, the sonarman notifies the officer of the deck, announcing the object's bearing, and immediately starts concentrating his pinging in that direction so as not to lose contact. At the same time, the officer has the helmsman turn the ship directly toward the object. Quickly the echo is evaluated, for sometimes an echo may come from a whale or even a school of fish. If it is sufficiently solid to suggest a submarine, our ship begins its attack.

By now another instrument in the sonar compartment, the range recorder, has been switched on, showing each echo as a short trace on a steadily moving roll of paper. The bearing and range of the target are constantly being called out, while the range recorder also reveals the rate at which the range is closing. By listening to the "doppler effect" (difference in pitch between the PING and the Bung) the officer may also be able to tell whether the submarine is advancing toward our ship or retreating from it. In short, he integrates all of the information flowing from the sonar compartment in order to form an impression of the submarine's course and speed, while constantly keeping our ship aimed directly at the target. As the range inevitably closes (no World War II submarine, when submerged, could outrun an antisubmarine vessel), the bungs follow closer and closer upon the PINGs, creating a sense of increasing, intensifying action building toward a climax: PING————Bung; PING————Bung; PING——— Bung; PING—Bung; PING–Bung. As soon as the sonarman calls out "Range— seven double-oh" (700 yards), the officer brings the ship to a new course so that it will pass *ahead* of the moving target. The reason for this is the time required for the depth charges to sink, for if they were to be dropped from directly above the submarine, the latter would pass well clear before they could reach their depth and explode. With the attacking ship applying a lead angle from 700 yards in, if all has been calculated correctly the submarine will advance directly into the pattern of sinking depth charges, and will be in their midst when they explode.

As the range gets down to about 300 yards the PINGs and the Bungs almost merge, and then, at a range of something less than 200 yards, we lose contact altogether. The range recorder indicates the optimum instant to begin dropping the pattern, the order is given, and off the rack the depth charges roll, one after the other at set intervals. Whether or not the attack is successful depends on many factors, including the skill of the antisubmarine officer, the skill of the submarine commander, the actual depth of the submarine at drop time, and pure luck.

One of the great differences between our training at Miami and at Key West was that now we began exercising at sea with "tame" subs, that is, American submarines based at Key West. This enabled us to become thoroughly familiar with actual echoes from a real submarine, and to conduct realistic practice attacks. A tame sub, running submerged as a target, usually towed a buoy on the surface to help ship commanders keep track of its location. During practice attacks or "runs" the officer trainee was supposed to be stationed where he could receive and react to the constant flow of information from the sonar compartment, but not see the submarine's buoy bobbing along through the water ahead. I tell you this so that you will understand the meaning of a little verse that went the rounds among us, sung to the tune of "School Days":

> Sound School, Sound School, dear old hang around school.
> Pinging and training and listening too—
> Pick up the sound of the submarine's screw.
> We keep our marks from being low
> By watching the buoy as we go.
> We ping off the girls with "No echo!"
> When we were in good old Key West.

In completing an attack on a tame sub, our ship would drop not depth charges but a dye marker staining the water at the drop point. At the moment of drop the sonarman would send a special signal down to the submarine, which in turn would release a bubble or "slug" of air. The slug, rising to the surface, would reveal the accuracy of the drop. Sometimes we did fairly well, even without sneaking a look at the buoy. But trying to keep one's mind focused on the constant flow of information from the sonar stack and the range recorder, and quickly calculating the correct response, all the while fighting down the persistent nausea of motion sickness, could be quite a challenge. On more than one occasion I looked forward most earnestly to the moment in the afternoon when the officer in charge would terminate the day's exercises and order the submarine to surface. Soon after that order was transmitted by sonar, the black conning tower of the submarine would break the surface, cascading white water, and our undersea friend would join us for the run back to Key West.

Once I volunteered to spend a day aboard a tame sub, so that I might have a better understanding of the submariner's ways in the contest between us. After proceeding out to sea with our surface escorts, we submerged and remained below the surface for more than six hours while the antisubmarine vessels carried out their practice attacks. How very different everything is down there. With considerable interest I listen to water drip, drip, dripping somewhere within the ancient hull, but none of the crew shows any degree of concern. Next we hear the sound of distant pinging from an approaching antisubmarine vessel, coming closer and closer, propellers steadily throbbing. Her sonar searches systematically, relentlessly—and suddenly finds us. Now the attack begins. The pinging continues, lapping up our echoes, while the ship bores in. The sound of her engines and propellers steadily mounts to a heavy rumble and then, as she passes overhead, a menacing roar. Thank goodness there will be no actual depth charges, only a score on the record of some ASW trainee! I never ceased to be impressed with the steely courage of all men who served in submarines.

At the conclusion of our course at Key West I emerged, unaccountably, at the head of my class. Happily I rode the bus back up to Miami, where I settled into assigned quarters to await further orders. My fond hope was to be sent to a destroyer escort under construction somewhere in New England, an assignment that would give me some opportunity to visit with family and friends at home before finally shipping out. Each day I stopped in at SCTC to inquire if my orders had arrived, and each time came away no wiser. At last, on 9 June, the news came. I was to be antisubmarine warfare officer of the U.S.S. *Elden* (DE 264), a ship under construction at the Charlestown Navy Yard, Boston. It was exactly what I wanted.

Arrangements soon were made for an introductory meeting of those of the

Elden's officers then in Miami. About half a dozen of us met with our new captain, the man who would hold all our lives in his hand, Lt. Comdr. George F. Adams. Tall and wiry, taut and very businesslike, he appeared to be in his late forties or early fifties. I noted a pair of piercing eyes, a prominent and sharply chiseled nose under which was displayed a nicely clipped mustache, a firm mouth and jaw—obviously the features of a no-nonsense commander. In a brief, informal speech Captain Adams outlined his policies and told us exactly what he expected—a clean ship, a happy ship, a fighting ship. That sounded good. As for my other new shipmates, I liked what I saw and heard. We would become a team.

My orders actually directed me to report to the Naval Operating Base at Norfolk, Virginia, where most of the *Elden*'s crew would be assembled, but allowed me a few extra days beforehand when I could be at home. So, at long last, I boarded a train and began rolling north. It was a long ride in a coach, but I enjoyed it all. Mother and Dad met me at the Union Station in Providence for a happy reunion; it was great to be home again. Marilyn, whose husband Bill Schmid was serving in the Coast Guard, now had a baby daughter to display, and I was delighted to make the acquaintance of my first niece. Mother, of course, regaled me with my favorite food.

During those four wonderful days at home I tried hard to recapture at least a slight taste of former times, an effort that was aided by a happy coincidence. Tom, like myself now headed for imminent sea duty, also was home on leave, as was Yeoman Mary Noyes. So there was tennis (ensign against yeoman), and a sailing party, and a session of party games. Dad proudly took Tom and me to have lunch with some of his friends in downtown Providence. Tom and I also stopped in for a weekday visit at Calvary, where we enjoyed a chat with our good pastor, Earl Hollier Tomlin, and his secretary, Trudy Kraus. On my last day of freedom I went sailing and swimming at Gaspee Point with a group that included Clara and Ethel, Roger and Tom. But when evening came, I was at home with family. Soon it was time to pick up my suitcase and depart; my train for New York pulled out of Providence about midnight. Ahead lay my future on board the *Elden,* a whole new adventure whose outcome nobody could foretell.

2

SHAKEDOWN

On 3 July 1943 I arrived at the huge Naval Operating Base at Norfolk, gaining my first impression of a major naval facility complete with docks, warehouses, repair shops, rows and rows of wooden barracks, mess halls, a huge drill field, areas for recreation, and an officers' club. Everything seemed highly organized and busy. I was duly impressed, but had little time to reflect on this new world, for the *Elden*'s men were being assembled here, and I immediately became a part of that process.

Captain Adams, together with a few key officers and petty officers, was already in Boston overseeing the final preparations at the shipyard where the *Elden* was being readied for commissioning. At Norfolk the responsibility of the other officers, headed by the executive officer or second-in-command, Lt. Frederick C. Hartman, was to receive the enlisted personnel and get them organized for sea duty. Fred Hartman proved to be an experienced, highly competent officer, generally relaxed and always likable. I felt comfortable working under his direction, and buckled down with a will. At the same time, I was making the acquaintance of all the other *Elden* officers then at Norfolk, with whom I soon would be sharing very close quarters, and we were becoming friends.

The greater part of the crew, having been assembled at Norfolk from various ships and training stations, was turned over to us in a body and duly installed in a pair of wooden barracks. Many of these young men were from the South, speaking with a soothing drawl that somehow seemed to spring more from the soil than the sea. Actually, though, the *Elden*'s crew hailed from nearly all parts of the United States, and friendly banter between "Yankees" and "Rebels" soon became a familiar part of their life together, lending a particular spice to the necessarily close teamwork in which they were becoming engaged.

One of the major tasks for the officers was to draw up what is known as a "Watch, Quarter, and Station Bill," assigning to each member of the crew his posts in a variety of circumstances, including routine watches under way, emergency (General Quarters), and enemy action (Battle Stations). On the *Elden,* General Quarters and Battle Stations were virtually identical, so the two terms will be used interchangeably here. The crew also was divided according to training into firemen (engineers), the deck gang, and various specialized groups such as the cooks and bakers, signalmen, quartermasters, radiomen, radarmen, and sonarmen. Several trained sonarmen had been assigned to the *Elden,* but I needed more actual operators to make up three rotating watches, any one of which had to be able to operate the sonar equipment effectively during a sudden first attack while the ship was going to Battle Stations. Knowing the importance in sonar work of a good ear for sound, especially pitch, I chose from among the seamen a few who claimed to have musical ability, and began training them in the fundamentals of "Ping, train, listen." Soon they were able to take their places with our regular "ping jockeys," filling out the three watches.

During the last week of July our preparations at Norfolk were completed. On the afternoon of Saturday, 31 July, under a blistering sun, the *Elden*'s officers and men underwent a formal inspection, after which we headed for Boston by train to join our ship. On 2 August I reported in at the Charlestown Navy Yard directly across the river from the office building in which I had downed the bananas and water nineteen months earlier. Naturally, I was eager to gain my first view of the brand-new ship in which I was to serve. Named in honor of Ralph Waldo Elden, executive officer of a destroyer lost in the Battle of Midway the previous year, she was one of a number of *Evarts* class short-hull destroyer escorts being turned out by the Navy Yard at a rate of one per week, or better. The *Elden* had been constructed from the keel up in a little over five months, the last to be completed of a group of six DEs comprising CortDiv (Escort Division) 16: *William C. Miller* (DE 259), *Cabana* (DE 260), *Dionne* (DE 261), *Canfield* (DE 262), *Deede* (DE 263), *Elden* (DE 264).

Making my way past the old weathered brick and cut-stone buildings, the newer fabrication sheds, and the tall traveling cranes, I soon found the *Elden* moored to a dock, awaiting the official ceremony that would put her in commission. As I approached at dock level through all the bustle of yard workmen and navy personnel, I noticed first the looming gray superstructure, mast, and stack. Then, advancing to the dock's edge, I could take in also the long, lean hull from sharp bow to rounded stern.

She wears the usual coat of navy gray, shiny new, with three small white numerals at the bow—264. Displacing slightly more than 1,300 tons when fully loaded, she is 289 feet long overall, with a beam of 35 feet, in other words, not quite as long as a football field and only five feet wider than the end zone. Her main or weather deck is flush, that is, running unbroken all the way from the 20-foot-high bow to the 10-foot-high stern. Piercing either bow is a hawsepipe bearing a large, double-fluked anchor. The bridge superstructure, containing four deck levels including the flying bridge at the very top, rises 42 feet above the waterline. Amidships are three additional sections of superstructure, each only one deck level high, containing the galley (kitchen), workshops and storage compartments, and access hatches to the crew's quarters below. Just abaft the bridge superstructure stands the tall, slightly rakish mast, bearing near its peak the antennas for the ship's two principal types of radar—SA (sky search) and SL (surface search). The single low stack is amidships. Watertight integrity being a vital consideration, there are no ports (round windows) anywhere in the hull or even in the main deck level of the superstructure. Beautifully proportioned, this trim fighting ship gives an overall impression of purposeful grace. She seems in perfect repose at the dock and yet, like all her kind, reveals only too clearly the fact that her mood of tranquillity is feigned, as though only her mooring lines prevent her from surging forward, cutting the water with her sharp prow.

This fighting machine is to become the home—one might almost say the world—of the more than two hundred navy personnel assigned to manage and fight her. In wartime, once a navy man is ordered to a ship and has reported aboard for duty he becomes, in a sense, *attached* with an invisible chain of obligation under authority. Thereafter he can depart from his steel world only occasionally for temporary tasks elsewhere, or rare liberty ashore. Sailormen live on board day and night, week after week—standing watches in rotation, eating on schedule in crowded messing compartments, working at various assigned tasks, standing alert at Battle Stations, sleeping in narrow bunks one above another in dimly lit belowdecks quarters. At times of occasional leisure they drink strong coffee, chat, read—or simply stand at the rail, gazing out across the surface of the ever-changing, seemingly boundless deep. Lurking in every mind is the grim thought that the ship can very quickly become for all on board a tomb. But enough of reverie.

As I walk slowly along the dock I gain a good first view of the *Elden*'s potential punch. She carries thirteen mounted guns, all dual purpose, that is, effective against both surface and air targets. Forward are two 3-inch guns, the first of which is mounted on the main deck and the second on the superstructure deck abaft and above the first. A third 3-inch gun is mounted aft on the superstructure deck overlooking the fantail. Each is partially surrounded with a solid fencelike barrier nearly four feet high, within whose sheltering perimeter are located the ready-ammunition lockers. About thirty feet forward of the after 3-inch gun, and mounted at a level somewhat above it for a clear field of fire, is a quadruple-mount (four-barreled) 1.1-inch rapid-firing gun. The remaining nine guns are single-mount 20-millimeter Oerlikon machine guns, easily identifiable by the pair of curved shoulder braces into which the gunner is strapped and also the rectangular steel plates mounted nearly vertically on either side of the long, slender barrel. Two of these highly effective guns are located forward on the superstructure deck a few feet abaft the second 3-inch gun. A third is mounted on the deck above just forward of the wheelhouse. The remaining six are ranged atop the superstructure amidships, three on each side.

As for weapons to be employed against submerged submarines, in that category too the *Elden* is well equipped. Located at the very stern, on the fantail, are two long sloping racks for depth charges. When the safety bar at the after end of the rack is removed, the charges can be dropped one after the other at spaced intervals. In addition, there are four K-guns on each side of the main deck aft. Each of these is able to hurl a depth charge forty yards outwards from the side of the ship, thus creating a broad pattern in which to trap a submarine. Finally, just aft of the Number One 3-inch gun forward is a heavy rectangular mount known as a Hedgehog because of its bristling appearance when loaded with twenty-four antisubmarine missiles, each weighing thirty-two pounds. All twenty-four are thrown in a single simultaneous volley 200 yards ahead of the bow, to fall in an oval-shaped pattern approximately 120 feet by 140 feet. This weapon has a considerable advantage over depth charges in that the pattern is delivered before the sonar loses contact with the target. Also, unlike depth charges, the Hedgehog projectiles are not set to explode at a predetermined depth; rather, they explode on contact with any solid object. Thus a well-directed pattern may destroy a submarine even if the target's actual depth has been misjudged.

Now I go aboard, striding up the gangplank to the main deck. Moving forward along the port side, I walk beneath the 26-foot motor whaleboat, slung on davits, and pass by the port-side watertight door leading into the bridge superstructure. Continuing forward, I walk under a life raft stowed on an overhead rack, pass by the Hedgehog and the Number One 3-inch gun, and arrive on the forecastle. Here I note the pair of anchor chains extending forward

Forward 3-inch guns of destroyer escort moored at SCTC, Miami, in March 1943. In the background, under the palms, may be seen the bullet-riddled lifeboat, a reminder to all sailors. U.S. Navy.

along the deck to the port and starboard hawsepipes, and the engine-driven capstan by which either anchor may be raised. When I stand at the very stem of the ship and look aft, the *Elden* appears slim indeed and, with the high bridge superstructure, even a little topheavy.

Next I walk aft along the starboard side, passing under another quick-release life raft. The steel deck itself, I notice, is overlaid with spaced rectangles of non-skid material for sure footing in wet weather. At each topside battle station is a metal rack holding a supply of gray steel helmets stacked one on top of the other, ready to be grabbed as needed. Nearby is a watertight metal box containing a sound-powered set of earphones and mouthpiece. Such headsets at all battle stations make possible a quick flow of verbal communication between the battle stations and the captain's "talkers" on the flying bridge. Arriving on the fantail, I notice at the very stern, between the pair of depth charge racks, a set of smoke generators that will enable the *Elden* to lay a concealing barrier of thick smoke between a convoy and an enemy marauder.

Below the main deck amidships are the engine spaces, crammed with machinery and accessible only through manholes. A climb down a vertical ladder quickly brings me into a mysterious inferno—a place of motors, shafts, pipes, valves, gauges—the domain of the ship's engineering officers, motor machinist's mates, and firemen. The General Motors diesel-electric engines, turning twin screws, are able to drive the *Elden* forward through the water at a flank (top) speed of about 21 knots. Normal cruising speed, however, is 15 knots or the equivalent of about 17 miles per hour on land. Awed but feeling very much out of my element, I quickly climb back topside and drink in the harbor air.

But then it's below again, this time to visit the crew's berthing compartments still farther aft. Descending a steep ladder located just inside the after deckhouse, I immediately detect the pervasive odor of fresh paint. All compartments are immaculate and completely ready for occupancy. There is a compact but well-stocked sick bay in charge of a chief pharmacist's mate (the ship carries no doctor); a laundry about eight by fifteen feet in size with equipment for washing, drying, and steam-pressing the uniforms of all hands aboard; and several sizable sleeping compartments. In the latter the numerous hinged bunks, secured up out of the way when not in use, are arranged in tiers of three. On the steel deck directly below each set of bunks are three low, flat-topped, built-in lockers for clothing and other personal possessions. These also serve as seats. Aft of the crew's quarters, at the stern, is the after steering compartment, with its own manhole giving access to the open fantail. In case of a breakdown in the regular steering mechanism, the ship can be kept on course by the man stationed here. A visit to one of the crew's heads (washrooms) in the deckhouse topside reveals a compact arrangement of showers, wash basins, and—precisely implaced along the length of a metal trough through which sea water is run—a very unprivate row of seats.

Walking forward along the main deck, I discover the galley. Its dimensions are only about twelve by fourteen feet, but within that limited space are ranges and ovens, sinks, and a workshelf adequate for preparing three square meals a day for some two hundred hungry men. Indeed, every facility built into the *Elden* is amazingly compact and designed for efficiency.

Again proceeding forward, I enter the bridge superstructure, stepping over the coaming against which closes the heavy watertight door. Just inside is an open hatch with a steep ladder leading down to the crew's messing compartment. There most of the space is filled with a serving counter, long narrow tables and benches arranged in parallel rows, and, off to one side, a separate area with equipment for washing the compartmented, stainless-steel trays from which the men eat. Forward of the messing compartment, on the port side, is an exclusive berthing and messing compartment for the *Elden*'s small complement of chief petty officers—the experienced, knowledgeable, and respected "chiefs."

Now I'm ready to explore the four levels of the bridge superstructure, where I myself am to spend most of my time while aboard. On the main-deck level directly above the crew's messing compartment is "officers' country" consisting of a tiny pantry, the wardroom, five small staterooms, and a head. Here, as in all spaces belowdecks, the lighting is artificial and the ventilation by forced air. First I come to the tiny pantry containing an electric refrigerator and facilities for serving meals to a dozen officers. Immediately forward of the pantry and connected with it by a pass-through is the athwartships wardroom, an eleven-by-sixteen-foot rectangular compartment, where the officers work and dine. Entering this compartment, the first thing I notice is the rectangular table covered with a green baize cloth and surrounded by chairs for about ten diners, the whole occupying most of the center space. Just inside the door on the starboard side stands a four-foot-tall storage cabinet on whose flat top I see a ready silex of strong black coffee together with a supply of cups and saucers. Along the remaining length of the starboard bulkhead is a built-in padded divan. The port bulkhead opposite is broken by a curtained door giving access to a two-bunk stateroom. Firmly secured to this bulkhead stands a grilled metal bookcase containing our little library. The other four staterooms are situated two on each side of the narrow central passageway leading forward from the wardroom. Here, too, a curtain of flame-resistant material hanging across each open doorway provides a small degree of privacy for the occupants. Continuing forward along the short passageway, I find on the port side the officers' head, equipped with shower stall and single toilet. Convenient. In rough weather it will be only a short, direct dash from the dining table to the head. Beyond, a turn to starboard leads to a watertight door giving access to the open deck just below the Number Two 3-inch gun. Officers' country appears to be altogether a snug, tight little world completely sealed off from daylight, fresh breezes—and the salty wash of boisterous seas.

I enter one of the two-man staterooms on the starboard side, a compartment roughly nine feet square. The outer bulkhead is completely insulated with a light-green sheathing carefully fitted to provide unbroken coverage. An air duct and heavily insulated cables run along the overhead, and forced air is constantly introduced with a steady rushing sound that soon will become so familiar as to go unnoticed. A pair of bunks extend along the outer bulkhead fore and aft, each being neatly made up and covered with a regulation blue cotton spread. The lower bunk is a retangular metal box attached to the steel deck; the upper is hinged at the bulkhead, its outer edge suspended by a pair of chains near the head and foot. Also provided are a built-in desk, lockers for clothing, and a small wash basin below a mirrored cabinet. Simple luxury.

I resume my exploration of the bridge superstructure by stepping from the wardroom to the after passageway just outside the pantry. From there a steep interior ladder leads to the deck above, where I find the captain's cabin on the port side and the ship's office on the starboard. The latter is just large enough for two or three yeomen at their typewriters.

Climbing again, I arrive at the level of the navigating bridge. Here I step outside and make a complete circuit. Directly forward is one of the 20-millimeter guns overlooking the two forward 3-inch guns. On both the port and starboard rails are mounted a 24-inch searchlight and also a blinker light for transmitting messages in Morse code. Aft are the port and starboard flag lockers, each containing a full set of signal flags ready to be snapped onto the signal halyards and run up to the yard. Inside the superstructure at this level are three vitally important compartments, in addition to a very small "sea cabin" where the captain may snooze when he finds it necessary to remain close to the bridge. The forwardmost compartment is the wheelhouse, with a row of glass ports at eye level providing a view forward over the bow. Here I note the wheel, about twenty-four inches in diameter, by which the ship is steered. Within easy reach is the engine-order telegraph. Directly aft of the wheelhouse and connected with it by a doorway is the combined chartroom and radar compartment, where careful attention will be paid to the ship's position and the location of any other vessels or aircraft in the vicinity. Soon this interior compartment will become known as the Combat Information Center (CIC). Finally, the third compartment aft is the radio shack. Here the radiomen on watch, wearing earphones and sitting at typewriters, will handle all incoming and outgoing

OFFICIAL PHOTOGRAPH
NOT TO BE RELEASED
FOR PUBLICATION
NAVY YARD MARE ISLAND, CALIF.

RESTRICTED

Evarts class destroyer escort, showing superstructure and flying bridge, with 3-inch guns forward and 20-millimeter guns amidships. U.S. Navy.

radio messages, whether in plain English or cipher. Both here and in the radar compartment I am struck by the odor of newness—not only of fresh paint but also the dry, pungent aroma of brand-new electrical equipment. Everything is new, assembled here from hundreds of manufacturing plants across the nation, and all ready to be tried out. Innumerable switches wait to be thrown, buttons to be pressed, wheels to be turned. And we twelve officers, together with our chiefs and petty officers, are in charge of—and responsible for—all of it. Furthermore, as we well know, our lives will depend upon our skill in using this equipment.

My final climb is to the well-named flying bridge, where the ship will be conned at sea, either by the captain himself or by his direct representative, the officer whose turn it is to be on watch as OOD, Officer of the Deck. Emerging at the top of the interior ladder, I find myself now in an area about sixteen feet square, enclosed on all sides but completely open to the sky, with unobstructed views in all directions, for I am above the top of the stack. On either side of this flying bridge are lookout stations where men equipped with binoculars will constantly search their assigned sectors of sea and sky. Directly forward is a flat-roofed enclosed compartment entered by a sliding door. Here the several teams of sonarmen will spend their successive watches, operating the sonar stack and listening intently to the monotonous PING-PING-PING-PING of their ever-questing gear.

The OOD and his Junior Officer of the Deck (JOOD) normally will stand on the raised platform in the center of the flying bridge just aft of the sonar hut. Mounted on this platform is a binnacle with a gyrocompass and an azimuth circle for taking bearings. Near at hand are two metal speaking tubes, one communicating directly with the helmsman in the wheelhouse below, the other with the chartroom and radar compartment. A rudder indicator on the forward bulkhead reveals the position of the ship's rudder at any moment, while an inclinometer shows the extent of the ship's roll (which may be of no comfort to the observer). Sound-powered phones give direct vocal access to "talkers" at various stations, including the ready guns and the depth charge racks. Another telephone is connected directly with the captain's cabin and the wardroom. Within easy reach, I note, is that ever-important lever which can bring the entire ship to instant life and action by activating the General Alarm, calling all hands to General Quarters with an insistent and persistent BONG-BONG-BONG-BONG-BONG-BONG ringing throughout the ship.

My inspection of the ship is interrupted by the loudspeakers blaring forth an order—"Now hear this! All officers report to the wardroom. All officers report to the wardroom." I hurry back down the series of ladders to find the group already assembling around the table, awaiting the arrival of Captain Adams. There is our executive officer, Lt. Fred Hartman, already familiar from Norfolk days. Four of the other officers, by virtue of rank and experience, will rotate as officer of the deck whenever the ship is under way. The first of these is our gunnery officer, Lt. John T. Rickard, a quiet-spoken lawyer and rancher from California, with some previous experience at sea. Next is our first lieutenant (officer in charge of the deck force), Lt. Russell O. Morrow, a thoughtful, conscientious lawyer from Florida. The third is Lt. (j.g.) Leo Miller, stocky, moon-faced, and somewhat excitable, but above all a man with a strong sense of responsibility. Completing the foursome is tousle-headed, sleepy-eyed Lt. (j.g.) James K. Neill, the ship's communication officer and my division head. Also present, I note, are the two engineering officers responsible for the operation of the ship's engines and other belowdecks machinery, Lt. Paul E. Pontius and Lt. (j.g.) Edward W. Lee. Our complement of officers is completed with four very young and quite inexperienced ensigns. One of these is our supply officer, S. H. Bernstein. Rotating as junior officer of the deck when under way will be two others besides myself—John W. Leggett, a clean-cut, highly intelligent Ivy Leaguer with a carefully cultivated air of nonchalance, and Dexter B. Hill, who will join us subsequently. None of the officers, including the captain, is regular navy; all are naval reserve, brought in from civilian life. Rapid training must count!

As Captain Adams enters the wardroom, we all spring to attention, remaining rigid until he says "At ease, gentlemen" and takes his place at the head of the table. We all find seats and await the captain's remarks. As he talks earnestly about preparations for the *Elden*'s impending commissioning, I mark again the piercing, darting eyes, the hawkish nose, the neatly clipped mustache, the firm jaw, all of which together convey a distinct impression of inner intensity and external authority. This man is determined to perform well, and expects everyone under him to do the same. In Miami he had told us that he wanted a clean ship, a happy ship, a fighting ship. Of this I am now certain—he will command a taut ship.

Altogether there are twelve officers, a fact that raises a mystery. The five wardroom staterooms contain all told only nine bunks, for the first one on the port side forward of the wardroom is a single-berthed room reserved for the executive officer. The captain has his own cabin a deck above. That still leaves two officers without a place to sleep. Where will the unlucky pair bed down after coming off watch? Certainly not on the wardroom divan or, worse yet, the dining table, for a better place has been found. Adjacent to the crew's quarters aft and not far above the rumbling port propeller shaft is located the ship's brig, a tiny compartment with a lockable grilled door and exactly two bunks. This has been proclaimed to be no longer a brig or place of ignominious confinement for delinquents, but rather an officers' stateroom aft! Pairs of junior officers, myself among them, will take turns residing in stern luxury, emerging periodically, of course, to eat meals, stand watches, and perform all other required duties. Thus the *Elden* is a ship without a brig.

Every navy man will understand me when I testify that the *Elden* could not have operated without her enlisted personnel, the roughly two hundred men in blue denims upon whom we all depended so heavily. A few were seasoned veterans; most were relatively inexperienced and innocent of the wide world, a fair cross-section of America's male youth sucked into a war none of them had wanted. They differed from the commissioned officers mainly in lacking the advantages of higher education. Fortunately, we were well furnished with experienced chief petty officers who knew the game forward and backward, with a knack for getting the most out of ship and crew. One of these was Chief Boatswain's Mate Jesse E. Prewett, an old hand with deck gear and lines, winches and davits. Whenever Prewett growled, the deck gang paid attention.

Boss of the engine spaces below was CEM Joseph A. Breau, a master of marine machinery. On the navigating bridge the "exec" would have the expert assistance of Chief Quartermaster's Mate Martin H. Lariscy, who tolerated "Ninety-Day Wonders" like me because he had to, while conveying very subtly his firm opinion that the old navy was the real navy. Upon such as these, and our own best efforts, depended the life of every man aboard.

Each man who served on the *Elden* made his own particular contribution. Lariscy's principal assistant in the wheelhouse and chartroom was Quartermaster James F. Brehm. The man immediately summoned whenever any of the ship's electronic equipment misbehaved was unflappable Radio Technician James A. Hampton, who usually was able to put things right in fairly short order. Our rotating radar watches included a number of young seamen who didn't qualify for specialist ratings until later—J. B. Duke, Harry U. Levie, Richard J. Little, Alan E. Loeffler, and Glady E. Pruitt. The radio shack was under the quietly efficient supervision of Radioman Lester L. Harris, a very able and responsible petty officer, assisted by radiomen Ralph E. Glew, Stanley L. Reynolds, Louis A. Rhodes, and Robert L. Wesner. My rated "ping jockeys" were sonarmen Robert J. Donovan, Frederick J. Hyde, Jr., Edward W. Mihaly, Frank L. Ottaway, and Carl J. Tatum, but I also must mention one of my young trainees on the sonar stack, Seaman Charles W. Wray, who learned well. Leader of the signal gang at the flag hoists was Signalman Martin B. Molinero, quick to pick up with his telescope a distant signal and get the message to the OOD. In the ship's office, adjacent to the captain's stateroom, the efficient keeping of the ship's records and the typing of all official correspondence were managed by yeomen Edward J. Carroll and Eugene J. Gray. There were a number of other key enlisted men whose conscientious work I came to appreciate, among them Pharmacist's Mate Edward I. Stoneham, Storekeeper Nick Medica, and Carpenter's Mate Paul G. Kunze. Other names and faces also drift through my memory, and I just wish that I could meet them once again, someday, somewhere.

On commissioning day—Wednesday, 4 August 1943—the *Elden* lay moored at Pier 8, Charlestown Navy Yard. A set of bleachers had been erected on the dock alongside the ship to accommodate the throng of invited guests, among them Mother, Dad, and my sister, who had come up from Edgewood for the occasion. The ship's company, all in spotless white, was drawn up in formation on the main deck wherever the ranks could be fitted around K-guns and depth charge racks—rigid, expectant, a little proud. At 1635 the captain of the Navy Yard strode up the gangplank and the brief ceremony began. The decisive moment came when Captain Adams read aloud his orders from the navy directing him to assume command of the U.S.S. *Elden*. At that moment he

Commissioning ceremony for U.S.S. *Elden* (DE 264), 4 August 1943. Captain Adams reading his orders; Executive Officer Fred Hartman at left; Mrs. L. K. Elden and her young son behind the microphone; Ensign Leach second from right. U.S. Navy, courtesy of Boston National Historical Park.

acquired enormous authority over every man aboard. Indeed, the commanding officer of a navy ship is, within certain defined limits, virtually a dictator, for the hazards of the sea together with the extraordinary perils of war require that his word be taken as law.

At the precise moment when the *Elden* was placed in commission, the union jack was raised at the stem and the national colors at the stern. Also the first watch was set. Then the assembled guests were invited aboard for refreshments and an opportunity to explore some parts of the ship in which their husbands, sons, and lovers were to confront the enemy at sea. It was a brief, pleasant interlude of relaxation and sociability, a time when every member of the ship's company fortunate enough to have guests aboard could show off his ship and introduce his new shipmates. When it was over, the guests trooped ashore and we turned back to the urgent business at hand.

For the first time in my experience of just under a year I found myself serving not in a navy school or training station but in a seagoing ship to which I belonged and where I bore very definite responsibilities. It felt a little like being called up to the first team. This was emphasized by the issuing of certain items of personal equipment—a gray steel helmet with the letters ASW stenciled in red on the front; a Colt .45-caliber semi-automatic pistol with web belt and cartridge pouch; a sheath knife; an inflatable lifebelt to which could be fastened a whistle and a small electric light to facilitate rescue; a comfortable navy watch jacket. Foul weather gear, including sou'wester, oilskins, and rubber boots, also was at hand, a reminder of what the Atlantic Ocean could be like when aroused.

The next few days at Charlestown were filled with a constant bustle of continuing preparations, a multitude of little problems to be solved, often in consultation with yard personnel. One such supervisor very kindly provided each of the *Elden*'s officers with a personal stainless-steel napkin holder in which were incised the owner's initials and the name of the ship. Thereafter these attractive and practical souvenirs were routinely laid at our places for every meal in the wardroom. I had long since stowed my personal gear in the portside stateroom just off the wardroom, where I slept in the upper bunk above Russ Morrow. That proved to be the beginning of a cherished friendship with a splendid shipmate considerably older and more experienced than I.

Two days after the commissioning the *Elden* received and stowed her allotment of ammunition, some of it being distributed to the ready-ammunition lockers on deck near the guns, the remainder in the magazines below. We also had ample supplies of diesel fuel, fresh water (and the equipment to make more from sea water), and food. The ship was ready to go. Naturally, all of us aboard hoped that the *Elden* would be a lucky ship; none of us could foresee how incredibly lucky she actually would be.

On the morning of 7 August the *Elden* was scheduled for her first brief excursion out of Boston Harbor. A few minutes ahead of time the special sea detail was set, which meant that working parties of seamen under the immediate supervision of the chief boatswain's mate were on deck to handle the mooring lines. Belowdecks the engineers had the engines humming smoothly, causing a slight vibration on all decks. As the last of the mooring lines splashed into the murky water, the union jack at the stem and the national colors at the stern were removed; at the same instant the national ensign was run up the gaff amidships. The *Elden* was under way and about to log the very first of her tens of thousands of miles.

One prolonged blast of the ship's whistle gave warning to all other craft that we were moving away from the dock and out into the channel. Finding the correct heading, we slowly gained speed, slipping smoothly past the wharves of South Boston, past historic Castle Island whose guns dominated this very channel in the seventeenth century. Then, as we passed through the open gate of the barrier protecting Boston Harbor against U-boats, Captain Adams ordered the General Alarm sounded, bringing all hands to General Quarters on the double. My battle station, as ASW officer, was on the flying bridge near the sonar hut, so I was in a position to see or know much of what was going on.

The *Elden*'s first tentative venture into open water was fairly brief, the objective being mainly to test the ship's responses. Speaking very personally, the response in which I was most immediately interested was that relating to the surge of the ocean swell. How would this particular ship behave? In retrospect, I must say that I was neither disappointed nor particularly reassured. Upon our return to the Navy Yard, gangs of workmen descended upon the ship in successive shifts, to make all needed adjustments and repairs. By 12 August the *Elden* was proclaimed complete and ready.

The next day we took her out for structural firing, to see how well she would stand up to the jarring effect of heavy explosions. Naturally, the captain was tense, and his tension inevitably filtered down through the successive OODs to each watchstander on the flying bridge. Those eagle eyes were on everything, demanding top performance. And as the skipper was testing us, so were we assessing his qualities and skills. We launched a pattern of Hedgehog projectiles over the bow, watching them fly off through the air like a volley of arrows, to descend and mark the water with a sudden oval of splatting splashes. We stuffed wads of cotton batting in our ears and began test firing all guns. Every blast from a 3-inch gun jarred the entire ship; the 1.1-inch and the 20s made rapid drumbeats and broken ripples of fast, sharp explosions. Additionally, we tested all the K-guns and the two depth charge racks, expending a number of charges in the process. After putting on such a noisy show, the *Elden* turned her bow back toward the harbor, and by 1730 was moored port side to Pier 9, with the liberty party eagerly contemplating the prospect of a few free hours in Boston town.

Strangely, our first threat of enemy action came not while we were coursing the briny deep off Boston but snugly moored to our pier at Charlestown. It happened at 1841 on 15 August when the ship suddenly was notified of an air raid alert for the Boston area. Two minutes later all hands heard the compulsive sound of the General Alarm. Instantly there began a staccato pounding of many feet racing along decks and up ladders. Reaching battle stations topside, every man buckled his inflatable lifebelt around his waist and clapped a steel helmet on his head. The gun crews readied all guns for action, with ammunition at hand. Belowdecks were other teams on the alert—engineers making all preparations for getting under way, ammunition passers near the magazines, damage control parties ready to douse fires or shore up collapsing bulkheads. At the same time, every other ship in the Navy Yard was making the same preparations, alert for the first sign of approaching Heinkels. After all, if American aircraft could bomb Tokyo, as they had done in April 1942, what was to prevent Hitler from pulling off some equally unexpected stunt? But of course no German aircraft appeared, and we secured from General Quarters at 1922.

The *Elden* again sortied on the afternoon of 17 August, with orders for our first extended mission, an offshore patrol that would serve as a sort of trial on our own—our first overnight run. Emerging from Boston Harbor, we proceeded south to the buoy off the entrance to the Cape Cod Canal, reversed course, and commenced zig-zagging northward toward Cape Ann. After sunset, when the order was given to "darken ship," watertight doors were closed and secured, and no illumination was permitted anywhere on the open decks, not even the glow of a lighted cigarette. Anyone moving from one part of the ship to another along the gently rolling main deck had to feel his way, seeing little but blackness on every hand, and hearing only the monotonous throbbing of the engines, the rumbling of the twin propellers, and the rush of salt water along the ship's side.

This first dark night at sea, feeling heavy responsibility as ASW officer, I slept in my clothes, ready to race up the three ladders to the flying bridge whenever any sonar contact was made. Fortunately, the U-boats were busy elsewhere, and the long night passed quite uneventfully. The next morning we conducted speed runs off Provincetown Harbor, where there was a measured mile. Then, after some gunnery and flag hoist drills during the afternoon, we returned to port feeling quite feisty.

Every new navy ship went through an initiation known as "shakedown," a period of systematic training and testing designed to make sure that the ship and her complement were in all respects ready for full operational duty. On board the *Elden* now were more than two hundred seamen, firemen, electricians, mechanics, gunners, yeomen, signalmen, radiomen, radarmen, sonarmen, radio technicians, storekeepers, pharmacist's mates, cooks, bakers, stewards, carpenters, quartermasters, chief petty officers, and commissioned officers. With shakedown, all would be melded into a team able to operate this one ship, with all its intricate equipment, effectively under combat conditions. Shakedown, in short, would make the *Elden* a full-fledged fighting ship.

At Bermuda, 800 miles off the East Coast, the United States Navy, with the expert cooperation of the Royal Navy, had established a four-week shakedown program, consisting of a series of practical training exercises, for newly commissioned destroyer escorts. Upon successful completion of the program, a DE would be certified as ready to begin her active role with the fleet. So Bermuda was the *Elden*'s first destination, and I had high hopes for another reunion with

Tom Buffum, who now was serving there on the U.S.S. *Partridge,* a fleet tug. Shortly before the *Elden*'s departure from Boston, without revealing where we were bound, I let Mother and Dad know that they should not expect any more home visits by me for at least a month.

The *Elden* was to make the voyage unaccompanied, and this was to be my first experience so far away from land, a real voyage through waters where U-boats might be encountered. On 20 August at exactly 1000 the ship got underway from Charlestown, passing through the gate about a half hour later. That afternoon, while pulling away from the coast, we went to Battle Stations and spent some exciting moments repelling mock air attacks by a squadron of twenty-one friendly aircraft. It gave the pilots good practice and us a sense of combat readiness as we swung and aimed our thirteen guns. Then the planes departed, leaving us to continue on our solitary way, farther and farther out onto the great sullen deep. Well did I recall the moving and somber refrain of the Navy Hymn we had sung so routinely in Divine Service at Midshipmen's School: "Oh hear us when we cry to Thee for those in peril on the sea!"

To the men aboard her a lone ship on the surface of the ocean seems a most conspicuous target, for she is the one object standing out clearly at the very center of a flat, circular, blue-green stage. One looks at the surface of the ocean all around and sees only the ship's long white wake trailing astern toward a distant horizon. Hour after hour, day after day, the ship seems transfixed in that conspicuous position, while at any point within a hundred square miles a cunning periscope may be watching, undetected. Only our speed gave us some advantage, for the *Elden* could run at a good steady 15 knots, or even faster if necessary, but a submerged submarine could make only 8 or 9 at best, and that only for a relatively short period of time. Should such a foe come within range of our sonar we would, of course, proceed immediately to the attack.

At sea the ship's daily routine was based almost entirely upon the sequence of the traditional rotating watches. Some members of the crew who had special responsibilities or performed specialized tasks, such as chief petty officers, pharmacist's mates, cooks and bakers, and yeomen, observed regular working hours during the day, and normally did not stand regular watches. The remainder of the men were divided into three equal groups which regularly rotated through the following sequence of watches:

2000 - 2400 (Midnight)	First or Evening watch
0000 - 0400	Midwatch
0400 - 0800	Morning watch
0800 - 1200 (Noon)	Forenoon watch
1200 - 1600	Afternoon watch

| 1600 - 1800 | First dog watch |
| 1800 - 2000 | Second dog watch |

The latter two might be combined to form a single four-hour watch for several consecutive days, after which the watch could be "dogged" (broken down into its two segments), so that in a regular sequence of watches the same men would not always be standing the fatiguing and unpopular midwatch. Also, a dogged watch made it easier to serve supper to all hands within a reasonable time.

The OOD and his JOOD, both equipped with binoculars, stood on the flying bridge and ran the ship. Also on watch at any given time were four lookouts, a sonar team, a radar team, a helmsman, a quartermaster (who kept a rough record of all significant occurrences), radio and signal teams, crews for the ready guns (which always included one of the forward 3-inch guns, the 1.1-inch gun, and three of the 20s), a depth charge team on the fantail, teams of engineers belowdecks, and a man in the after steering compartment — possibly fifty men all told. The OOD was directly in charge of the ship during his watch, with the heavy responsibility of seeing that all of the captain's standing orders were carried out and the ship's routine properly observed.

As the *Elden* pushed on toward Bermuda, the weather began a rapid and, to me at least, somewhat distressing change for the worse. The rising wind took on a seemingly malicious quality, kicking the surging gray waves higher and higher so that the slender little ship plunged and rolled more and more erratically. Many of us became seasick as never before. When not on watch or other required duty I sought the haven of my upper bunk, there to lie in misery. Russ Morrow in the bunk below was, if possible, even more sick than I. In order to maintain what bodily strength I could, I took to bed with me a slice of dry bread on which to gnaw. Lying on my back, bread on chest, I drifted off to sleep despite the awful gyrations of the ship, waking periodically to resume my sporadic nibbling. Then would arrive the dreaded time when I was required to drag myself up those three swaying ladders to the flying bridge for a seemingly interminable four-hour stint of swooping through the leaden sky with Jack Rickard or Russ Morrow or Leo Miller or Jim Neill.

In rough seas a watch on the flying bridge could be physically exhausting. I constantly shifted weight from one foot to the other, trying to maintain balance on a deck that surged and then fell away, surged and then fell away, frequently shuddering under the impact of a battering comber. Often I had to cling to the binnacle or the railing to avoid being thrown for a loss. Occasionally, when the bow slammed obliquely into a racing wall of water, the alert watchstander quickly ducked down in the lee of the sonar hut to escape the lash of flying spray that was sure to follow. But however deeply the *Elden* buried her nose in gray-green water she always surged clear, recovered, and headed for the next encounter. Someone had thoughtfully lashed an ordinary metal bucket by its handle to the railing of the raised platform, adjacent to where the OOD and JOOD stood. The bucket swung endlessly back and forth, back and forth, following the motion of the ship. From time to time one of the glassy-eyed watchstanders would stagger to that swinging receptacle and bow over it for minutes at a time in apparent obeisance to the god of the sea. Then, having made his sacrifice, he would grope his way groggily back to his place of duty. I was among the most persistent votaries, partly inspired, no doubt, by the example of my fellow sufferers.

When at last the incredibly long watch drew to its close and my relief arrived on the flying bridge, I gratefully stumbled back down the three swaying ladders and climbed into my bunk. Writing home later, however, I said that the voyage had been "pretty nice," marred only by a "gastronomical disturbance." The folks at home knew what I meant, and Dad was so kind as to send me back some folksy advice. "Stand out in the open and face the bow," he wrote, "spread your legs apart and let the wind part your whiskers in the middle." That was all well and good, but I had no whiskers.

At 1115 on 22 August we had the thrill of a landfall, sighting radio towers on Bermuda. Five minutes later Gibbs Hill Light came into view. Taking aboard the pilot who came out to meet us, we threaded our way along the channel while drinking in the picturesque beauty of pastel-colored houses set here and there against the green hillsides. Finally we came to our assigned anchorage in Great Sound among a considerable fleet of British and American naval vessels. Some time later we moored alongside the destroyer tender *Hamul* (AD 20), a large ship equipped to effect repairs and otherwise service destroyers and destroyer escorts. Capain Adams, no doubt pleased with our safe and successful passage from Boston, authorized an hour of swimming from the *Elden*'s side. The water was delightful, and we enjoyed the experience greatly.

The next evening, because of an approaching hurricane, the *Elden* was instructed to monitor our voice radio continuously for further orders. Great Sound itself was becoming very rough as the wind increased in force, causing the water to churn wildly between the two ships. We hoisted the motor whaleboat and made all other preparations for getting under way on fifteen minutes' notice. If there was to be a genuine hurricane, the open ocean was the last place I myself wanted to be, but the plain truth was that a ship actually would be safer at sea than in a harbor where she might snap her lines and be driven aground.

With the weather steadily worsening, on the morning of 24 August the dreaded order came—out to sea! At 0824, with a pilot aboard, the *Elden* got under way and took her place in the dismal line of departing ships. When, near the seaward end of the channel, the pilot climbed over the *Elden*'s side and nimbly jumped down onto the bobbing deck of the pilotboat, I felt a surge of fierce envy such as I had never experienced before. He was returning to a snug, dry, and completely motionless home somewhere on the island, while I—well, I had no choice but to undergo the wrath of Neptune yet another time.

As each vessel ahead of us sortied from the channel and entered the surging waters of the open sea, we could see her mast begin swinging ever more wildly from side to side, and eventually the ship herself would be virtually obliterated by the relentless, driving, gray waves, the spume, and the lowering darkness. We too advanced steadily into it, and felt ourselves lifted and battered by forces of incredible power. From now on, each of the ships was on her own; there was little attempt to maintain any kind of formation, for none was feasible. As soon as practicable, the *Elden* changed course in order to head directly into the racing combers, which was safer than taking them on the beam, and assumed a speed just sufficient to maintain course and headway. For the next twenty-four hours the *Elden* staggered on. The game little ship would climb the sloping side of an advancing comber, thrust forward over the foaming crest, hang there precariously for a long second or two as the wave surged on beneath her, and then drop her bow with breathtaking speed down, down until it plunged directly into the next great wall of water. At that moment the whole ship would shudder, while a sheet of flying spray went slashing up over the bow and past the flying bridge. She bucked like a bronco, slamming and shuddering until it seemed that her back would break. Meals, for those who were interested in such, featured sandwiches and coffee hastily consumed. We dragged ourselves up the three ladders to stand our successive watches, and then clumped back down again to collapse in our bunks. Trying to sleep, we had to hang on to avoid being thrown out onto the surging deck. Awake, we could only lie and listen to the incessant creaking and groaning of the ship in travail, the crashing of loose articles sliding from place to place, the thunderous slam of great waves against the hull. Eventually I would learn the trick of putting a twist in the two chains by which my bunk was suspended, thereby elevating the outer edge.

The open decks glistened with constantly renewed wetness. Men moved along the exposed main deck only when necessary, paying close attention to the ship's motion as solid steel underfoot heaved up and then fell away, grabbing for handholds along the sheltering sides of the superstructure, ducking in whenever a wave broke.

By the afternoon of 25 August the storm had passed, leaving only a vast expanse of slowly heaving ocean in its wake. Once again we sighted Bermuda, entered the channel, and dropped our anchor in Great Sound, a most welcome haven. That very evening, much as though nothing unusual had occurred, we enjoyed a movie on the fantail under the open sky, the enlisted men sitting on the deck or on lockers, the officers on chairs carried aft from the wardroom. It seemed that we had passed the ordeal by hurricane with flying colors, and most of us felt a little more like seasoned salts. It is tempting to suppose that the naval authorities at Bermuda routinely ordered up a hurricane as an initiation for each newly arrived DE.

After that we plunged immediately into the shakedown training program. We spent a number of days working with tame submarines, and a great deal of time at various forms of gunnery. Whenever we engaged in the latter, all hands were called to Battle Stations. Those men in exposed positions topside grabbed their steel helmets and rolled down their shirtsleeves as a precaution against flash burns. In company with other DEs we fired repeatedly at a sleeve target towed far behind a courageous and trusting airplane. Similarly, we pumped dozens of shells at a surface target towed behind an equally courageous tug. We fired by day and we fired by night, in the second instance illuminating the target with our searchlight or with star shells. The latter were made to burst high in the air above the target, illuminating the surface of the ocean with an eerie, greenish-yellow light as they slowly, slowly descended and then burned out.

Loading drill on a 3-inch gun (not *Elden*). U.S. Navy.

Occasionally one of the gun crews would report a hangfire or misfire. Then there would be moments of tension until the breech could be cleared and the offending cartridge extracted and thrown overboard.

Here I should say something further about the characteristics and capabilities of our three types of guns. The 3-inch dual purpose gun employed fixed ammunition, which simply means that the explosive projectile and the brass case containing the propelling charge were pre-fitted together in a single unit approximately twenty-eight inches long, weighing about twenty-four pounds. As this cartridge was driven forward into the barrel of the gun by the heel of the loader's hand, the breech mechanism automatically slid shut. Then the gun captain activated the firing mechanism, causing the gun to discharge with a terrific BLAM that was almost like a blow in the face to anyone standing nearby. Upon firing, the barrel recoiled and the breech mechanism slid open, ejecting the spent case. As the hot case flew out, it was caught by the "hot shellman" (who wore elbow-length asbestos gloves) and flung out of the way. Then the gun was ready for the next cartridge.

A well-trained gun crew of approximately seven, working in perfect coordination, could get off a shot about every five seconds. Maximum surface range was 14,600 yards or a little over seven miles, while maximum altitude when firing nearly straight overhead was more than 29,000 feet (approximately the height of Mount Everest), but always the 3-inch gun was most effective at closer quarters. Exploding in the sea, the shell sent up a sudden column of white water, enabling the gunners to adjust for the next shot. When fired into the air with a timed fuse, the bursting shell left a sudden brownish puff of smoke followed, seconds later, by the thud of the explosion. After a prolonged period of firing, the deck would be littered with spent cases rolling slowly back and forth with the ship's motion. Normally, these cases were picked up, stowed, and later turned in for salvage.

The quadruple-mount 1.1-inch gun aft, also with a crew of about seven, was capable of spitting out 150 explosive rounds per minute, each projectile weighing nearly a pound, to a range of 7,400 yards or an altitude of 19,000 feet. Usually this gun was fired in fairly short but heavy bursts, with the gun crew working fast to feed in fresh clips of cartridges for the four barrels.

Each 20-millimeter Oerlikon had a crew of three. The man who aimed and fired it was strapped into a curved pair of shoulder braces so that he could lean way back in aiming at high targets. A second crewman standing beside the gun was able to adjust the mount for the convenience of the gunner. The third man kept busy supplying the gun with fresh ammunition in pre-packed metal drums. This extremely effective weapon had a maximum surface range of 6,000 yards and a maximum altitude of about 6,000 feet. Firing more than 400 explosive

20-millimeter gun (not *Elden*). U.S. Navy.

rounds per minute, the 20-millimeter was a mainstay against close surface targets and low-flying aircraft. When all the 20s on one side as well as the 1.1-inch were firing simultaneously, the *Elden* seemed to erupt in fire, smoke, and blasting noise, with long lines of tracers stabbing off into the distance.

Each day the radio gang produced a mimeographed news bulletin announcing various occurrences around the world as they were picked up by radio. This was available at every breakfast in the wardroom, keeping us quite up-to-date on the progress of the war effort. It was early in September that we received the heartening news of the successful Allied landing in southern Italy, followed by the surrender of the Italian government—cause for lively commentary around the table, with rejoicing and cautious optimism. Another service contributed by the crew in the radio shack was to regale all hands with recorded music played over the ship's PA system. A sense of wistful longing was reinforced at Bermuda by repeated renditions of a leading song on the hit parade—Johnny Black's "Paper Doll." The tune was catchy, the lyrics appropriately woeful, and we heard them again and again, flung to the damp breezes of Great Sound.

The *Elden* rode out a second gale at sea, this one catching us while our ship and two other DEs, the *Gantner* (DE 60) and the *Douglas L. Howard* (DE 138), were escorting the tug *Choctaw*. Wind and waves mounted menacingly, with heavy rain squalls, as the barometer slumped to 29.32. Again for long hours the *Elden* labored in angry seas, with our men moving cautiously along open, water-drenched decks only when necessary as the watches came and went in dreary succession. Once the storm had spent its fury, we again returned thankfully to the anchorage in Great Sound, rejoining our sister ships and also some ships of the Royal Navy crewed by indomitable Britons who had been battling the U-boats since 1939 and who addressed their personal mail to such places as Belfast, Cardiff, Coventry, Glasgow, Liverpool, and Nether Poppleton.

If the ocean-going tug *Choctaw* was at Bermuda, so was the *Partridge* and so was Tom Buffum. Unfortunately, however, the business of the respective ships made our get-togethers rare indeed. Just as at Midshipmen's School, it seemed strange, unnaturally strange, for two such close friends to be so near and yet actually see so little of each other. Our most memorable day was Sunday, 29 August, when both Tom and I, along with another young officer from the *Partridge,* were able to get ashore for a few hours of recreation. The three of us went into Hamilton, rented bicycles, and spent a delightful day exploring the eastern end of the island. We ate ice cream, swam in luxurious, clear green sea water, visited the aquarium (where we noticed how human some of the fish faces seemed), and explored an underground cavern whose ceiling dripped with stalactites. Having brought with us a packed lunch, we sought liquid refreshment at a rickety old country store set back a short distance from the road. There the elderly black proprietor brought forth from his refrigerator a container of cool, true-flavored ginger ale that made our lunch complete. Later that day, after saying goodbye to Tom and his shipmate, I returned to the *Elden* much refreshed and ready for more sea duty.

Most days and some nights the *Elden* was out at sea conducting drills in one of the designated operating areas, usually in the company of one or more other escorts. We held fire drills, man overboard drills, loss of steering control drills, and depth charge setting drills. Our gun crews were increasing their rate of fire and sharpening their aim; our submarine attack teams were whetting their specialized skills; our damage control parties were improving their effectiveness in dealing with imaginary fires, weakened bulkheads, and gashes in the ship's hull.

On 8 September, while at sea for gunnery exercises, the *Elden* was notified by radio that a plane was down not far from our position. This was no drill. Immediately we headed for the indicated area and commenced searching. After nearly an hour and a half our lookouts sighted the aircraft floating about 5,000 yards ahead, in reasonably good condition after the forced landing. As the ship slowed for a cautious approach, the rescue party hastily prepared to lower the motor whaleboat. The plane's pilot apparently was uninjured and wished to remain where he was until towed, but his radioman had sustained a bad cut over one eye. So the injured man was quickly ferried to the *Elden,* where our chief pharmacist's mate expertly applied the required three stitches. Later the downed aircraft was taken in tow by SC 681, relieving the *Elden* of further responsibility. For us, the event had been a satisfying test of our efficiency in handling an unexpected emergency.

Destroyer escort dropping a full pattern of depth charges. U.S. Navy.

Always of most immediate concern to me as ASW officer was our drilling for actual attacks upon enemy submarines. If the *Elden* was about to drop a pattern of depth charges, the order would pass from the flying bridge to the fantail by sound-powered phone: "Set a 13-charge pattern, *shallow!*" (or medium, or deep, or any of three other settings). After repeating the command to indicate that they had understood it correctly, the men at the depth charge stations would hurry from charge to charge, wrenches in hand, making the prescribed settings. When this had been accomplished they would report to the bridge that the thirteen charges were set and ready.

On 15 September, after first conducting such setting drills, we actually dropped a full 13-charge pattern. At precisely spaced intervals the commands went out: "Roll One!——Roll Two!——Roll Three!——Roll Four!——Roll Five!" As those five charges were being dropped from the stern rack at spaced intervals, the eight K-guns were hurling their charges out to either side, thereby creating a diamond-shaped pattern roughly 200 yards long and 100 yards wide. When all thirteen charges had dropped into the water, our eyes focused on the *Elden's* lengthening wake. After a predictable number of seconds the antici- pated hammer blows began, and the geysers of white water burst from the deep, leaving in turmoil a great patch of the sea astern. That same afternoon, after conducting Hedgehog loading drills, we fired a full spread of twenty-four projectiles forward, watching them drop in their proper oval-shaped pattern. In this case, of course, there were no explosions, just quick splats and then silence. The *Elden* finished up by laying a smoke screen from the generators at the stern.

Two days later, operating with submarine R-7, we tracked our submerged friend by sonar, plowed ahead for the attack, and at the precise moment indicated by the range recorder fired Hedgehog projectiles that were loaded with harmless plaster instead of explosive powder. The sub could tell if she was struck by one or more of them, but would suffer no damage. This realistic exercise marked the conclusion of our at-sea training off Bermuda. All that now remained was a final inspection of the ship by the shakedown staff. We underwent that inspection early in the afternoon of 18 September while lying at anchor in Great Sound. As a result, the *Elden* was marked as ready for full operation with the fleet.

During the month at Bermuda we encountered no U-boats. Apparently they were not interested in bothering with our little games, and so we were able to carry on unmolested. The period of intense training had been a "shakedown" for individuals as well as the ship. I myself was beginning to become somewhat more tolerant of the *Elden's* incessant motion in a generally moderate sea, more accustomed to sleeping in an unsteady upper bunk to the lullaby of rumbling, creaking, and hissing in a vessel under way.

Before suppertime on the day of the final inspection we were on our way back to the States. The *Elden* was teamed up with the U.S.S. *Gantner* (DE 60) as escort for the transport *George Washington* bound for Chesapeake Bay. This was the *Elden*'s first real escort duty, and we took the responsibility very seriously indeed, maintaining a diligent patrol while constantly echo ranging. On this fairly short voyage, however, we discovered no prowling U-boats. Arriving at the sea buoy off the capes of the Chesapeake with some sense of relief, we watched the *George Washington* plow on towards the shelter of the Bay, while her former escorts turned their sharp prows northward for Boston.

During the forenoon watch on 21 September we found ourselves rounding the sandy arm of Cape Cod, happily "rolling home." At 1713 the *Elden* moored starboard side to the *Gantner*'s port side at Pier 4W, Charlestown Navy Yard. Exactly twenty-two minutes later the liberty party, in dress blues, was on its way to the streets of Boston. Some headed for the restaurants and theaters or the U.S.O. club, others for the bars and honky-tonks. As for me, I had the watch until 2000, and stayed aboard.

3
TO THE PACIFIC FLEET

The six DEs of CortDiv 16 had been assigned to the Pacific Fleet, which meant that before long our principal foe would be not Hitler's experienced and very aggressive U-boats but the Imperial Japanese Navy with its heavy fleet units and, in particular, its numerous I class and RO class submarines. By this time, however, the first critical turning point in the great Pacific War had been successfully passed. The awesome Japanese advance of 1942 had been stopped well short of Australia and New Zealand. Subsequently, the enemy had been thrown out of Guadalcanal by American marines and soldiers, and forced to evacuate the Aleutians by the U.S. Army. Nevertheless, the Imperial Japanese Navy remained a powerful force at sea, while tenacious Japanese garrisons held concentric perimeters of well-fortified island bases embracing much of the vast South and Central Pacific. The sea route to Japan itself, along which our Pacific Fleet was to advance, would be long, difficult, and extremely dangerous.

From 21 September until 2 October 1943 the *Elden* remained at Boston, taking on ammunition, fuel, and stores. Whenever we were to begin receiving a fresh supply of ammunition or fuel an imperative announcement blared from the PA system across all decks and through all compartments: "Now hear this! The smoking lamp is *out* throughout the ship. The smoking lamp is *out* throughout the ship." Thereafter no smoking was permitted anywhere on board until the loading had been completed and the smoking lamp again was "lit."

During the *Elden*'s stay at Boston most of our men enjoyed periodic liberty; those whose homes were in the Northeast naturally took maximum advantage of this opportunity for a last visit with family and friends. Some, indeed, found liberty so irresistible that they overstayed their allotted time. They were disciplined, after their eventual return, at a hearing known as "Captain's Mast," the sentence generally involving restriction to the ship for a stated number of days. Fair enough. I myself was able to get down to Providence on several occasions. Mother and Dad correctly perceived that the shakedown experience had "taken something out of me," but were buoyed (or so I hoped) by my apparent air of confidence. Also, of course, I was glad to give the senior Buffums a good report on Tom. When at last the time came for me to make my final departure, my loving and loyal family, plus ever-buoyant Clara, saw me to the Union Station. There had been many previous departures—this, at last, was the real thing. So I boarded the late evening train for Boston and the *Elden,* with a last wave toward the little party left behind, all of us realizing that I probably would not see them again for many long months, perhaps years—possibly never. That parting wasn't easy.

At 0745 on 2 October the *Elden* finally got under way for a voyage that would take us across 9,000 miles of ocean, with stops at Norfolk, the Panama Canal, San Pedro, and San Francisco, before reaching Pearl Harbor in the Hawaiian Islands. As we steamed slowly past the wharves of South Boston, we found a dense fog blanketing the outer harbor, which forced us to anchor in President Roads for about an hour until improved visibility enabled us to pass through the gate with safety. After that, the first leg of our long voyage went well. En route we held man overboard drill, and exercised the boarding and salvage party as well as the fire and rescue parties, in our ceaseless effort to be well prepared for any emergency.

By this time, of course, I had become fully acquainted with all my fellow officers. Almost certainly, in the aggregate, we were typical of corresponding groups in virtually all of the navy's destroyer escorts. Hailing from all sections of the country, we were ex-students and young professionals straight out of civilian life. Some were married, some single. None had a career commitment to the navy, but all were in for the duration of the war. Whatever our individual background, preparation, type and level of training, we knew that we were fully involved in a deadly contest whose outcome would shape the future of the world for generations to come. Therefore, each in his own way was determined to perform as well as possible, playing on the navy team until the essential victory had been gained. Then we could go home.

Fortunately, too, each of us remained a distinct individual, recognized and appreciated as such. Captain Adams was efficient, crisp, tense, and a little starchy—no one ever took him lightly, least of all myself. He commanded respect. Fred Hartman, although businesslike and thorough, was more easy-going and friendly—the kind of "exec" a junior officer would feel able to approach for advice or support, knowing that he would get a fair and sympathetic hearing. Our two attorneys—Russ Morrow and Jack Rickard—were something of a contrast. The former was energetic, friendly, and anxious to please; the latter a bit more deliberate and reserved. Each had complete integrity and a fine sense of duty. Each also on occasion revealed what all of us so much needed under the circumstances of our taut existence—a sense of humor, the ability to chuckle at ourselves and others and the minor absurdities of life afloat. Leo Miller, Jack's assistant gunnery officer, provided yet another contrast. Dark and chunky, quick and energetic, Leo seemed most intent not to commit even the slightest fault that could bring reproach from on high, and also to permit among his own subordinates no slackness that might reflect upon himself. So, despite his general affability, he was quick to rebuke any delinquent sailor in a tone whose height increased with the intensity of his displeasure. Leo could be described as aggressively conscientious.

The *Elden*'s communication officer and my immediate superior, Jim Neill, was a quite different type. Slow moving and slow speaking, he seemed always, entirely, and almost excessively relaxed, often giving the rumpled impression of having just arisen from inadequate slumber (which indeed was often the case). Jim proved to be a boyish foil for Ned Lee, our assistant engineer, who was dark and rangy, with piercing eyes and a determined set to his jaw. Sometimes at the tag end of a day, in the privacy of the wardroom, Jim and Ned would go for each other in rough but friendly horseplay, much like college roommates, while the rest of us egged them on. As for us mere ensigns, we were trailing on behind our more experienced colleagues—trying hard to perform well, coping with the paperwork and other routine requirements of a huge bureaucratic system, standing our watches, dealing with the enlisted men under our immediate supervision (in my case, the radarmen and sonarmen), learning by experience, joking over whatever could be turned into momentary humor, and often reflecting the lingering aura of the campuses from which we had so recently come.

Standing into Chesapeake Bay on the afternoon of 3 October, we secured the sonar, unloaded the Hedgehog, and made certain that all depth charges were set on "Safe." It was about 1900 when the *Elden* arrived at the Naval Operating Base, Norfolk. As Captain Adams gingerly eased the ship in toward Pier 5, a boatswain's mate stood poised on the forecastle, coiled heaving line in hand. At just the right moment he sent the line snaking through the air to the dock, where willing hands grabbed it and began hauling in the first heavy mooring line. At the same time, a sharp blast from a police whistle gave the signal for the simultaneous lowering of the national ensign from the gaff amidships, and the raising of the union jack and the national colors at bow and stern respectively. Was it only three months ago that our crew had first assembled here at Norfolk and been assigned their individual stations on the ship? Bermuda, it seemed, had made us feel like veterans.

The *Elden* had come from Boston without a supply officer on board, Bernstein having been transferred off because of chronic seasickness. At Norfolk we acquired our new supply officer, Ens. Raymond C. Hartung, a handsome and happy-minded young officer, obviously very capable, a welcome addition to the wardroom mess. Mail came, too. I received a letter from Dad advising me to conserve my strength for a long pull. "Sunday I went to church," he continued, "and many people asked about you. Howard Goodchild was shipped out somewhere to parts unknown and many of the boys are far from Providence now. Looked at the flag in the church [representing members in the armed forces] and it is almost full of stars. It will be quite a parade if they should line up when they come home."

We spent the next nine days within the broad confines of Chesapeake Bay, making one-day cruises and, on several occasions, serving as a training ship for other groups. This latter duty made us feel all the more like seasoned salts as we leaned languidly on the ship's rail and, with just a faint air of disdain, contemplated the latest contingent of landlubbers shuffling up the gangplank for a day's training on board.

In midafternoon on 9 October, after a day of exercising in the Bay, the *Elden* was proceeding along the buoyed channel to Norfolk with Jim Neill "at the con" as OOD, giving the orders to the helmsman for course and speed. I happened to be on the flying bridge at the time, along with the usual lookouts— and Captain Adams, tense as always when following a channel. Suddenly Jim noticed that the ship was heading toward nun buoy number 2, and in his own quiet way called down through the speaking tube for the helmsman to make a change of course so as to avoid striking the large metal marker. At the same moment the captain became aware of the danger and, even as the *Elden*'s stern was beginning to sweep sideways in response to Jim's order, grabbed the speaking tube and shouted down for an opposite change of course. The obedient helmsman instantly spun the wheel in the opposite direction, our stern reversed its swing, and the *Elden* went plowing directly into and over the buoy.

Every good junior officer knows instinctively those times when it is well for him to maintain what, in present-day jargon, is known as a low profile, or what

Mark Twain, with greater elegance, labeled a "fine inspiration of prudence."
That was such a moment, and I remained unobtrusively in the background,
watching the whole scenario unfold and keeping a very sober face despite a
Vesuvian sense of amusement. Jim, feeling completely innocent, stood round-
eyed and weak-kneed, wondering just how sharp the knife would be when it
came. The captain was like an overloaded rocket with a lit fuse, eyes darting
here and there, teeth clenched, mustache aquiver, ear cocked to the dreadful
clangor of the heavy steel buoy as it scraped and banged along the underside of
the *Elden*'s hull from stem to stern. At last the awful thing bobbed up into view
astern, apparently little the worse for its rough keel-hauling, whereupon the
captain turned upon poor Jim and unloaded his wrath, undoubtedly fortified
with a good deal of personal embarrassment.

The ship still was proceeding toward the base, twin propellers churning the
water astern, when everyone became aware of an unfamiliar vibration that
spoke only too eloquently of damage to at least one of the shafts or propellers.
As a result, the *Elden* moved the next day to the Navy Yard at Portsmouth, on
the Elizabeth River, where she went into drydock for repair. This unexpected
experience, in turn, deprived us of the dubious pleasure of an escort mission to
New York and back, with a storm at sea thrown in for added flavor. Anyway,
our ship soon was as good as new and ready for her next assignment.

We resumed the long voyage to the Pacific on 13 October when, in company
with the *Canfield* (DE 262), the *Deede* (DE 263), and the *Cloues* (DE 265), we
formed the screen for a group of several transports en route to the West Coast.
In formation we forged steadily southward, each ship trailing a long, gradually
dissolving wake.

During the long night watches, one of the duties of the JOOD was to make
periodic inspection tours to see that the ready gun crews were alert, that no
lights were showing on the open decks, and that watertight integrity and fire
security were being properly maintained belowdecks. I made many such tours,
groping my way in blackness along the surging deck with the dark water hissing
by just below, swinging open and then dogging shut behind me the heavy
watertight doors, passing quietly through dimly lit belowdecks compartments
where the air was heavy with the smell of sweat and multiple exhalation. I
concluded each such inspection with a climb back up to the flying bridge where
the fresh night air whipped by.

The hour just before sunrise traditionally has been considered a time of
enhanced peril, presumably because it was the time when a lurking enemy
might choose to strike. In the navy, this threat was countered by the highly
unpopular "dawn alert." Shortly before the first pale glimmer of light appears

like a faint blush along the eastern horizon the OOD activates the General Alarm, causing all hands, even those who have stood the recent midwatch, to slide out of their bunks, throw on their clothing, and race to their battle stations. Then, for perhaps three-quarters of an hour, we all stand sleepy-eyed and poised for action in full battle array, until rosy-fingered dawn provides enough visibility all around to justify a resumption of the regular watch. By now it is too late to return to the sack, for breakfast soon will be served. After that comes the morning muster of all divisions on the main deck. There, as the blue-denimed ranks stand balancing casually against the slow rise and fall of the deck, the division officers call the roll and make necessary announcements. And so to work.

During daytime working hours men off watch are kept busy at such routine tasks as hosing and swabbing decks, cleaning heads and other compartments, and chipping paint in a seemingly endless round of preparation for repainting. In fact, the metallic tattoo of chipping hammers is one of the most familiar sounds on the *Elden,* while the pungent smell of fresh paint is our daily perfume. The battle against rust never ceases—never can cease—if the ship is to remain in tip-top condition. This much I can say without exaggeration and with lingering pride—the *Elden* was a clean ship.

Breakfast, lunch, and dinner are served on schedule, with the off-watch members of the crew lining up on the ladder leading to the messing compartment below, the line extending along the starboard side of the main deck, while the officers gather in the wardroom. As the captain enters the wardroom to share the meal, somebody calls out "Ten-Shun!" The captain takes his seat at the head of the table, with "At ease, gentlemen," and we all sit down.

Each day precisely at noon, while we are at lunch, occurs a small ceremony in which the captain is officially informed of the time. Shortly before that hour the OOD sends the quartermaster down to the wardroom door. At precisely the correct moment the quartermaster knocks, enters, draws a breath, and recites, "Captain, the officer of the deck reports 1200, chronometers wound!" As the last word falls upon our ears, the captain breathes a quiet "Very well" into his cup of coffee, the quartermaster makes good his escape, and we all resume the interrupted meal. That the chronometers have indeed been wound, I might add, is a fact of great importance, for without their accurate timekeeping a ship cannot compute longitude.

The tropical sun, combined with the warm, salty sea air, can produce a lively thirst. As navy regulations forbid the consumption of alcohol on board ship, the *Elden*'s men drink a variety of other beverages. Coffee is the most common, consumed at all hours of the day and night. At meals, cold milk is a welcome treat, but on long voyages we must be satisfied with the kind made from powder. Canned fruit juice, kept cold in the refrigerator in the wardroom pantry, is especially refreshing after a long watch under the glaring sun.

In the evening, as the sun drops below the horizon, the ship again routinely goes to General Quarters, this time for "evening alert," after which the regular rotating watches are resumed. Plowing on in total darkness, the *Elden* continues across the watery waste, most of her officers and men now asleep in their bunks, trusting their lives to the vigilance and skill of their shipmates on watch.

Standing on the flying bridge in the darkness of a night watch, one may be able to discern off to either side the faint dark blur of other ships in the formation, all similarly on watch. It is wonderfully reassuring to know that only one deck below, in the radar compartment, each individual ship is continuously revealed on the radarscope as a small blob of light, with bearing and range quite precisely indicated. Furthermore, should any strange ship intrude upon our circle of ocean, or any submarine break the surface within a radius of five miles, that too will be instantly revealed. If an enemy appears, the OOD will sound the General Alarm and then direct the ready guns, as needed, while the ship is going to Battle Stations. "Action starboard, action starboard! Pick up surface target bearing zero-eight-zero!" The captain arrives on the flying bridge, is quickly briefed by the OOD, and takes control. Within three minutes every station is reported fully manned and ready for action. Grouped around the various guns are their crews looking, in their steel helmets, like clusters of blue-gray mushrooms. The *Elden* is prepared to throw everything she has—fast. If it proves to be a false alarm, the men take off their helmets and lifebelts, and resume their previous activity—watch-standing, working, or happily sleeping.

By noon of 15 October our formation had reached a point 545 miles east of Stuart, Florida. About an hour later the *Cloues,* on the port side of the screen, suddenly announced a sonar contact. Immediately the transports changed course to starboard as an evasive maneuver, and the *Elden* went to Battle Stations. Our lookouts intently studied the surface of the ever-restless sea with their binoculars, searching for the curling white wave that trails a moving periscope and the thin darting streak that marks the path of a speeding torpedo. Our sonarmen carried on a diligent search, eager to catch an echo from any stalking U-boat. Members of our depth charge team on the fantail gripped their wrenches, prepared to make any settings ordered. Our gun crews had their weapons ready, ammunition at hand, in case any conning tower broached. In the meantime, the *Cloues* was busy developing her contact, while I stood at my station awaiting further developments.

Suddenly an echo from the sonar stack, faint but repeated again and again. "Contact bearing 355!" That put the ball squarely in my court for the very first time, bringing into immediate play all my training from Miami, Key West, and

Bermuda. Of only one thing could I be certain—this was no *tame* submarine. As I stood at the door of the sonar hut evaluating the echoes, Captain Adams ordered the helmsman to swing the ship around to course 355, heading directly toward the target. Responding quickly to the change of rudder, the *Elden* heeled as her stern swept sideways. PING———Bung, PING——Bung, PING— Bung. Was it a U-boat? The echoes were not entirely convincing. Should we attack? With vulnerable transports present we dared not take time to evaluate the contact more carefully. I made a quick decision and recommended a 13-charge pattern set for medium depth; the order was sent aft to the fantail by sound-powered phone. As the range diminished, with the echoes coming in faster and faster, the captain made his decision—attack.

At 700 yards we changed course to take our lead angle, just as we had done so many times at Bermuda. Then, when the moving line of echo traces on the range recorder arrived at exactly the right place, I yelled out "Roll One!" Again the right moment—"Roll Two!" (Thump-Thump of the K-guns)—"Roll Three!"—"Roll Four!"—"Roll Five!" All thirteen were gone, and now the *Elden* was pulling steadily away from the spot, while our fellow escorts stood clear. Suddenly the heavy hammer blows began, with the sea astern erupting in a cluster of white geysers. We swung around sharply to regain contact, stern sweeping sideways, while all guns able to bear concentrated on the great patch of disturbed water, ready to open fire should a damaged U-boat break the surface. Our sonarmen resumed their search of the indicated area, but could obtain only mushy echoes, a result of the explosions. We had lost contact. Soon the *Cloues* made the same report, and we agreed that whatever had caused the echoes was not a submarine. Securing from General Quarters, the captain ordered "all engines ahead flank" so that the *Elden* could regain her station in the screen as quickly as possible.

At 1540 on 17 October we sighted the mountains of Hispaniola some forty miles to the west. Two hours later Cape Engaño Light was visible on our starboard bow at a distance of twenty-three miles as we entered the Mona Passage between Hispaniola and Puerto Rico. Soon the *Elden* changed course to head southwesterly for the Panama Canal. For the next three days we cruised serenely across the blue Caribbean under sunny skies. Nights were now so warm that many of the *Elden*'s men chose to sleep on deck instead of below where the air all too readily became fetid. I was fortunate in having the use of a folding cot which I set up on the superstructure deck near the mast. There I slumbered in sheer luxury under the brilliant stars of a tropical sky, lulled by the gentle rolling of the ship, the caress of balmy air, and the swishing of the water rushing along the ship's sides.

Our days were filled with music, piped through the ship's PA system. One day, having grown somewhat weary of the steady diet of popular hit tunes, I asked the radio gang if they could favor us with an all-Victor Herbert concert. They seemed happy to oblige. So at dinnertime we enjoyed some glorious melodies of a happier day when our world seemed bathed in romance, moving Captain Adams to remark approvingly, "Now that's the kind of music *I* was brought up on." Needless to say, it wasn't many evenings later when the experience was repeated, though not by popular request of the crew.

We made our landfall at 0809 on 21 October, sighting the coast of Panama due south at a distance of sixty-three miles. That afternoon all the ships of our group passed through the antisubmarine net and entered the harbor at Cristobal, Canal Zone. Before long, with a pilot aboard, the *Elden* began her transit through the canal toward the Pacific Ocean. Never had I seen such a heavily fortified and defended area, including numerous gun emplacements. After passing through the Gatun Locks, Pedro Miguel Locks, and Miraflores Locks, we moored very early in the morning alongside the *Canfield* at Pier 18B, Balboa. There we received replacements for our thirteen expended depth charges, and also more than a ton of meat, including the turkeys for our Thanksgiving dinner.

While in the Canal Zone we also received a welcome delivery of personal mail, which demonstrated how remarkably effective the Fleet Post Office generally was in getting a particular ship's accumulation of mail to the right point at the right time. Eagerly I opened a letter from Mother, and read that Howard Goodchild, after only a few weeks of duty as a navy pilot aboard the escort carrier *Card,* was listed as missing, his plane having failed to return. This news came as a real shock. Howie had been my patrol leader in Troop 37 and one of the best-liked, most respected boys in Cranston High School. He was, as I recall, the first of the Calvary men to lose his life in the war.

Late in the afternoon of 22 October the *Elden* nosed out into the Pacific Ocean, our destination California. Now we had with us as fellow escorts only the *Canfield* and the *Deede,* shepherding the attack transports *Bolivar* (APA 34), *Elmore* (APA 42), and *Wayne* (APA 54). In a very real sense, we had passed from one war to another. Behind us in the Atlantic were the German U-boats, while now, far off to the west, were the Japanese submarines. For the present, then, we were cruising in relatively safe, indeed peaceful, waters. Nevertheless, we continued our constant vigilance, never knowing when we might suddenly encounter a lone raider.

Rounding Point Mala, our formation headed northwest to parallel the coast of Central America and Mexico. In traversing the broad mouth of the Gulf of Tehuantepec we encountered an extremely heavy offshore swell which we had to take broad on our beam, with rolls up to 55 degrees. High on the *Elden*'s flying bridge such drastic rolling from side to side flung us back and forth through the air, first one way and then another, with the watchstanders clinging hard to binnacle or rail to avoid being tumbled. Despite this heavy rolling, however, to my enormous personal satisfaction I retained every meal. I had acquired my navy-issue sea legs!

I was also becoming much better acquainted with many of the crew, especially those in C-Division. They were proving to be a good group, as varied as the America from which they came, nearly all accepting with mild cheerfulness the cramped quarters, fatigue, wetness, and boredom. Gradually, thanks to the sometimes profane but always stimulating influence of the *Elden*'s veteran chiefs, inexperience and uncertainty were giving way to competence and confidence. At Battle Stations our men appeared as tough and ready as any crew afloat. When going ashore on liberty they approached the quarterdeck in dress blues or whites, as the order might be, caps squared just above eyebrows, black shoes gleaming below bell-bottom trousers, with a smart salute for the officer of the deck and the colors aft. In their spare time on board, the men read magazines and books, wrote letters home, studied for promotion, discussed sports and the ever-fascinating subject of women, daydreamed about the past and the future. They wanted home and family as much as did the officers; that was obvious from the mail we had to censor.

Some of the men remain especially vivid in my memory. Take, for example, the *Elden*'s leading radioman, Lester Harris. A clean-cut, quiet-spoken, self-respecting Southerner, Harris ran the ship's tiny radio shack with its earphoned personnel like an efficient office. Always thoroughly dependable, he performed his vital duties without ostentation or complaint, held the respect of his radio gang, and worked in close cooperation with the communication officer. Our leading storekeeper was Nick Medica, so short and stocky as to be overlooked in a crowd, but a big man when it came to responsibility. Medica's biggest visible problem was motion; hardly had the *Elden* pulled away from the dock when he could be found bending over the lee rail or gagging in the crew's head. Yet I never heard him complain, and I suppose he simply accepted this affliction as a part of his personal contribution to the war effort. One who paid a different price, with equal grace, was Elton Davis, a black steward's mate who served in the wardroom. This deep Southerner was tall and handsome, his usually serious demeanor occasionally lightened by a broad and infectious grin. Davis cleaned our rooms, made our bunks, and served our meals at table with a quiet courtesy that translated into personal dignity. Because of his race, he had no real hope of moving along to other duties, although he did gain well-deserved promotion. Whenever the ship went to General Quarters, Davis hurried to a station belowdecks where he helped pass ammunition from the magazines up to the guns.

Crewmen such as Harris, Medica, and Davis simply illustrate the quality and diversity of personnel assembled in the *Elden* by the navy from its various training facilities across the country. By and large they were able and qualified. They were also brave and dedicated, prepared to confront a tough and resourceful foe whenever the opportunity came, and nearly all, I suspect, would have performed creditably in the supreme test. They were dedicated to victory in what they understood to be a good cause. And so were we all.

Shortly after noon on 1 November the *Elden* stood into the harbor of San Pedro, the port of Los Angeles. There our congenial wardroom coterie was further reinforced with the addition of Ens. Charles Smart, a slow-moving officer of sandy complexion and somewhat bulky proportions whose arrival stretched our already crowded berthing facilities to their extreme limit. In addition, we received a fresh supply of mail, including some early Christmas packages—weeks before Thanksgiving.

Having refueled, the *Elden* pulled out of San Pedro on the afternoon of 2 November, joining up with the *Canfield, Cloues,* and *Deede.* As the transports no longer were present, the four DEs simply formed a column and steamed steadily northward up the coast toward San Francisco. That evening Jim Neill, who had managed to survive the captain's wrath after the collision with the buoy, was happily taking a shower in the officers' head when our brace of engineering officers, Paul Pontius and Ned Lee, pulled shut the door and secured it with a length of stout line, imprisoning Jim inside. Under the small grilled window in the door they then posted a hastily prepared sign reading DO NOT FEED THE ANIMALS—ELDEN ZOO. This accomplished, our inspired engineers were pleased to share with all and sundry the intriguing spectacle of the wet, naked beast that, when provoked, hurled water through the grill. An enjoyable half hour went by in this fashion before Jim finally was released, muttering threats of vengeance. Our new ensign must have wondered what kind of ark he had joined.

The next afternoon the column of ships advanced into a bank of heavy, low-lying fog that reduced visibility to less than 500 yards. As an extra precaution the captain had lookouts stationed on the forecastle. A half hour later we emerged in the clear, and soon entered the swept channel leading eastward to San Francisco Bay. Again we encountered heavy fog, and again emerged. At 1732 the *Elden,* third in the column of DEs, passed under the magnificent Golden Gate Bridge. Immediately all hands topside began drinking in the unforgettable first view of San Francisco on the starboard bow. Proceeding to Treasure Island, site of a naval base, the ships moored at the North Pier.

Ahead was the delightful prospect of liberty in the enchanted metropolis of the West.

Frisco was a week of magic before sailing off to the real war. The lights, the crowds, the busy stores and varied restaurants were exciting, making the loneliness of the ocean seem like a dream that was suddenly interrupted. I managed to do all my Christmas shopping for the folks at home, mostly in the stores along Market Street, arranging to have each item mailed. Also I succumbed to the temptation of a very smart-looking gray gabardine work uniform, offered by one of the outfitters. Months earlier, presumably in Washington or goodness knows where, some board of naval bureaucrats had decided that the standard khaki work uniform worn day in and day out by navy officers and chief petty officers should be gradually superseded by gray, presumably on the grounds that gray would be less conspicuous aboard ship. Such a change seemed to us an unnecessary complication, but gray it was to be, with the changeover taking nearly all the remainder of the war.

One evening I went down to Fishermen's Wharf with Leo Miller and Ray Hartung. We wandered in to a seafood restaurant named Exposition Grotto and were shown to a table. There, each of us protected by a huge yellow bib snug under the chin, we feasted on ice-cold cracked crab, a delicacy that seldom appeared on the *Elden*'s menu. That dinner was to become for us almost a legend. Months later, in the glare and heat of the equatorial zone, one or another of us would conjure up the memory by inquiring, "How would you like to be at Exposition Grotto right now eating ice-cold cracked crab?" The question needed no answer.

While the *Elden* was at San Francisco, Paul Pontius and Dexter Hill were detached, which left us short one officer, the list now reading: Adams, Hartman, Rickard, Morrow, Miller, Neill, Lee, Leach, Leggett, Hartung, and Smart. Our executive officer, Fred Hartman, had established himself as a trusted and respected link between the captain and his officers, being both the captain's loyal right-hand man and a congenial friend in the wardroom. Most of us had come to feel very comfortable with each other, which was essential, considering the crowded conditions in which we lived.

At 0730 on 11 November (Armistice Day of the First World War) the *Elden* set the special sea detail, and twelve minutes later hauled in the last line to the dock. In company with the *Canfield, Cloues,* and *Deede,* we were underway for Pearl Harbor and the war against Japan. As our column of four passed under the Golden Gate Bridge and set course toward the southwest, all hands knew that it was farewell to the States. Among the fighting forces in the Pacific theater at that time a rather pessimistic prediction of homecoming had become current— "Golden Gate in '48," which certainly did not portend for the *Elden* an early return. Our last view of land faded gradually, after which we saw only our three slim gray sisters and the restless sea.

By this time I was taking my turn at residing aft in the "brig." One night I was awakened by a rasping command from the loudspeaker, "Now hear this! Relieve the watch! Relieve the watch!" Knowing that I was scheduled to stand the morning watch starting at 0400, I crawled sleepily out of the sack, got dressed to the heavy rumble of the port propeller shaft just below, and headed forward toward the ladder leading up to the main deck. Then, miraculously, a clock on the bulkhead before me made a simple gesture that won my instant gratitude—its hour hand pointed not to 4 but to 12, which meant that the correct time was midnight and I could go back to bed for another four hours before beginning my watch! Some weeks later, incidentally, in a sensible effort to smooth off one of the rough edges of life at sea, we adopted a more humane method of arousing the oncoming watch at night, sending one or more men of the offgoing watch to awaken individually the members of the next watch without disturbing other sleepers.

The night watches on the flying bridge, or any of the topside stations for that matter, usually were deadly monotonous. To help the men remain alert, a pair of messcooks was assigned to go the rounds once each watch, lugging a large pot of bitter black coffee (known as "joe") and a bucket of warm water containing a few thick, handleless, navy mugs. Their coming was eagerly awaited early in the watch, but of course it took time for the men at each station to finish sipping the hot brew and then drop the mugs back into the bucket for the use of the next station. The various ready gun stations came first, which meant that the watch on the flying bridge often waited with growing impatience. Finally one of the lookouts would press the button on his sound-powered phone and begin inquiring of the various stations, "Where are the joe boys now?" When at last the long-delayed pair did arrive with coffee pot and bucket, we each fished a mug out of the tepid water, eyed the black beverage as it was poured, and then sipped appreciatively, enjoying the warmth and stimulation.

One night when Russ Morrow had the watch and I was his JOOD, with Captain Adams slumbering peacefully below, Russ began singing some songs to pass the weary hours. I was especially intrigued when he began working his way through all the many verses of "Abdul Abulbul Amir" a mock-heroic ballad whose intricacies had previously escaped me. By the time he had finished I was eager to learn all the verses for myself, so on subsequent nights when we had the watch together Russ served as my tutor, both of us passing the time in lusty song. Our tones, for the most part, were quickly snatched away by the wind passing across the flying bridge, so even the nearby lookouts heard little. As for the sonarmen in the hut forward of the bridge, they were concentrating on their pinging, not our singing.

Very early in the morning of 17 November, six days after we had taken our departure from San Francisco, the *Elden's* radar picked up the island of Molokai bearing 205 degrees, distant 61 miles, and the island of Maui bearing 175 degrees, distant 78 miles. Later, the morning's bright sunshine revealed the lush green beauty of Molokai to the south and Oahu to the west as our little formation approached the Kaiwi Channel. Oahu, with its steep-sided green hills and deeply indented valleys, seemed a place not only of natural enchantment but also of peculiar, tragic import with respect to the war itself. As the site of the great American military and naval base in and around Pearl Harbor, the setting for the navy's most terrible disaster and the home base of the now rapidly expanding Pacific Fleet, Oahu became, as we made our approach, the inevitable focus of attention.

The naval authorities at Pearl Harbor knew of our coming, of course, and had planned a special and most practical kind of welcome. Out came a plane towing a sleeve target, requiring our four DEs to spend a good hour or more demonstrating their proficiency at anti-aircraft gunnery. We went to Battle Stations and stuffed wads of cotton in our ears. The plane approached our formation on a parallel course, the towed sleeve following well behind. Each ship, as the target came within range, opened fire. Now it was the *Elden's* turn. "Action starboard! Action starboard! All guns—pick up target bearing zero-three-zero! Commence firing!" A second's pause, and then the ship suddenly erupted in a pandemonium of rapid explosive bursts, jarring the decks underfoot. The bright lines of the tracers stabbed out into the blue sky like streams of water from a battery of hoses, seeking out the rapidly passing sleeve. Dirty brown puffs of smoke from the 3-inch shells blossomed ahead, behind, and—sometimes—alongside that target. Then the sleeve was past. "All guns—Cease firing!" The sudden silence was welcome, enabling us to prepare for another pass while listening to the drumfire of the next ship astern.

Once the exercise was over, the formation began its final approach to Pearl Harbor on the south coast of Oahu. As the *Elden* cautiously advanced, we on the flying bridge saw spreading out before us a long sweep of predominantly hilly terrain, in some places a veritable jumble of steep-sided hills, green and brown all over. Off to the left loomed the jagged ridge of the Waianae Range. To the right of that, behind Pearl Harbor, extended a broad sloping plain. Off to the right, behind the city of Honolulu, was another mass of irregular hills twisting up into jagged ridges—the impressive Koolau Range. Still farther to the right we could almost see the famous rolling combers advancing relentlessly upon Waikiki Beach, with the unforgettable backdrop of Diamond Head standing like an ancient sentinel, heavily fortified.

The narrow entrance to Pearl Harbor, directly ahead, was guarded by Fort Kamehameha, where an alert watch stationed in an observation tower routinely challenged every approaching vessel. As the interrogatory flashes from a blinker light began, the *Elden*'s signal watch aimed one of our rail-mounted signal lights shoreward and began flapping the handle that controlled the shutter, sending off dots and dashes of light that identified us properly to the fort. Only after the fort, in turn, had expressed its approval by giving us clearance did the *Elden* presume to nose her way into the approach channel. Now, on both sides, a long line of white breakers warned us not to stray from the set course as Captain Adams, characteristically taut, conned the ship toward the haven. On the land ahead we could begin to distinguish masses of scrub growth, groups of graceful palm trees, and buildings of various sorts, while in the vicinity of the harbor itself we could discern the characteristic features of every major naval base—barracks, shops and warehouses, and the masts of numerous ships topped with radio and radar antennas. Fortifications with barbed wire and bunkers guarded each side of the narrow entrance; an antisubmarine net, now drawn aside, contributed to the security of this once-ravaged base. Entering with all the martial dignity we could muster, the *Elden* and her three sister DEs sought their assigned moorings amidst a great variety of gray ships. The long voyage from Boston had been completed, and the *Elden* was out in the war zone as a member of the growing Pacific Fleet.

All of us were understandably curious about the famous base to which we had come. Was any of the devastation of 7 December 1941 still visible? Just off Ford Island lay the blasted hulk of the U.S.S. *Arizona,* little more than her masts showing above the calm surface of the water—still the tomb for a thousand of her crew. Another sunken battleship was under salvage. Later I was to observe the badly damaged U.S.S. *Oklahoma* in drydock, her steel side ripped as though by a gigantic can opener. But the huge, sprawling base itself, with its dozens of piers and hundreds of buildings, appeared to be in excellent condition, a busy complex designed to provide nearly every conceivable form of service needed by the fleet, from ammunition and fuel to repair, training, and recreation. Tractor-drawn passenger vehicles with room for large numbers of standing riders moved slowly along established routes, providing efficient if not very exciting transportation through most sections of the base. Liberty boats operated frequently between the various ships in the harbor and the fleet landing, where buses waited to carry officers and men to Honolulu. I noted also the long, thin barrels of numerous anti-aircraft guns pointing skyward from well-constructed emplacements, evidence of our readiness for any further attempt the Japanese might make.

One of the important aspects of the Pacific War about which we on the *Elden* as yet knew very little was the technique of resupplying ships while under way at sea. This technique, requiring special equipment and a high level of skill on the part of deck officers and crewmen, actually was one of the navy's most important achievements, for it enabled task forces to operate at sea far from established bases for weeks at a time, the ships being resupplied periodically with fuel, ammunition, and food by fleet service vessels at prearranged rendezvous. The *Elden,* as a "new boy on the block," was about to be initiated into this critical aspect of naval operations.

On 19 November, after only one full day in Pearl Harbor, the *Elden* was sent out to sea as sole escort for a brace of fleet oilers, the *Cacapon* (AO 52) and *Saugatuck* (AO 75), our destination an area about 350 miles northeast of Oahu, not far from the track along which we had so recently come from the West Coast. With the *Elden* echo-ranging ahead of the two deep-sitting oilers, in a fairly rough sea, our formation proceeded on its mission, zig-zagging in accordance with Plan 6. Zig-zagging meant a precisely prescribed sequence of course changes calculated to enable a ship or formation of ships to advance along a selected base course while making frequent, irregular changes of heading, a procedure intended to thwart a submarine trying to maneuver into firing position. All fleet vessels carried a book of numbered zig-zag plans, which enabled a task group commander to specify any plan to commence at any designated time. In all these plans the course changes occurred precisely at specified minutes of the hour. For example, Plan 6, which we were using, might have required all ships to change course 15 degrees to port at six minutes past the hour, 40 degrees to starboard at fourteen minutes past the hour, 30 degrees to port at twenty-four minutes past the hour, and so on. Obviously, the OOD in every ship had to keep close track of the time and make his turns correctly, lest he surge out of station in the formation and risk a collision.

In midafternoon on 20 November our group made rendezvous with the U.S.S. *Honolulu* (CL 48), a light cruiser of the *Brooklyn* class, one of the ships damaged during the Japanese attack of 7 December. She was the most powerful combat ship with which, as yet, the *Elden* had had any business. Almost immediately the *Honolulu* began her approach to the *Cacapon* for the purpose of refueling. We on the *Elden* watched the process, fascinated.

The oiler steamed slowly and steadily on a prescribed course selected for minimum roll, screened by the escort. Carefully the ship to be refueled approached from astern and gradually overtook the oiler until in position alongside, with only about forty yards of space between, almost close enough to throw a football from one to the other. Course was maintained and the speed adjusted so that the position of the two ships remained as nearly constant as possible, even as both were plunging through the water at a speed of perhaps eight or ten knots. The bow waves of both ships incessantly smashed into each other, sending wild, turbulent water racing through the narrow channel between the steel hulls. Both helmsmen had to use all their skill at the wheel to avoid any dangerous veering. It was a time of great tension. Skillfully, with the aid of the oiler's cranes, the heavy fuel hoses were passed across the gap and secured on the intake valves of the fuel tanks. Then the oil was pumped across. For as long as necessary, sometimes half an hour or more, the two ships remained in that precarious situation, one drinking from the other. Finally, when satiated, the receiving vessel relinquished the hoses and carefully maneuvered clear of the oiler. As soon as one ship had been refueled another could move up to take its place, and indeed, as we later saw, it was common practice in the fleet for an oiler to refuel two ships at a time, one on either side.

When the *Honolulu* had drunk her fill of diesel oil she drew away from the *Cacapon,* built up speed, and took off on her own affairs, soon disappearing from view. The next morning our two oilers conducted a fueling exercise of their own. Then, early that afternoon came the *Elden*'s turn, with the ship at General Quarters and the deck gang poised to haul aboard the oiler's hose. Gingerly but skillfully Captain Adams brought the *Elden* creeping up on the port quarter of the *Cacapon* until we were close alongside in fueling position. The massive bulk of the oiler, stolidly cleaving the waves, now loomed close beside us while her well-trained deck gang, working as a team, sent the hose across to our main deck. The entire procedure went well, and our initiation was successfully completed. On 22 November all three ships returned to Pearl.

Jim Ederer QM3/c at the helm. The voice tube from the flying bridge is visible above the helmsman's head.

While we were away, exciting news had broken. Powerful army and marine units made assault landings on the low-lying, Japanese-held atolls of Makin and Tarawa in the Gilbert Islands, the extreme southeastern corner of Japan's vast fortified perimeter some 2,100 miles southwest of Oahu. This invasion and speedy, though very bloody, conquest marked the real beginning of America's long, difficult amphibious advance across the Central Pacific toward Japan itself, paralleling the other great drive already underway from the Solomons and New Guinea toward the Philippines.

On 24 November we went to sea again, this time for intensive and realistic gunnery practice in company with the three DEs with whom we had voyaged from San Francisco, plus the U.S.S. *Martin* (DE 30), joined later by a high-speed minesweeper, the *Zane* (DMS 14). It was quite a show. Altogether the *Elden* expended 178 rounds of 3-inch ammunition, 686 of 1.1-inch, and 2,109 of 20-millimeter. As usual, after the concussive blasts had ceased, the crew gathered up the valuable brass cartridge cases littering the decks and stored them away for salvage.

The next day was Thanksgiving, but our formation remained out overnight, steaming through a sea that seemed almost as placid as one of the lakes in Roger Williams Park back in Providence. A number of the ships were ahead of the *Elden* in column, and keen noses on our flying bridge detected a most pleasant aroma wafting down the line—the smell of turkeys roasting in the galley ovens as the cooks prepared the coming feast. On Thanksgiving morning, as we approached Oahu, a formation of friendly aircraft appeared and subjected us to simulated horizontal bombing, dive bombing, and torpedo attacks, roaring over and past us with realistic ferocity while we tracked them with all our guns. That exercise completed, we headed directly for Pearl.

Moored alongside the *Canfield,* the *Elden* joined all the other ships and units at the base in Thanksgiving. Our cooks outdid themselves in laying before all hands a most excellent repast—roast turkey and dressing, potatoes, lima beans, salad, cranberry sauce, several kinds of dessert, nuts, and candy. We enjoyed it thoroughly, even as our thoughts turned to home, where the dishes had long since been washed and put away.

Having eaten my fill, I took a few minutes to write a letter to my family. After describing our holiday dinner, I attempted some levity by drawing attention to the wry humor implicit in some of the traditional titles accorded certain functionaries on a navy ship. There was an "Oil King" and a "Water King." The man in charge of the provision issue room was known as the "Jack-of-the-Dust." Most ironic of all was the grandiose title "Captain of the Head," with concomitant duties that may readily be imagined. "As usual," I concluded, "work is calling me, but time passes quickly when I am busy. I keep trying to guess when I shall be home again for good, because that's what I look forward to. I don't fool myself about its being soon, but anyway the longer you wait for something the more you enjoy it. In the meantime I'm trying to do a good job, and have as much fun as possible."

4

OPERATION FLINTLOCK:
The Marshall Islands

ntil Thanksgiving Day, 1943, the *Elden*'s role in the war was only
incidental—shakedown training, a long voyage to the home base
of the Pacific Fleet, an exercise in fueling while at sea. Now,
having feasted on turkey and all the fixings, and having fed the *Elden*'s
magazines with fresh ammunition from the destroyer tender *Black Hawk*
(AD 9), we made all preparations for getting under way in the late afternoon of
25 November for "out there"—which meant the area of the Pacific far to the
southwest where American forces were actively challenging the Japanese after
the successful invasion of the Gilbert Islands. In short, for the very first time the
Elden was about to head directly into the war, and one could hardly do that
without feeling some combination of excitement and apprehension.

The moment when a combat ship, her water and fuel tanks topped up, her
magazines full of ammunition, her food lockers crammed, sets off for a combat
zone is marked inevitably with a dark sense of foreboding. As she starts to back
cautiously into the channel, the ship blows one prolonged blast on her whistle.
Men on the dock watch her slowly gathering speed; they wonder where she is
bound, how she will fare, whether she will return. The ship's company, trying to
look both efficient and nonchalant, drinks in the last close view of docks,
buildings, vehicles, and shore-bound humanity. We, too, are asking ourselves
questions. How will it go with us? Will we see land again? Only one thing is

certain—out on that vast blue deep the potential for disaster is everywhere and ever present.

Soon the *Elden* joined her sister ship the *Canfield* as escort for the fully laden fleet oilers *Kaskaskia* (AO 27) and *Cacapon* (AO 52), heading southwestward. Other similar groups were slipping out of Pearl at about the same time, proceeding at first independently, later to combine into larger groups. Our little group of four, once formed up, began zig-zagging. As darkness enveloped the broad Pacific south of Oahu, we darkened ship and steamed on in total darkness until, about 2145, our lookouts began noticing erratic signal flashes from an unknown source astern. Directed to investigate by the task unit commander, the *Elden* went to General Quarters, dropped out of station in the screen, and headed toward the mysterious flashes. Quickly we closed the range, all guns at the ready, and flashed a challenge. Every friendly ship anywhere in the Central Pacific was supposed to know the correct code response for that particular date, but the reply we received was not the correct one, only AA-AA-AA, which was an ordinary uncoded inquiry. Again our signalmen challenged, with the same result. We had the target on our radar; one of our 24-inch searchlights was aimed directly along the indicated bearing so that whenever the captain gave the order to illuminate, the intruder would be locked squarely in its powerful beam; our gun crews stood ready to open fire. Finally, forty-five minutes after the mysterious flashing had begun, the stranger deigned to identify himself as "P 483," which presumably meant PC 483. Other information being received from a secret source convinced us that the intruder was indeed "one of ours." So ended our first tense alert of the voyage, and the *Elden* hastened to catch up with the formation and resume her place in the screen.

As every passing hour brought us closer to enemy bases, we continued to maintain a high degree of readiness for any eventuality. On the afternoon of 29 November, with the ship slicing through rough water, Captain Adams finally addressed all hands, revealing the nature of our mission and leaving no doubt that the *Elden* was fully into the war at sea. American forces were involved in extensive fleet activity against the Japanese-held Marshall Islands. At that time the Marshalls meant little to me except as a name being seen more frequently in the news dispatches. A scattered group of low-lying coral atolls several hundred miles northwest of the Gilberts and a little over 2,000 miles from Pearl Harbor, they had been held by Japan since the First World War. Now the enemy was dug in on Jaluit, Mili, and Majuro in the southern part of the group, Kwajalein in the center, and the important atoll of Eniwetok off to the northwest. Until the Marshalls had been wrested from the enemy, there could be no further American advance across the Central Pacific, and so the Marshalls were next on our shopping list. Their Japanese defenders, however, saw the situation at least as clearly as we did, and were determined not to let our forces peel off any more of their outer defensive perimeter.

It was common practice to designate each distinct operation by a code name; the impending attempt against the Marshalls would be Operation Flintlock. Deciding to bypass Jaluit and Mili, the American high command had set 31 January 1944 as the date for the landings on Majuro and Kwajalein, which would allow sufficient time for the assembling and training of the necessary forces and for thorough pre-invasion reconnaissance and bombardment. The terrible lesson of Marine losses on the beach at Tarawa had been well learned. This time the preparation was to be even more thorough. Then, if all went well at Majuro and Kwajalein, the invasion of Eniwetok would follow in due course. The navy's part in Operation Flintlock was assigned to Adm. Raymond A. Spruance's Central Pacific Force (later to be known as the Fifth Fleet), to which the *Elden* now was assigned.

Why were we heading toward the Marshalls so early? Fast carrier attack groups were about to commence a systematic pounding of Japanese positions there to soften them up for the amphibious landings at the end of January. Those task groups would need fresh supplies of fuel to enable them to make repeated and prolonged attacks without having to go all the way back to Pearl Harbor. Consequently, the *Elden*'s first major operational assignment was to help escort the fleet oilers to an area roughly five hundred miles northeast of the Marshalls, where the attack groups could be refueled at sea. There was a distinct possibility that enemy aircraft or submarines operating out of the Marshalls might discover our activity in that area and attempt to interfere. Should our sonar team detect a submarine, I would be needed immediately on the flying bridge, and so I slept in my clothing night after night, ready to race up those three ladders to my station.

Every ship involved in Operation Flintlock, and there were hundreds of them, was given its own code name for use in voice radio communications, so as to conceal from Japanese listeners the identity of participating units. In order to make identification easy for our own forces, on the other hand, all these various code names were listed alphabetically, together with the corresponding ship's name and hull number, in a classified book issued to all ships. Under this system a voice radio exchange might sound like this: "Hello Creampuff, this is Tenderloin. How do you read me? Over." "Hello Tenderloin, this is Creampuff. I read you loud and clear. Over." "Hello Creampuff, this is Tenderloin. Proceed on previously assigned duty with Dashboard and Tackhammer. Over." "Hello Tenderloin, this is Creampuff. Willco [Will comply]. Out." An eavesdropping Japanese would have no way of knowing whether Creampuff was a battleship and Tenderloin a destroyer, or vice versa.

One evening we listened fascinated to the regular English-language propaganda broadcast from Tokyo. The program was introduced by an obviously Japanese voice, but the various items of "news" which followed were read in flawless English by "Tokyo Rose," whose cultured enunciation would not have been out of place in a student debate at Vassar. With an air of gracious elegance combined with sly taunting she destroyed American aircraft carriers right and left, emphasizing how they broke in two and sank "instantaneously." Interspersed with such choice items were recorded messages from American prisoners of war, each introduced in a bluff, good-humored style designed to suggest humanity and friendly tolerance. The effect of all this, if anything, was to reinforce our distaste for the Japanese, especially in their clumsy exaggeration of American losses and their blatant exploitation of helpless prisoners.

At last, on the morning of 30 November, our group made rendezvous with units of Task Force 50, which included carriers, heavy and light cruisers, and destroyers. For the first time, in support of a major operation, the *Elden* found herself linked with the first team, the big combat ships which had been active in promoting America's beginning counterdrive across the Central Pacific and now were about to strike new blows against enemy-held islands. Such a rendezvous far out at sea was to become for the *Elden* almost a routine experience, but it never entirely lost a certain element of excitement and drama. Typically, at the break of dawn only our own familiar formation of oilers and escorts would be zig-zagging across an apparently empty sea, all hands at General Quarters. Suddenly our radar would detect a friendly aircraft twenty or more miles distant, and soon our lookouts would spot the lone plane, a scout from the approaching carrier force. Before long, just over the distant horizon, we would begin to make out the tiny black objects that gradually enlarged to become the masts and superstructures of fighting ships approaching the rendezvous. They would come in precisely ordered groups, the great gray ships, heavily armed and all business. Our formation then would come temporarily under the command of their senior admiral, who would designate the base course and speed for fueling. The destroyers and other escorts would form an extended screen, while the oilers prepared to service the heavy ships first, one on each side simultaneously. In some later fueling operations involving very large forces and numerous oilers, the whole ocean as far as one could see would be dotted with groups of ships all moving in the same direction in the carefully choreographed fueling operation.

With speed so low and no possibility of rapid maneuvering, not even zig-zagging, the fueling groups were dangerously vulnerable throughout the long process, and remained very much on the alert. It was a time of heightened tension. Far overhead, in the bright blue dome of the sky, the fighters of the combat air patrol maintained constant vigilance against Japanese aircraft. The destroyers and DEs echo-ranging ahead of the fueling groups carefully re-adjusted stations as necessary when one or more of them dropped out of the screen to go alongside one of the oilers. Finally, after all ships had drunk their fill, the attack force would head off on its next combat mission, gradually disappearing beyond the horizon. Then the oilers and their escorts, again alone, would proceed to a designated waiting area, there to cruise back and forth for several more days until it was time for another rendezvous and more refueling. At last, when the oilers were nearly empty, they would return to Pearl for replenishment, being replaced in the forward area by other similar ships with fresh supplies for the fleet.

On 3 December the *Elden* received provisions and 23,800 gallons of diesel oil from the *Cacapon*. As the now nearly empty oiler was about to depart for Pearl, we gave her in return a good supply of *Elden* mail for the folks back home. A letter of mine sent off at sea in this way was delivered in Rhode Island just ten days later—remarkably good service! On 4 December aircraft from the carriers we had fueled opened the Marshalls operation by blasting enemy positions on Kwajalein. Two days later we made our second rendezvous with the attack groups for more fueling. From about 0800 until 1845, for nearly eleven hours, the fueling went on, after which the *Elden* and her companions headed back toward the Hawaiian Islands, our immediate task completed.

We sighted Mt. Kaala, Oahu, at 0712 on 10 December, and by early after-noon were comfortably moored alongside the *Cabana* in Pearl Harbor. Since leaving port fifteen days earlier the *Elden* had steamed continuously for at least 4,000 miles, equivalent to a voyage from Pearl Harbor to Tokyo except that our reception at the end was more friendly. It felt good to have the ship quiet and at rest, to drink a glass of cool fresh milk, to undress and enjoy a full night's sleep between sheets. There was time for needed repairs to equipment, general sprucing up, and some liberty in Honolulu. Also we gained a new companion in the wardroom when Ens. W. G. Carden reported aboard for duty.

While awaiting our next assignment in the continuing operation against the Marshalls, we were kept fairly well occupied at Pearl. Small ships such as destroyers and DEs often were moored side by side in nests of two, three, or more, which made a rather cozy community, with ready visitation from one to another. During daytime working hours parties of sailors in blue denims scrubbed, scraped, painted, and chatted back and forth over the rails like housewives at a back fence. Occasionally a detail of men worked like ants, transferring supplies from dock to ship. Above all this activity, from time to time came blaring forth some urgent command from the loudspeakers: "Now hear this! Sweepers, man your brooms!" or "Seaman Antonelli, lay up to the quarterdeck on the double!" or "Relieve the watch!" It was noisy, it was busy and sometimes even hectic, but it was also neighborly.

With supper over and darkness lowering, gradually blotting out the lush green backdrop of Hawaiian hills, lights winked on all over the huge base, on ships and in buildings, while the distant slopes began displaying whole clusters of house lights. It was then that the men began crowding onto the ships' fantails for the evening film show—a different feature film on each ship, to be enjoyed under the stars. With several ships in a nest, we had a choice of several different films, and it was not uncommon for a discriminating fan to go from ship to ship inquiring what film was about to be shown, until he found one to his liking.

The *Elden*'s officers and men had long since become a team, with a high level of morale fortified by the contribution we now were beginning to make to the drive for victory in the Pacific. A few of our men, on their own initiative, had started to produce a chatty little newspaper which appeared occasionally quite apart from the mimeographed sheet of world news prepared daily by the radio gang. Also helpful to morale were recreational facilities ashore. The navy maintained a picnic area and beach near Barbers Point to which, by prior arrangement, whole groups of officers and men would be transported by bus for a few hours of carefree recreation. On 15 December half the *Elden*'s men enjoyed this facility, and the following day the other half. We ate a barbecue lunch, played catch, pitched horseshoes, swam in the ocean, and loafed on the beach. A few days later we drew softball equipment from a base office; the *Elden*'s officers—Carden on the mound, Neill at first, Hartung at second, Hartman at shortstop, Rickard at third, with Morrow, Leggett, Smart, and Leach guarding the outfield—suffered a humiliating 11-7 defeat at the hands of the enlisted men. Nor did the subsequent issue of the ship's newspaper neglect to report the outcome.

One evening in mid-December I was reveling in a long and luxurious shower when the General Alarm sounded—BONG - BONG - BONG - BONG - BONG - BONG—while a rasping, metallic voice ordered "All hands to General Quarters! All hands to General Quarters!" Grabbing a towel, I gave myself a couple of quick swipes and raced into my stateroom, where I jumped into a pair of pants and thrust one arm into the sleeve of a shirt (more to insure that the shirt would go along with me than anything else). Suddenly I remembered that I had left my slippers in the head, so I darted back for necessary footwear. Back in my room once more, I buckled on my pistol belt and then, ignoring the dampness that already was permeating my attire, went dashing up the ladders to the flying bridge. All around me men were preparing for action. In the darkness I groped for my gray steel helmet, clamped it on my head, finished donning my shirt, buckled on my lifebelt, and stood ready for the first Japanese attack on Pearl Harbor since the fateful seventh of December. The whole base and all ships were at Battle Stations; off in the distant sky we could see the sharp burst of anti-aircraft shells. Within minutes, though, it proved to be a false alarm—there were no enemy aircraft in the vicinity—and so we secured from General Quarters.

On the morning of 17 December the *Elden* got under way to conduct engineering trials south of Oahu. While still at sea late the next afternoon, we received orders by radio to begin searching for an OS2U observation-scout plane reported down. Immediately we headed eastward toward the designated location at flank speed. Two-and-a-half hours later we were in radio communication with an assisting patrol plane which gave us valuable coaching as we conducted our search, with the result that at 2038 we sighted the lights of the floating cripple. Moving close, we lowered our motor whaleboat and brought the plane's two officers safely aboard. The OS2U, they told us, was from the battleship *Mississippi*, and had been forced down about eleven o'clock that morning. Relaxing in our small wardroom, the flyboys enjoyed our hot coffee and the other comforts we were able to provide. Early the next morning, while the *Elden* was patrolling near the still-floating seaplane, the heavy cruiser *Wichita* (CA45) arrived on the scene and relieved us of further responsibility, enabling us to return to Pearl.

The *Elden* joined with the U.S.S. *Sederstrom* (DE 31) and the U.S.S. *Tisdale* (DE 33) on 21 December for a brief workout with submarine S-41 some distance off Barbers Point. On the next afternoon we headed for the island of Maui to participate in amphibious landing exercises with the U.S.S. *Dempsey* (DE 25), the troop transports *Leonard Wood, President Polk,* and *Pierce,* and the cargo ship *Thuban.* Later, at Maalaea Bay, Maui, where the landing exercises were taking place, we were joined by the transport *Heywood* escorted by PC 487. During the next few days, while the troops "invaded" Maui, the escort vessels maintained barrier patrols as a guard against intrusion by unfriendly submarines. A barrier patrol involved the repeated tracing of a course shaped like an elongated figure eight lying between two designated points, always echo ranging, and turning outward at each extremity to begin the next leg. It was hour after hour, watch after watch, of repetition. During such a patrol the principal concern of the OOD was to check his bearings on land frequently and adjust his course accordingly, so as to make the end turns at the correct places. We did find some interest in observing through our binoculars the activities of the troops practicing their assault techniques. More inspiring, however, was the magnificent view of the lush island of Maui with the enormous cone of Haleakala rising more than 10,000 feet out of the sea, nearly twice as high as Mt. Washington, which Tom Buffum and I had climbed together during our last summer in New England.

On Christmas Eve, as a golden sun settled down into the dark blue sea, many of the *Elden*'s men gathered on the fantail to sing carols. I had the watch as JOOD on the flying bridge from 2000 to midnight, and was there when Christmas Day actually arrived because my relief, Jack Leggett, slept happily on past the hour (dreaming, no doubt, of sugarplums). While I was waiting for him to appear the engine room watch phoned up to wish the watch on the flying bridge a Merry Christmas, after which I went onto another circuit to send similar greetings to the ready gun watches, with a caution not to shoot if they saw a sleigh with reindeer coursing through the night sky. About twenty minutes past midnight my relief finally emerged at the top of the ladder, quite cheerful, and permitted me to go below. So began my first Christmas at sea.

After breakfast I opened my gifts from home, which had been accumulating for weeks. Those of us who received eatables put most of them out on the wardroom table for all to share. At 1030 that morning the church pennant was hoisted and the *Elden* experienced her first official worship service. Aft on the fantail had been placed a portable lectern, constructed for the occasion by the carpenter's mate. There we gathered on the open deck in brilliant sunshine and fresh sea air, with the beautiful island of Maui as a backdrop, to celebrate the coming of the Prince of Peace. After the singing of "Oh Come, All Ye Faithful," there was a Christmas prayer followed by the Lord's Prayer, a reading of the Christmas story as recorded by Luke, and the singing of "Silent Night." Then Captain Adams delivered a brief sermon whose theme I cannot now recall. The service was brought to a close with more prayer, the singing of "Onward Christian Soldiers," and a benediction. To be in worship in such circumstances, with such a remarkable setting, was most satisfying, and I was grateful for a deepened sense of fellowship with many shipmates. Later all hands enjoyed an excellent Christmas dinner in surroundings as festive as could be contrived in a man-of-war. There was even a Santa Claus candle on the wardroom table. Yes, it was a very good day for the *Elden,* one to be remembered and cherished. Three days later our group of ships concluded the pre-invasion rehearsal and set course for Pearl Harbor, where we arrived during the afternoon of 29 December.

Happy New Year! One thing the *Elden* could never afford to neglect was further training in antisubmarine warfare; fortunately, ways and means were provided. For one thing, at Pearl Harbor (and many other bases) ingenious training devices known as "attack teachers" enabled ASW officers and sonar teams to sharpen their skills in simulated attacks, with results precisely reported. Think of an electronic game in an arcade and then multiply its size and·complexity by ten. Such an "attack teacher" could be installed in a building ashore or even aboard a destroyer tender afloat, making it available wherever destroyers and DEs congregated. We used these devices frequently. In addition, several times during the first part of January the *Elden* sortied for exercises with tame submarines—*Skipjack* (SS 184), *Angler* (SS 240), *Flier* (SS 250), *Jack* (SS 259), and *Sunfish* (SS 281). These boats all were sleek, black, and deadly— primed for the grim game of preying upon Japanese shipping. One of them, the *Flier,* later would be lost off the coast of North Borneo.

On the afternoon of 10 January we ventured out with the *William C. Miller,* the *Canfield,* and the *Deede* for intensive gunnery exercises lasting several days. These included not only the familiar firing at a towed sleeve, but also illumination of other ships by means of star shells, firing at a radio-controlled drone plane, and bombarding shore targets on Kahoolawe Island. In addition, our group made rendezvous with a tug towing a radar sled target for what was called "surprise battle practice." The idea was to familiarize all hands with conditions when an enemy vessel is suddenly encountered within immediate gun range, the ready guns opening fire while the ship is in the process of going to Battle Stations. During night battle practice, as the DEs in column ahead of the *Elden* fired on the sled target, getting the range by radar, their 3-inch shells looked like glowing ping-pong balls arching across the black sky. During our return to Pearl on 13 January the group underwent a simulated surprise attack by friendly aircraft, with our ships breaking formation and maneuvering radically to evade the stinging hornets.

One interesting aspect of navy life was the occasional meeting up with some friend of former days—an old chum from high school or college, or a fellow midshipman at Columbia, or perhaps a classmate at SCTC Miami. Alan Grimes, one of my close friends at Key West, was ASW officer on the *Deede,* so we saw each other fairly often when our ships were together. But encountering a friend from home was more rare. Long before the fateful 7 December 1941, one of the Y.P.F. boys, Austin Aker, had joined the navy to see the world. What he did see, as a gunner on board the U.S.S. *Selfridge* (DD 357), was the Japanese attack on Pearl Harbor. Now, in January 1944, I discovered that the *Selfridge* was again at Pearl, and so I ambled over to see Aut. His ship was a sorry sight, fitted with a blunt temporary bow after having had her entire forecastle mangled by a Japanese torpedo in the Battle of Vella Lavella. Aut himself was fit enough, but he hadn't been home since 1940, and looked considerably older than I had remembered. It was good to get together and talk, even for a short time. After such long, hard service Aut was more than ready for some home leave; only sixteen days after our reunion at Pearl he was attending morning service at Calvary in Providence. Naturally, Mother and Dad probed eagerly for whatever he could tell them about me, which was little more than the fact that I was well and apparently thriving. But such personal contacts across the miles were invaluable.

During the first half of January, while American aircraft operating from newly constructed airstrips in the captured Gilbert Islands were continuing the process of softening up Japanese defenses in the Marshalls, ships of the various task groups then in Pearl Harbor were completing preparations for their assigned missions in Operation Flintlock. Such an amphibious operation in the vast Pacific was a bit like a circus on the move. Various components assembled and proceeded separately, with all eventually converging on the objective in accordance with an elaborate timetable. Some were scheduled to arrive sooner than others, but all were expected to fit into place and perform their assigned functions. Always, however, the commanders had to be prepared for the unexpected, adjusting plans to meet changed circumstances. We found it challenging and exciting to participate as one small member of the mighty team.

The *Elden*'s part in the impending invasion actually began on the morning of 16 January with a prolonged blast from the ship's whistle as we hauled in the last line, hoisted the colors to the gaff, and slowly eased out into the channel. Other ships, too, were getting under way or preparing to do so at about the same time. What was different about this particular voyage was the company the *Elden* would be keeping. True, our primary responsibility, as before, was to shepherd a pair of fleet oilers, the *Cimarron* (AO 22) and the *Ashtabula* (AO 51), but we three were to be part of a much larger group of major combat vessels. From time to time during the voyage some of the ships would be detached and others would join up, but for much of the next ten days our companions included the formidable aircraft carriers *Enterprise* (CV 6) and *Yorktown* (CV 10), the light carriers *Belleau Wood* (CVL 24) and *Cowpens* (CVL 25), the heavy cruiser *Wichita* (CA 45), the light cruiser *Oakland* (CL 95), and a bevy of *Fletcher* class destroyers including the *Ingersoll* (DD 652), *Knapp* (DD 653), *Cotten* (DD 669), *Gatling* (DD 671), and *Healy* (DD 672).

Whenever any convoy sortied from harbor, it was always the escorts that went out first, immediately fanning out to establish a perimeter of barrier patrols behind which the larger, more vulnerable ships, emerging one by one, could form up. Once the heavy ships were in formation, the escorts scurried to form the antisubmarine screen ahead and on the flanks. This procedure was reversed when entering a harbor, with the escorts always the last to go in. One can readily see that a major sortie needed to be carefully planned in advance, each ship having its assigned time of departure, so as to avoid undue clogging and confusion. Like so much that was done in the navy, success depended heavily upon timing and teamwork.

So our group formed up and set its course, with the green mountains of Oahu slowly dropping below the horizon astern. Our course was to take us south-westward across an enormous expanse of nearly empty ocean, passing a thousand miles east of the threatened Marshalls, five hundred miles east of the newly won Gilberts, and down across the equator. Then we were to turn westward, pass around the southern end of the Gilberts, head northward towards the equator, and fuel the carrier attack forces that were to begin pounding the Marshalls on 29 January.

This long voyage proved to be, on the whole, rather pleasant, although operating in such close conjunction with major units of the fleet inevitably generated an air of tension on the *Elden*'s flying bridge. Day after day the sun grew more brilliant and hot. Sometimes I stood my watches stripped to the waist, head protected by my tropical helmet, eyes by a good pair of polaroids. Always I had my binoculars suspended from my neck and often in hand searching the surface of the sea. There were a few sonar contacts made by some of the destroyers, and on one occasion the *Oakland* even laid a pattern of depth charges, but no enemy ever put in an actual appearance. On 21 January the *Elden* fueled from the *Ashtabula*.

Some of our people amused themselves (and others) during the long voyage by cultivating various forms of facial hair. For some reason full beards were prohibited, but that still left plenty of leeway for chin brushes, handlebars, and other exotic growths. Jack Leggett, always debonair, looked especially distin-guished in a neatly trimmed Van Dyke, while Ned Lee claimed the champion among drooping handlebars. Somehow I wasn't much interested in trying it myself, but I did retain my keen delight in vocal harmony. One evening, strolling aft to the fantail in balmy weather, I found a couple of the loungers harmonizing on some favorite old songs, and couldn't resist making it a trio. For the next half hour or so we had a grand time together near the depth charge racks, two sailors and a junior officer, blending voices above the constant rumbling of the twin screws below.

A little before noon on 22 January the *Elden* made her first crossing of the equator, when all "pollywogs" of the ship's company became transformed into "shellbacks" (even though the traditional rites of initiation were cancelled by Captain Adams because of premature horseplay on the part of a few overzeal-ous crewmen). If you want to gain an impression of what we missed, consult Comdr. Edward P. Stafford's book *The Big "E"* (New York: Random House, 1962) for a vivid description of the initiation on board the *Enterprise* during the same crossing. Soon we also crossed the 180th meridian (international date line), thereby losing a day from the calendar.

On 24 January we started up the west side of the Gilberts. The following day occurred the final refueling before the attack group left us and began its run-in to the Marshalls. As the *Elden* was being fueled on the *Cimarron's* starboard side, looming just beyond the oiler was the massive bulk of the carrier *Yorktown* being fueled on the port side, all three of us (small, medium, and great) promenading together in precisely adjusted coordination. Then the *Elden* and the two oilers turned southward for the atoll of Funafuti, where we were to await further orders. En route we were joined by other DEs and oilers, some of which subsequently left us again, with the result that when we nosed into the lagoon at Funafuti on 28 January our group consisted of the *Elden,* the *Emery* (DE 28), the *Cimarron* (AO 22), the *Platte* (AO 24), the *Sabine* (AO 25), and the *Kaskaskia* (AO 27).

Funafuti was our first atoll, which is a special kind of place. An atoll is simply the crater rim of an undersea volcano protruding slightly above ocean level. This uneven rim forms a ring of low islets enclosing a lagoon (the water-filled crater). Funafuti's lagoon, bordered by about thirty such islets, proved to be ten miles wide and more than thirteen miles long. With a clear passage between two islands, such a lagoon could serve as a relatively secure anchorage for an entire fleet. When approaching an atoll by sea, often the very first objects sighted will be the masts of any vessels in the lagoon and the dull-green foliage of coconut palms that appear to be growing in the ocean, because the islets are so very low, seldom rising more than a few feet above sea level.

American forces had set up an advance base at Funafuti, and other vessels were there ahead of us. The *Elden* took on additional fuel, and then settled down to a period of riding quietly at anchor while awaiting the word that would summon us with our oilers to the Marshalls. It was at this time that Rear Adm. Mark Mitscher's carriers began their series of daily strikes against selected Japanese positions, effectively destroying enemy air power throughout that extensive group of islands. On 31 January, the designated landing or "D" day, our amphibious troops went ashore on Kwajalein, which was heavily defended, and Majuro, which was not. Other atolls in the Marshalls—Jaluit, Mili, Maloelap, Wotje, and Eniwetok—were left in Japanese hands, at least for the present.

Our group of oilers, consisting now of the *Cimarron, Kaskaskia,* and *Platte,* escorted by the *Emery* and the *Elden,* got under way for the Marshalls on the afternoon of D-Day. At 0337 on 3 February, almost as we were crossing the equator northbound, we received definite orders to proceed to Majuro Atoll some 425 miles to the north. Our course would take us between Jaluit and Mili, both still held by the enemy. Twice during that afternoon we went to General Quarters when unidentified aircraft were detected by radar, but each time they proved to be friendly. That evening the *Emery* made a sonar contact, causing the formation to execute an emergency turn to starboard, but this alarm too was a false one. As ASW officer I thought it wise to spend the entire night in or near the sonar hut, which I suppose was like carrying an umbrella to prevent rain. We encountered no Japanese aircraft or submarines as we passed about fifty miles east of Jaluit.

The next morning at 0945 our lookouts sighted the palms of Majuro, green in the forenoon light. Approaching nearer, we encountered a small American craft lazily patrolling off the entrance to the lagoon with one of her men calmly tending a fishing line trailing astern—apparent confirmation that all was well. Although the Japanese had begun to develop Majuro as a base with barracks, an observation tower, and hangars for seaplanes, they had decided to abandon it well before American troops arrived. Consequently, the small landing force at Majuro had found only three Japanese still there, and this beautiful atoll with its more than fifty coral islands and twenty-one-mile-long lagoon, had fallen into our hands without a fight. In the days to come Majuro was to serve as a commodious haven for Admiral Spruance's fleet, a place where the task forces could be comfortably and safely resupplied for further missions.

When the *Elden* finally entered the lagoon on the afternoon of 4 February, we found a considerable number of ships already there. Among them were the battleships *Indiana* (BB 58) and *Washington* (BB 56), both badly damaged from a collision at sea three days earlier, always a danger when ships were maneuvering in close proximity. Sixty feet of the *Washington*'s bow was crumpled back and skewed at a ludicrous angle; the steel plating of the *Indiana*'s starboard quarter was ripped open. For the time being, the *Elden* moored alongside the U.S.S. *Reynolds* (DE 42).

A ship really was a compact community on the move, with its own individual qualities and character—even personality. Operating in close conjunction with another ship soon made that vessel seem almost like an old friend, or at least an acquaintance. Inevitably, though, ships went their separate ways on distant missions, and might not see each other for long periods of time, might even be operating thousands of miles apart. Then, unexpectedly, they would find themselves together again at some unforeseen location, each eying the other with interest, an acquaintanceship renewed. Majuro, with so many ships constantly coming and going, was the kind of place where that could happen.

In the tropics ice cream was a rare treat for us, as the *Elden* lacked the equipment needed to make it. So, whenever we had occasion to go alongside a large vessel such as an oiler or other supply ship we habitually asked if they had a few gallons of ice cream they would sell. More often than not the answer was the one we wanted to hear. One time, though, when our supply officer tried to make such a purchase, he lacked the required amount of hard cash. Immediately the word was passed throughout the ship for voluntary contributions to a worthy cause. You never saw a line form so quickly. In no time the transaction was completed to everyone's satisfaction.

Mail from home arrived in irregular batches—sometimes a feast, sometimes a famine—according to our location and movements. Such mail had to be addressed simply to U.S.S. *Elden* (DE 264), F.P.O., San Francisco, California. That put the letter into the Fleet Post Office system which was constantly being apprised of every ship's impending ports of call (information which, of course, had to be kept secret). The Fleet Post Office dispatched the letter accordingly, doing its best to get it to the right destination in time to intercept the ship. One of our first thoughts upon entering a haven such as Majuro at the end of a voyage was "Mail!" The captain would send an armed officer together with the ship's postmaster off in the motor whaleboat to the base post office, typically a Quonset hut. There the officer would take custody of any official classified dispatches ("officer messenger mail"), while the ship's postmaster collected one or more bulging sacks of ordinary personal mail to be hurried back to the *Elden* and distributed. In general, the system worked amazingly well, greatly supporting morale. Inevitably, there were some delays and mix-ups, and indeed it was not unusual for a man to receive letters from home out of sequence.

Mother wrote to me regularly each week, Dad nearly as often, and my sister Marilyn occasionally. I also enjoyed cheerful letters from some of the Y.P.F. girls both at home and in the service, and fairly regular issues of *The Odyssey*, often marked with a personal note from "Uncle George" Jones. As for Tom Buffum, I suspected that by now he and the *Partridge* were somewhere in the British Isles. On 16 January he wrote:

> Looks like I might see guns fired in real action before you do. We are going to be in on the start of anything that comes. . . . We only learned it ourselves the other day, and it was a sobering piece of news. I don't have my fingers crossed, as I have always had good luck, but I do hope it stays with me now.

To both of us, Brown University and even Midshipmen's School were beginning to seem far in the past. A letter from Dad, himself a combat veteran, turned briefly and somewhat uncharacteristically to philosophy:

> I think of you so much day and night and do a bit of praying for you also. It has always been so through the ages—wars and the young men must go off and do the fighting. I suppose it is too much to ask that this be the war to end wars, as that was the theme song of the last war. But like each day we live we never know what it will bring so it is well to take the view that life is a pattern and what is our lot will be. Each morning the sun comes up even in a storm and even the storm will pass.

After our safe voyage from Funafuti to Majuro I wrote home: "Give my regards to all, and don't worry. Things are looking good."

The chaplain of the crippled *Washington* invited all navy personnel from the smaller ships to attend Divine Worship on Sunday, 6 February. Somebody once remarked that there were no atheists in the foxholes, a considerable exaggeration, of course. But it was equally true that there were few atheists among those Americans who went down to the sea in ships. On that bright Sunday morning in Majuro lagoon, ship's boats converged on the great battleship from all directions, bringing officers and men of diverse religious backgrounds, grateful for the opportunity to assemble for worship. Stepping onto a main deck that in comparison with the *Elden*'s looked like a plaza, we were ushered below into narrow passageways where many men were waiting patiently for a chance to crowd into the compartment where the service was to be held. When it came time to receive Communion, a long line moved slowly forward. I was glad to be there.

That same afternoon all ships suddenly received a warning from SOPA (Senior Officer Present Afloat) that unidentified aircraft were approaching—in other words, Condition Red. The *Elden,* along with all the others, went to Battle Stations. There was no doubt that such a fleet, immobile in the lagoon, made a tempting target for the Japanese. Eventually, however, the approaching aircraft were found to be our own, so back we went to Condition Green—all hands secure from Battle Stations, resume normal watches.

On the evening of 7 February the *Elden* and the *Emery* sortied, to make rendezvous early the following morning with Task Unit 50.17.2 consisting of five fleet oilers—the *Lackawanna* (AO 40), *Neosho* (AO 48), *Tallulah* (AO 50), *Neshanic* (AO 71), and *Saugatuck* (AO 75), escorted by the *Greer* (DE 23), *Whitman* (DE 24), *Brackett* (DE 41), and our old friend the *Deede.* Relieving the *Deede* and the *Greer,* we assumed stations in the screen for a return voyage to Funafuti. This time we passed about forty-five miles northeast of Mili and well east of the Gilberts. At 0820 on 11 February the *Elden* picked up Funafuti on her radar at a distance of seventeen miles, and by midafternoon our entire group was at rest in the commodious lagoon. The *Elden* proceeded to obtain 4,000 gallons of water from the *Lackawanna,* diesel oil from the YOG 82, ammunition from the *Cascade* (AD 16), and thirty gallons of frozen milk from the *Pastores* (AF 16). In addition, we were able to replenish our supplies of ice cream and candy. It was almost a foretaste of the now ubiquitous shopping center.

After supper on 13 February, with our departure scheduled for the next day and, if possible, mail to be gotten off beforehand, Fred Hartman came through officers' country calling out "Censors!" which meant an urgent task for all available officers. Letters from the crew came pouring onto the wardroom table, and we sat reading them, occasionally seizing a pair of scissors to delete some forbidden piece of information. In particular, no one was permitted to reveal our location or any details of our official activity. One letter was found to contain a solicitous inquiry about the well-being of a certain "Uncle Marshall." The amused but unrelenting censor penned in the margin a further inquiry about "Aunt Kwajalein," and returned the entire missive to its author for rewriting.

Getting under way at 1049 on 14 February, the *Elden* and the *Emery* sortied and established barrier patrols to cover the subsequent sortie of the *Lackawanna, Neosho,* and *Neshanic,* laden with more fuel for the fleet. By early afternoon we were on our way to Majuro. Our course took us within sight of tiny Tamana Island, and during the afternoon of the seventeenth we passed north of Mili as we swung westward toward our destination. Entering Majuro lagoon at 0800 the next morning, the *Elden* refueled from the *Caliente* (AO 53). Before noon we were at sea again, this time to make rendezvous north of Majuro with the *Dionne* (DE 261) and the merchant vessel *Quebec.* Having thus relieved the former so that she could proceed to Majuro, we went close alongside the *Quebec* in order to give the master his instructions. Taking station ahead, we then escorted the vessel as far east as the 180th meridian. From there the *Quebec* proceeded toward the Hawaiian Islands alone, while the *Elden* returned to Majuro. Amost immediately we were ordered to perform the same service for the S.S. *Mission Purissima,* which we accomplished with reasonable expedition and a minimum of grumbling, returning finally to Majuro on 25 February, ready for a little rest.

By this time American assault forces had seized Eniwetok, 350 miles northwest of Kwajalein, thereby denying to the Japanese a potential springboard for counterstrikes against Kwajalein and Majuro, and providing our fleet with another splendid anchorage that much closer to the Marianas. As for other enemy garrisons in the Marshalls—on Jaluit, Mili, Maloelap, and Wotje—they were simply pounded into impotence and left to survive as best they could.

Virtually every evening while anchored in the lagoon we enjoyed a motion picture on the fantail, with a large screen specially rigged for the occasion, the films routinely available through a navy exchange on base. Shortly before our movie was to begin one evening, a small navy landing craft containing three sailors, on the loose from goodness knows where, came roaring up to the *Elden*'s side. What movie were we going to show, they shouted. Given the answer, they gunned their motor and went roaring off, like hometown kids in a car, going the rounds until they found a film that captured their interest.

The daily care of the wardroom and officers' country was the responsibility of the *Elden*'s Filipino steward, Francisco Manzala, and steward's mates Elton Davis, Edwin Flowers, and Sylvester T. Franklin. It is painful to recall that during the Second World War the navy remained rigidly segregated. With few if any exceptions, black recruits were shunted automatically into the stewards' branch, to be trained and then assigned as servants for groups of commissioned officers. Manzala saw to the preparation of our meals, and in general supervised the work of his subordinates, who served our meals in style, made up our bunks with meticulous care, kept the wardroom tidy, and periodically carried our soiled clothing to the laundry aft. Because of their almost constant contact with white officers, the steward's mates were more vulnerable to bullying than other members of the crew, but I am happy to be able to say that in general, at least on the *Elden,* these men were treated with fairness and decency. The fact remains, however, that the system itself was grossly unfair and degrading. Although the steward's mates wore the navy uniform and were risking their lives like all the rest of us, they were quartered in a separate compartment aft, and their battle stations were never topside but always belowdecks as ammunition passers between the magazines and the guns.

Toward the end of February several of the officers, myself included, had an opportunity to go ashore on one of the low, palm-fringed islands. It was the first time in six weeks that I set the soles of my shoes on solid ground; believe me, it felt good. Near the water's edge I picked up a souvenir of the former occupants —a small glass bottle, possibly a container for medicine, with Japanese characters molded in its side. Occasionally, as at Bermuda, the ship's company enjoyed a swim along the *Elden*'s side while the motor whaleboat patrolled a short distance off, ready to pick up any floundering swimmer. Some of the more daring tried high diving from the upper deck levels, without winning any prizes for form.

By this time the navy had conveyed to Majuro a floating drydock large enough to service moderate-size ships of the fleet. The *Elden* entered this high-sided, rectangular facility on the last day of February for minor repairs and painting of the hull. After we had cautiously floated into the dock, the solid gates were closed behind us, the water was pumped out, and our ship was left sitting high but hardly dry on a row of keel blocks, her bottom fully exposed. All available hands were put to the task of scraping and wire-brushing the hull below the waterline, after which a coat of anticorrosive paint was applied from stem to stern.

But more important than a fresh coat of paint was the promotion of our executive officer, Fred Hartman, to full command of the *Elden.* Captain Adams, who had whipped us into shape as the crew of a fighting ship and conducted us safely thus far, relinquished the ship to Captain Hartman in a brief change-of-command ceremony on 3 March, and left us for a new assignment. Already on board was a new executive officer, Lt. Edgar Sneed. Two days after this change of command the fleet at Majuro underwent two successive air raid alerts, both proving false. Captain Hartman's quiet good humor during these episodes gave us an even greater appreciation for the quality of leadership displayed by this man who so recently had been casting dice with us around the wardroom table to determine who was to pay for an after-the-film round of fruit juice or coke. It is no exaggeration to say that every officer on board was pleased with the new command and optimistic about the future.

Every man aboard, too, was anxious to make a voyage back to the Hawaiian Islands, where we might enjoy some rest and liberty. At last the order came, and on 6 March the *Elden* began her voyage back to a friendly port. Forming up with the fleet oilers *Neosho* (AO 48), *Tallulah* (AO 50), *Pecos* (AO 65), and *Neshanic* (AO 71), together with the destroyers *Newcomb* (DD 586) and *Halsey Powell* (DD 686), we headed northeastward.

At 0330 the following morning the *Elden*'s sonar watch announced a contact at a range of 1,200 yards, but because at that very time our formation was just swinging to a leg of the zig-zag plan that would bring some of the oilers across our wake, we dropped no depth charges. Instead, the group took evasive action while the *Elden* investigated, regained contact, and decided that our target was a school of fish. Some hours later the *Halsey Powell* had a contact, also false. Then, at 1224, not to be outdone, the other destroyer announced a contact, made a run, and laid a pattern of depth charges. That seemed to inspire the *Halsey Powell*'s sonarmen, who soon developed a contact of their own, resulting in still more blasting. For a little over an hour nothing else happened. Then, at 1458, the *Elden*'s ping jockeys again heard echoes, which we very quickly evaluated nonsub. Seven minutes later the *Halsey Powell* announced a new contact and again unloaded a pattern. The sad fact is that our echoes all were coming from creatures of the deep, many of which must have lost their lives as a result. One of the *Elden*'s lookouts actually reported seeing a whale blow, which perhaps tells the whole tale.

When we reached the 180th meridian on the morning of 8 March, the two destroyers turned back toward Majuro, leaving the *Elden* as sole escort for the four oilers. Assuming station 3,000 yards ahead of the formation, we continued on our way, rolling gently in a tranquil sea. A school of dolphins arched gracefully above the surface, sampling at brief intervals the fresh breeze; flying fish occasionally shot out of the water and skimmed just above it before plunging out of sight, as though for the sheer joy of soaring in sunshine.

At 0245 on 13 March our radar detected the island of Oahu bearing 025 degrees, distant 30 miles. With the coming of daylight all hands could see the jumble of green mountains, a truly refreshing sight after the monotonous flatness of atolls and ocean. Routinely we covered the entrance of our convoy and then steamed proudly into Pearl Harbor ourselves, feeling like veterans back from the war zone, even though we had seen no action against the enemy, who had always been elsewhere. ComDesPac (Commander Destroyers, Pacific Fleet) now granted the *Elden* one week's "availability" for needed repairs, which meant that for that period of time we were exempt from being sent out to sea. Also, to our great joy, we found a large accumulation of mail awaiting us, the officers' letters being lugged into the wardroom in a wastebasket! The ones I received had mostly been written in January and February, with one piece dated as far back as December.

Shortly thereafter I submitted myself to a navy dentist who, as it turned out, should have been dressed in a red suit with horns and a forked tail. He grabbed at my jaws like a horse trader, and I began to feel that the whole of my face had somehow been taken over by my incredibly distended mouth. It wouldn't have surprised me at all if he had thrust his entire head inside for a better view. Next he began to probe my teeth with a sharp pick. *Jab*—there's one. *Jab*—another. *Jab*—and another. In no case did I have grounds to demur. Then he made sure of hitting only the offending teeth by cramming all other space in my mouth with cotton bolsters, which left only a tiny, irregular channel for the occasional passage of air into my lungs. Grabbing his electric drill, he began finding out what was at the bottom of it all, while I gurgled and squirmed, by now thoroughly convinced that he had financed his correspondence course in dentistry by working on the streets with a pneumatic drill. When that dentist finally released me, pleased no doubt with his handiwork, I arose from the chair and departed gladly. Thereafter, having been duly tested, I dreaded not the enemy's inquisition.

5

HUNTER-KILLER

That March of 1944 we settled in for a brief period of repair, routine work, training, and recreation, while awaiting our next assignment. My promotion from ensign to lieutenant (junior grade) had been processed, entitling me to add a second gold stripe to the sleeves of my dress blues and a new pair of shoulder boards to my dress whites, neither of which I had had any occasion to wear since leaving San Francisco. As for my living quarters, I now was residing comfortably if not capaciously with Jack Rickard, our gunnery officer, in the first stateroom on the starboard side just forward of the wardroom.

Oahu was yet to be fully savored. On 16 March I teamed up with Leo Miller for a day of liberty. After enjoying a meal in the gracious old Moana Hotel at Waikiki Beach, we rented bicycles and began a delightful exploration of the shady lanes and open country roads leading away from Waikiki. It was pure joy to inhale the scent of fresh green grass, and listen to the chattering and warbling of countless birds—like drinking a wonderful, invigorating tonic. Making our way up to the spectacular height called the Pali, we rested while watching the Pacific waves rolling in far below, and then went coasting on down the road leading back toward the beach. Leo and I had decided to take a room for the night at the Moana Hotel rather than return to the ship that evening, making this my first night away from the *Elden* since Boston. But it was hardly a bargain. In

Lieutenant (j.g.) Douglas E. Leach on Oahu, 1944.

order to be sure of getting back to the ship in time for morning muster we had to rise at 0545, which took the edge off an otherwise happy diversion from navy routine.

The *Elden*'s week of "availability" expired on 20 March, which meant that we were again fully available for missions at sea any time thereafter. On 21 March we received on board a group of student officers from the 3-inch gunnery course at Camp Catlin, and took them out for a day of practical experience during which they supervised the operation of our main battery. Beginning with 24 March we divided our time at sea between exercising with tame submarines and sharpening our gunnery. One day, for example, the *Elden* screened the U.S.S. *Florikan* (ASR 9) while the submarine *Salmon* (SS 182) made simulated torpedo runs. The next day we joined the destroyer *Boyd* (DD 544) for training exercises with the submarine S-28. Later the *Elden* had two days of gunnery in company with the *Harold C. Thomas* (DE 21) and the *Wileman* (DE 22) south of Oahu, putting ourselves through a variety of simulated action including anti-aircraft, day battle, and night battle. Then on the twenty-eighth we resumed our interest in submarines, working out with the *Reynolds* (DE 42) and the submarines *Salmon* (SS 182) and *Tilefish* (SS 307). The following day we again screened the *Florikan,* attempting to protect her from simulated attacks by the *Salmon* and the *Gudgeon* (SS 211). On this occasion, the *Elden* was allowed ninety minutes for making simulated depth charge attacks, during which time we made seven runs and scored six hits. Such frequent and intensive exercises were necessary to maintain a high level of combat efficiency. The great danger in the submarine service, incidentally, is dramatically illustrated by the fact that of the four submarines mentioned above, both the S-28 and the *Gudgeon* were lost later that same year.

The *Elden*'s next assignment, different from anything we had done before, came immediately. In the harrowing struggle to overcome the menace of German U-boats in the Atlantic, the navy had begun to enjoy considerable success with what were called hunter-killer groups, each consisting of an escort carrier (CVE) accompanied by several destroyers or DEs. The carrier's fighters and bombers would conduct systematic daily searches over large segments of ocean. If they sighted an enemy submarine on the surface (most World War II submarines had to surface periodically to recharge their batteries), the planes would immediately attack, either destroying the submarine or forcing it to submerge. In the latter case the planes would keep the submarine down while calling in the escort ships to sink her with Hedgehog missiles or depth charges. It was while engaged in this very kind of mission, flying off the U.S.S. *Card* (CVE 11), that Howie Goodchild had lost his life.

Now that we had established important forward bases in the Marshall Islands, the high command at Pearl Harbor, anticipating that Japanese submarines would become active along the vital supply route stretching from the Hawaiian Islands to the Marshalls, had decided to counter the threat with hunter-killer groups. The *Elden* was one of the ships assigned to this important duty. Now, instead of sashaying from base to base as an escort to fleet oilers, passively waiting for Japanese submarines to find us, we were told to go searching for them, literally looking for trouble. It seemed a mission particularly appropriate for a ship with our training and capability, and we liked the idea. What we did not know at the time was that the navy, having achieved the ability to decipher Japanese radio transmissions, was receiving frequent information about the actual location of enemy submarines on patrol, which meant that our searching would not be quite so random as it appeared to us.

The hunter-killer group to which the *Elden* now was assigned, officially known as Task Group 11.1, consisted of the escort carrier *Altamaha* (CVE 18), and the destroyer escorts *Harold C. Thomas, Wileman, Cabana,* and *Elden.* Departing from Pearl Harbor on the afternoon of 30 March, we assumed cruising formation with the four DEs screening the carrier, and headed for an area 600 miles northeast of Majuro between the two sets of sea lanes connecting Pearl Harbor with Kwajalein and Eniwetok. Our carrier was one of a type constructed rapidly during the war by superimposing a rectangular flight deck on a hull originally designed for a cargo vessel, with a very small island well forward on the starboard side. For our kind of mission her complement of aircraft consisted of roughly two dozen planes—Grumman Wildcat or Hellcat fighters together with Grumman TBF Avenger torpedo bombers.

Daily, as dawn approached, wc on the *Elden* were awakened by a raucous voice coming over the ship's PA system: "Now hear this! The ship will go to General Quarters in about five minutes!" It was a rude awakening, not as jarring as the sudden unheralded ringing of the General Alarm, but rude nonetheless. About the first of April, Jack Leggett, on watch when the time for dawn alert drew near, decided to try a different technique. On that particular morning we were awakened not by a raucous but an almost syrupy voice, like that of the announcer in a radio commercial: "Cheerio—Do you find it hard to get up in the morning? Are you logey, dull, listless? If so, try General Quarters, spelled G-E-N-E-R-A-L Q-U-A-R-T-E-R-S. You may try it in about ten minutes." Jack's cajoling invitation caused more chuckling than snorting on the *Elden,* but that particular experiment was never tried again.

Sleep was always welcome but often insufficient; whatever of it we had, we cherished. The accompanying dreams, of course, were quite unpredictable. For example, on this particular voyage I became aware that the *Elden* was carrying three passengers, a trio of attractive young women, one of whom even identified herself as a recent graduate of my own high school back home! Now this rather astonished me, to say the least, for most navy ships at sea carried only men and a cargo of wishful thinking. But these three young women, I was given to understand, were members of an auxiliary organization devoted to aiding the war effort by bolstering military morale, and that's exactly what they were doing by coming along with us on our voyage. At the time, this struck me as a most laudable endeavor. Moreover, I actually was becoming quite chummy with the girl from Cranston when Leo Miller woke me up from that dream to stand the midwatch! Alas, I never encountered her again.

The *Altamaha* commenced flight operations on 2 April when our group was about 850 miles southwest of Oahu. A carrier about to turn into the wind to launch planes always gave advance warning to all the other ships in company by hoisting the "Fox flag." As soon as our signal watch saw this, they immediately called out "Fox flag!" to the OOD, so that he could prepare to shift station as necessary. When the carrier "two-blocked" the Fox flag (hoisted it all the way up to the yardarm), she immediately swung into the wind and the entire formation reoriented, with the screening escorts hurrying to change station accordingly. In addition, one escort always was required to drop out of the screen and assume plane-guard station a short distance off the carrier's starboard quarter, in case one of the aircraft went into the drink.

Each aircraft about to be launched revved up its engine with an excited roar. Then it began its short run along the flight deck, passed over the forward edge, and dipped briefly down toward the hungry sea before gaining the lifting power needed for its gradual climb. One plane after another roared off in this manner at spaced intervals, following the leader up into the blue sky, where they closed up into operational formation and proceeded on their mission. We on the ships might not see them again for several hours. Later, after the patrol was completed, the planes reappeared, the Fox flag went up, and the carrier turned into the wind in preparation for recovering them. Again the escort serving as plane guard slid into her station, affording all hands topside a grandstand view of the always-tense spectacle of the landings. In a rough sea the flight deck of the "jeep carrier" would be rolling and pitching as though wantonly trying to deny haven to the circling planes, which made every landing a critical test of the pilot's skill.

We could see the landing officer take his stand at the after port corner of the slowly heaving flight deck, a signal paddle in each hand, ready to coach and coax each pilot into perfect alignment for a successful landing. The planes, spaced at lengthy intervals, proceeded in single file on reverse course parallel to the carrier's port side, their leader describing a gradual curve around so as to approach from astern, wheels and flaps down, hook dragging to catch one of the arresting cables stretched across the after portion of the flight deck. As the first plane slowly and almost gingerly drew near, the landing officer motioned with his paddles, the pilot responding with slight adjustments of position. Then, at the last moment, if all was not right, the landing officer waved him off and the pilot, gunning his motor, had to pass over the carrier and take a place at the end of the line for another try. A good approach, however, enabled the pilot to touch down squarely on the after part of the flight deck where, as his plane raced forward, its hook caught on one of the arresting cables, bringing him to an abrupt halt. Immediately, well-trained gangs of plane handlers rushed from the sides of the flight deck, released the hook, and got the plane moved forward well out of the way of the next aircraft just coming in to land. The speed and efficiency with which all this was accomplished, through careful training and teamwork, was truly impressive. When the last plane was safely aboard, the tension dissolved, the carrier resumed her normal course, and the other ships scurried back to their previous stations.

On the first day of flight operations the pilots practiced their gunnery by making strafing runs on a spar being towed behind the *Altamaha*. As each plane began its firing run, those of us observing from the ships saw first a sudden eruption of flashes along the leading edges of the wings, with long strings of white smoke puffs trailing behind; next, almost immediately, an angry eruption of multiple white splashes all around the moving spar; and then the sharp stuttering chatter of the aircraft's guns. One after another the planes roared down across the target and zoomed off toward the horizon in a sequence of angry attacks. It was an impressive show of skill and firepower.

Not until the afternoon of 4 April did our group have its first definite contact with the enemy lurking east of the Marshalls. Two of the planes on patrol sixty miles northwest of the formation suddenly sighted a Japanese submarine, radioed its position back to the *Altamaha,* and began to attack. At 1411 the task group commander dispatched the *Harold C. Thomas* and the *Wileman* to the scene of action. Arriving there in about three hours, the two DEs began a sonar search and hold-down operation while the planes, whose supplies of gasoline were getting low, returned to the carrier for the night. That same afternoon a second submarine also was sighted and attacked. But despite all efforts, contact was not regained with either of the submarines; both probably escaped. The *Harold C. Thomas* and the *Wileman,* frustrated, rejoined our formation at 1012 the next morning.

After four more days of flight operations without major episode, our group arrived at Majuro on the morning of 10 April, and slipped gratefully into the quiet lagoon. There we fueled, the *Elden* taking 40,000 gallons of diesel oil from the U.S.S. *Guadalupe* (AO 32). Fuel was our main reason for entering port, and once we had it we were able to resume our hunting. Accordingly, wasting no time, Task Group 11.1 sortied on the morning of 11 April, and the *Altamaha* resumed flight operations as before.

For five days we scoured the ocean northeast of the Marshalls without result. Were there no Japanese submarines left in the area? On 15 April, about 1800, Jim Neill went up to the flying bridge to begin the second dog watch. I retired to my stateroom, sat down at the desk, and began writing a letter. The *Altamaha* completed flight operations for the day at about 1827, turned to base course 250 degrees, and began zig-zagging, while the four DEs increased speed in order to re-orient the screen to the base course. It was during this maneuver, with the *Elden* on course 210 degrees, that our lookouts sighted a torpedo on the port bow racing toward the carrier beyond us. Grabbing the voice tube, Jim yelled down to the helmsman to bring the ship left to course 140, opposite and roughly parallel to the torpedo's course, rang the General Alarm, and had an immediate warning sent by voice radio to the carrier and our fellow escorts. Responding quickly, even as the broaching torpedo passed across the *Elden's* bow, the *Altamaha* swung off to the right and began retiring out of harm's way. The fact that the torpedo already was broaching when it passed us indicated that the enemy submarine had fired from nearly maximum range, apparently in a desperate attempt to score a hit. A close call, but our luck was continuing—so far.

At the moment when the General Alarm sounded throughout the ship I was in midsentence in my letter. Dropping the pen and leaping to my feet, I grabbed my pistol belt, tore out through the wardroom, and dashed up the ladders to the flying bridge. There I quickly learned what was going on. Already we were starting to run back along the torpedo's track, searching intensively with our sonar, eagerly listening for a tell-tale echo. The *Elden* plowed five miles out in that direction while the other DEs searched elsewhere. No contact. Turning left to course 60 degrees, we advanced another two miles. Still no contact. Next we turned left to course 320 degrees and searched for about four miles in that direction. Still no contact. There was one moment of sudden excitement when the *Cabana* announced a contact and made a Hedgehog attack—without result. In the meantime, the *Harold C. Thomas* had headed off to the northwest in order to protect the retiring carrier, leaving the *Wileman, Cabana,* and *Elden* to continue the search.

At 2000 the three DEs, spacing themselves at intervals of 2,400 yards in line abreast, commenced a systematic box search, expanding outward, which gave us the best possible chance of making contact with the elusive submarine. All during the hours of darkness the search went on, with our radar watch straining to pick up any indication that the quarry had come to the surface. I remained in or near the sonar hut all through that night, hoping for a solid echo, but neither our sonar nor our radar made any contact. The next morning at 0917 the task group commander, now many miles beyond the horizon, ordered all escorts to rejoin him. Less than two hours later we sighted the *Altamaha* and the *Harold C. Thomas,* and by noon all ships were back in normal formation, zig-zagging in accordance with Plan 9. Just when it was that I finally sat down at my desk to complete that broken sentence I don't recall.

On the morning of 17 April the carrier was conducting flight operations as usual, with the *Cabana* in plane-guard station. An incoming flight made the usual slow, circling approach for landing. One of the torpedo bombers made a bad touch-down, bounced off the port side of the flight deck, fell into the sea, and sank almost immediately. There was no possibility of a rescue.

Late the following afternoon our formation rendezvoused with another escort carrier, the *Fanshaw Bay* (CVE 70), together with her escorts, the U.S.S. *Coghlan* (DD 606) and the U.S.S. *Preble* (DM 20). The *Fanshaw Bay* relieved the *Altamaha,* which then departed for Pearl Harbor screened by the *Coghlan* and *Preble.* Our four DEs formed a 3,000-yard circular screen around the newcomer, and resumed the now familiar routine of the hunter-killer group.

On 19 April the carrier sent out four successive patrols of six planes each, without turning up any submarines. One of the torpedo bombers made a bad landing, slithering over into a portside gun position with nose and wing overhanging the water below. Fortunately, quick work by the carrier's deck gang effected a recovery.

The following afternoon we sighted the coconut palms of Majuro ten miles to the south. After all ships had entered the lagoon, the *Elden* fueled from our old friend the *Cimarron* (AO 22). On 21 April we took on needed provisions, and a navy paymaster came aboard with the wherewithal to bring all hands up to date in the matter of cash.

Between 22 and 29 April the *Fanshaw Bay* and her four escorts made another broad sweep toward the northeast, without positive result. For some reason the Japanese submarine force, although potentially quite formidable, was refraining from making any determined attempt to sever the long supply line connecting Pearl Harbor with the Marshalls. On 29 April our group reentered the fleet anchorage at Majuro, where the *Elden* fueled from the *Kennebago* (AO 81) and then moored alongside the *Cabana.* For many days our ships had been maneuvering at sea, reorienting the formation, changing stations in daytime and Stygian darkness, without ever coming close to a collision. Now we were at anchor in a tranquil lagoon, safe from any such peril—until a lowly garbage scow, coming alongside the *Elden* to collect refuse, managed to punch a hole in our starboard quarter eighteen inches above the waterline. Fortunately, the fissure was a small one, and our own welders were able to close it expeditiously.

We enjoyed only one night in port. Then out we went again, very early on Sunday morning, with the *Fanshaw Bay* and the other three DEs, under orders that lifted our spirits appreciably. Destination—Pearl Harbor. Scarcely had we pulled away from Majuro, however, when a plane from one of the landing strips on the atoll, towing a sleeve, came out to put us through some gunnery practice. Sighting the plane, the four escorts broke from their bent-line screen ahead of the carrier, went to Battle Stations, and formed a fairly tight circular screen around her. As the plane made repeated runs overhead, we blasted away at the fast-moving sleeve with all guns, shattering the quiet of a Sunday morning. With the exercise completed, the plane headed back for base, while our group continued its voyage to the northeast.

Some time previously a few of the *Elden*'s men, with the encouragement of Russ Morrow, had sought and gained permission to plan for fairly regular religious services on board. As the planning proceeded, I was asked to sing tenor in a quartet whose other members were Harris, Kunze, and Medica. The space we used for our brief rehearsals was the tiny carpenter's shop aft, where our harmonizing on old favorite hymns was in competition with the loud rumbling of the propellers below. The *Elden*'s first worship service since Christmas was held on the fantail during the forenoon of our departure from Majuro, providing an interesting contrast to the recently completed exercise in gunnery. Those who participated, sitting on benches in the fresh sea air, found it an uplifting experience that called up personal memories of hometown churches large and small.

The next morning our group was joined by another escort carrier also bound for Pearl, the *Kalinin Bay* (CVE 68), which made it possible for the two carriers to alternate flight duty, one sending out routine search patrols and the other employing her planes to make simulated attacks upon our formation as we forged steadily eastward, farther and farther from the war zone. We arrived at Pearl on the morning of 6 May, at which time our hunter-killer duty, which had proved to be fairly routine but strenuous, came to an end. Out of a total of thirty-eight days the *Elden* had been at sea thirty-five, always in company with one or more carriers. Understandably, our men were feeling some real sense of fatigue and a need for both rest and recreation.

My own relaxation, however, was temporarily shattered by a totally unexpected development. Upon our arrival in Pearl we received a sizable harvest of mail, and among my letters was one from a young woman in Norfolk, Virginia, where the *Elden* had tarried briefly seven months earlier, an interval of no little significance. Although I was certain that I had never met the girl, she addressed me as "Dearest Doug," and tenderly reminded me of "that last night we said goodbye to each other." Soon, she went on to inform me, she would be giving birth to our child, and was in great need of a regular allotment from my pay. Well, I did remember having been at Norfolk in October, the time indicated, but I also knew for absolute certain that I was not about to become a father! Why, at Norfolk I had not even had a near miss! Was this letter a joke, a shakedown, or a case of mistaken identity? What to do?

After confiding in Russ Morrow and pondering the strange problem overnight, I climbed ruefully to the deck above and knocked on the door of Captain

Hartman's stateroom. I briefly apprised the captain of what I had received in the mail, and handed him the girl's letter. Solemnly he perused the document and then, reaching into his own pile of mail, handed me two others on the same theme—one from the girl herself and the other from the Family Welfare Society in Norfolk, both asking him to use his influence with me on the girl's behalf. The Captain permitted me to read and digest these alarming letters while he sat impassively. Then, and only then, did he produce one final item which had been enclosed in one of the letters—the trump card. It was a photograph of the kind taken by professional photographers going the rounds of the tables in night clubs. It showed very clearly a happy couple seated at a nightclub table in Norfolk in October—the girl who had written to us and her male companion Doug. I saw instantly, as had the captain earlier, that the Doug in the photo-graph, although dressed in a navy officer's uniform, most definitely *was not I.* He was a naval aviator whose bright metal wings were clearly visible on his left breast. In short, it had to be a case of mistaken identity. The unfortunate girl, in trying to trace her departed lover through navy channels, had arrived at the wrong berth—mine.

Captain Hartman, obviously relishing my discomfiture, had played his part with a perfectly straight face, withholding the decisive photograph until the very end. Then he enjoyed my relief even more. And the story quickly spread. For some time thereafter I was called "Poppa" by wardroom wags who shook their heads sagely in remarking that "still waters run deep." A captain from another DE, dining with us on one occasion, felt free to comment loftily upon my moral laxity; indeed, the Norfolk affair, if I may call it that, even came to the attention of the commander of an escort division. To cap it all, when I took a refresher course in Antisubmarine Warfare on the base, one of the instructors at the school made a point of speaking personally with the *Elden* officer who had "left a trail of broken hearts in the States." *Sic praemium virtutis!* I have often wondered what did eventually happen to that girl and her baby—and if she ever did get an allotment from her pilot.

For all of us on the *Elden,* those days at Pearl Harbor were mostly very busy ones, with innumerable errands to be run and tasks to be completed. Officers checked on equipment and supplies, sweated over paperwork, examined can-didates for advancement in rating, and censored mail. A navy ship, as I have said before, is a community and, like any town ashore, its membership is in almost constant flux. Virtually every time the *Elden* completed a long voyage, some of our people were detached with orders to other stations, while new men came trudging up the gangplank, white canvas seabags on their shoulders, to fill the vacant billets. There was a gradual turnover among the officers as well. Nine months after the *Elden*'s commissioning, four of the original twelve officers—

Adams, Bernstein, Hill, and Pontius—no longer gathered at the wardroom table with Hartman, Lee, Leggett, Miller, Morrow, Neill, Rickard, and myself. We had been joined by others—Hartung, Smart, Carden, and Sneed. Early in May a young officer specially trained in communications, Ens. Leroy F. Werges, reported aboard as replacement for Jim Neill, who departed a few days later. As a result of this change, I took command of C-Division, with Roy Werges as my assistant.

Plans and preparations for the next giant step toward Japan were by this time approaching a climax, so our period of repose in Pearl Harbor was brief. On 19 May the *Elden* departed from Oahu with a group of transports carrying the Twenty-seventh Infantry Division, minus artillery, for amphibious landing exercises at Maalaea Bay, Maui. It was during this voyage that I began standing "top watches" at sea—in other words, I ceased being somebody else's JOOD and became OOD in my own right. The OOD was directly responsible to the captain for the conning and general operation of the ship during his watch, and was expected to take whatever action was required in any emergency, including a sudden encounter with the enemy, which meant that the lives of all hands were dependent upon his skill and judgment. It was an awesome responsibility, but after so many months of watchstanding as a JOOD I felt reasonably confident.

Shortly before 1600 on the day of our departure from Pearl I climbed up to the flying bridge and stood with the off-going OOD, Jack Rickard, while he explained the current situation, including the *Elden*'s course and speed, the specified and actual bearing and distance to the guide ship in the formation, the location of any nearby groups of ships or land, and any standing orders from the captain. When satisfied that I had all the information needed to carry on, I threw a salute while uttering four significant words—"I relieve you, Sir." From that instant the responsibility was all mine, until such time as the captain or the executive officer should come to the bridge and take over. At about the same time, my JOOD was relieving the off-going JOOD. And so the watch commenced.

Immediately I sent my JOOD to inspect the ship for watertight integrity, making sure that all was correct. At 1610 we tested the range recorder and at 1714 the ship's whistle and siren. Five minutes later our formation began zig-zagging, which meant that I had to make precisely timed changes of course every few minutes, in coordination with all the other ships. Frequently I took a bearing on the guide, and obtained her range from the radar watch below. If I discovered that the *Elden* was gradually falling off station, I had to adjust either course or speed, or both, in order to rectify the situation. It was marvelous what a brief change of five degrees in course or a few added revolutions of the propellers could accomplish if skillfully applied. An OOD who was lax in station-keeping might expect to receive a peremptory message by voice radio from the task group commander: "Hello, Featherbed. This is Grumpy. Get on station immediately! I say again—get on station immediately! Over." To which the chagrined OOD could only reply: "Hello, Grumpy. This is Featherbed. Willco. Out." I found the experience of having full control of the ship exhilarating, but was relieved, in more ways than one, when Leo Miller, the next OOD, arrived on the flying bridge to take my place. Leo, as always, insisted on a thorough briefing. Then, at last, "I relieve you, Sir," he said, saluting. I returned the salute and went clumping down the ladder to the Combat Information Center, where I wrote up my brief report for the log. After that, I was more than ready for a good supper.

The next morning when we arrived at Maalaea Bay, the *Elden* took station off the beach as primary control ship, a role normally played by a PC. It was the control ship that served as a point of reference for the successive waves of landing craft heading for the beach, dispatching each wave at the designated minute. Even with the landing rehearsal, the overall scene was relatively peaceful and very beautiful. Beyond the intervening stretch of sparkling blue water, beyond the surf-fringed beaches, I again saw the massive bulk of Haleakala, looking as though some primeval giant had seized the entire south end of Maui and drawn it up toward the sky. How I longed to be over there and climbing up to what surely must be one of the world's most breathtaking views. So near and yet so inaccessible!

After completing the first day's exercises, our task group proceeded to the anchorage in Lahaina Roads, and the *Elden* spent the night patrolling a three-and-a-half-mile sector to the north and west. That same day, back at Pearl Harbor, occurred a disaster. A large amphibious landing ship of the type known as an LST had been engaged in loading ammunition when suddenly there was a blasting explosion that spread from vessel to vessel in sheets of flame. The fiery blast destroyed six LSTs and three smaller ships, killing 163 men and injurng nearly 400. Handling ammunition was a task that always required the most stringent precautions, and it is somewhat chilling to recall that in wartime every navy combat ship carried enough explosives to blow her sky high.

On 23 May our group made an early morning approach to the small island of Kahoolawe, used by the navy for live firing, where we were to complete our exercises. Aircraft supporting the operation strafed and bombed the beach, lending a touch of realism that had not been possible at Maalaea Bay. Then, after all exercises had been completed, the task group formed its cruising disposition for the short return voyage to Pearl Harbor, the screen commander being in the U.S.S. *Waller* (DD 466). We entered port the next afternoon.

After that, the *Elden* participated in several days of antisubmarine exercises off Oahu, operating at various times with the *Florikan* (ASR 9), *Lyman* (DE 302), and *Twining* (DD 540). Our tame subs were the S-41, *Plaice* (SS 390), and the ill-fated *Seawolf* (SS 197) which was to be lost seven months later.

Like nearly all servicemen in wartime, we yearned for home, and pursued victory as the surest way of eventually getting home for good. Thus we had a real vested interest in every success gained by any of the anti-Axis powers anywhere. On the Eastern Front, Soviet armies now were regaining large areas from the German invaders, and we cheered them on. In Italy, American and British troops were slogging slowly northward, finally capturing the commanding height of Monte Cassino 120 miles southeast of Rome. Increasingly, too, there was intense speculation about the imminence of the long-awaited cross-Channel invasion by powerful forces from Britain, to begin the liberation of France and the Low Countries. That would be an operation of enormous scope, difficulty, and danger, but we never doubted that our side could pull it off, eventually. Tom Buffum would be involved in that, no doubt, and I wished him well.

In the South Pacific, General MacArthur's forces were busily chewing away at the entrenched Japanese along the north coast of New Guinea, all the time edging closer and closer to the Philippines. As for the Central Pacific, *our* ballpark, we now had a firm grip on the Marshall Islands, including remote Eniwetok, with yet another major advance clearly impending. Whatever the *Elden*'s next assignment, we were ready to go.

6

OPERATION FORAGER:
The Marianas

By the spring of 1944 there could be no doubt about the fighting qualities of the Japanese foe. During 1942 the Imperial Army and Navy had shown their ability on the offensive, overrunning vast areas with determination, skill, speed, and a fearsome ferocity. Their air forces had been effective, their army tough and mean, their navy well trained and daring. The following year, Japanese garrison troops stationed in the Gilberts had demonstrated an almost incredible tenacity in holding well-prepared defensive positions against overwhelming attack, generally preferring death to surrender even after the situation had become hopeless. Capturing a firmly held Japanese position was never easy and often extremely costly to the attackers. Now, in the spring of 1944, American forces were about to undertake the next great jump toward Japan, to the Marianas a thousand miles west of Eniwetok. The Marianas were a chain of volcanic islands constituting Japan's next defensive perimeter. Starting with Guam in the south, this chain stretches northward along a shallow arc for some 425 miles to a point barely a thousand miles south of Emperor Hirohito's palace. Moreover, these islands were not mere low-lying atolls, but substantial chunks of land rising in some cases to heights of well over a thousand feet. They were liberally furnished with airfields and other critically important base facilities that Japan was determined not to lose. Wresting the Marianas from their Japanese defenders would mean a fight to the death at the far end of a very long, exposed line of supply stretching 3,200 or more miles westward from Pearl Harbor—equal to the width of the Atlantic Ocean.

The American high command had decided to concentrate its effort on the three principal islands, all located in the southern portion of the chain—Guam, Tinian, and Saipan. These three, if taken from the Japanese, would not only undermine completely the Marianas defensive line blocking the approach to Japan, but also provide space for major airfields from which the systematic bombing of Japanese industrial centers could begin. The campaign to capture the Marianas, set for June 1944, was given the code name Operation Forager, with naval responsibility being assigned to Adm. Raymond A. Spruance's experienced Fifth Fleet.

Guam had been American territory until lost to the rampaging Japanese in December 1941, and its native Chamorro people tended to remain pro-American—or strongly anti-Japanese. About a hundred miles north of Guam lie the two islands of Saipan and Tinian, separated only by a three-mile-wide strait. These had been Japanese since 1914, and were thoroughly "Japan-ized." Their inhabitants were mostly Japanese and Okinawan farmers who raised sugar cane, vegetables, and cattle. All three islands were defended in 1944 by strong garrisons of Japanese troops—more than 18,000 on Guam, nearly 9,000 on Tinian, and well over 30,000 on Saipan. In addition, they had a good supply of local air power.

In order to take these three important bases it was necessary to convey two marine divisions and two army divisions plus thousands of corps and garrison troops, together with vast quantities of supplies and equipment, from the Hawaiian Islands to the Marianas. Fortunately, Eniwetok provided an excellent springboard for the final stage of that long journey. Its commodious lagoon, 388 square miles of clear, sheltered water, became a haven for nearly every ship engaged in Operation Forager, so that sometimes the masts in the lagoon, seen from a distance, looked almost like a forest growing in the ocean. The principal threat to the advance by sea from Eniwetok to the Marianas consisted of lurking Japanese submarines, and aircraft operating out of Truk, Yap, Palau, and the Marianas themselves. In addition, the Imperial Fleet, largely based in the Philippines, posed a potential threat of no mean proportions.

Knowing that the *Elden* had been assigned a role in Operation Forager, I wrote home on 3 June, shortly before our departure from Pearl Harbor, "Don't be surprised if you don't hear from me for awhile." All parents having a son in the navy knew what that sentence meant—a long voyage impending. They could only wonder where and for what purpose. The *Elden* and her sister the *Deede* left Pearl on the afternoon of 4 June as escorts to a convoy of six merchant vessels carrying garrison troops for Saipan, units assigned to mop up and defend the island once it had been overrun. After dark the first night out the *Elden* circled once all the way around the convoy to make sure that no lights were showing. Two days later, at 2100, we made a hasty attack upon a sonar contact, laying a full 13-charge pattern of depth charges set shallow, which undoubtedly generated a little excitement for the troops. Our contact soon was classified nonsub, we secured from General Quarters, and the formation resumed its normal quiet advance westward across the lonely sea.

The necessary but ever-unpopular dawn alert was always a component of our routine at sea, beginning with the raucous announcement on the PA system— "Now hear this! The ship will go to General Quarters in five minutes. The ship will go to General Quarters in five minutes." Sleepily I roll out of my bunk and grope for my clothing. There is just time for a quick visit to the head. Then I gather up my cartridge belt bearing the Colt pistol in its holster, and ascend the steep ladders to the flying bridge. Emerging at the top, I am struck by the dank wind whipping past. There is a feeling of chill and dampness every-where. All around is darkness as far as one can see in any direction, except for the white wake receding from the *Elden*'s stern and the faint glow of dawn in the eastern sky. I exchange words with the off-going OOD, who apprises me of the current situation including our present course, speed, and position relative to the guide. All around me in the darkness other men are taking their stations, buckling on lifebelts and donning steel helmets wet with morning dew. On the gundecks the gun crews are removing the protective canvas coverings from their weapons. Soon a "talker" on the flying bridge informs the captain that all stations are manned and ready. Off in the darkness I can just begin to make out the blurred shapes of other ships in our formation, all of them also now on the alert. So we all stand ready, swaying easily on the throbbing, gently heaving deck while we watch the miracle of dawn gradually unfolding in the eastern sky. When at last it is fully light the captain gives the welcome order to secure from General Quarters, and the old watch takes over once again. The rest of us clump below for breakfast.

On such a voyage the days and nights succeed each other with endless monotony, marked only by the routine of shipboard activity and an occasional false alarm. The dark watches of the night seem long indeed and usually quite tedious. Yet one always has the obligation to remain alert and prepared for any occurrence. Perhaps a lookout reports the appearance of a flare on the horizon, or the sharp flashes of distant gunfire. The OOD studies the indicated bearing through his binoculars. Yes, he thinks he sees it also. But the flare can be a star, or the gun flashes distant lightning. Better not take a chance—better be sure. The OOD reaches for the telephone and rings the captain's stateroom. In a moment the captain, clad in pajamas, arrives on the flying bridge to see for himself. Everyone stands peering along the indicated bearing for several minutes—total blackness, nothing at all. The captain waits a few more minutes, yawning, then goes below to his bunk. Immediately, there it is again! Well—it's a star, or distant lightning.

On such nights I may indulge in a little fantasizing, symptomatic of my yearning for home. Perhaps my father is a visitor on the *Elden,* standing there with me on the flying bridge, fascinated by our mode of operation and reassured by our efficiency. Or perhaps the ship is steaming slowly up Narragansett Bay toward Providence on a clear summer day. A sailboat approaches, and I recognize it as the Browns' catboat *Elizabeth,* crammed with my family and friends. They see me way up there on the flying bridge and start waving excitedly; proudly I return the greeting. All right, Walter Mitty, remember where you really are—en route to the war zone.

Our long voyage to Eniwetok was mostly routine—except for the thrilling news of D-Day in Europe, the long-awaited opening of the Second Front that would finally squeeze Germany out of the war. As the naval historian Samuel Eliot Morison has noted, "Added together, 'Overlord' in Europe and 'Forager' in the Pacific made the greatest military effort ever put forth by the United States or any other nation at one time." And it all happened in June 1944. Of course the men of the Fifth Fleet were elated by the news from Normandy, even though it seemed to upstage our own impending surprise for the folks back home. Headlines were headlines, and all of us out there knew that soon we also would be making the front page.

As our formation steamed steadily westward we enjoyed calm seas and at night a beautiful but all-too-revealing full moon that lit up the ocean like a huge lamp in the sky. Our course took us past the largely neutralized Japanese-held island of Wotje in the Marshalls at a comfortable distance of about eighty-five miles. In the early hours of 14 June the *Elden* piled on extra knots and forged ahead in order to make radar contact on Eniwetok as soon as possible. Our radar watch detected the atoll at a distance of twenty-one miles, and by 0605 that morning we were off the Deep Entrance. As the troop ships slowly entered, one after the other, the pair of escorts maintained protective barrier patrols and then, when the convoy was safely inside, ventured in to the welcome haven.

As we entered the passage we could see on the nearby land ample evidence of the so-called "Halsey shampoo"—shredded palm trees reduced to gaunt stumps standing forlornly amidst acres of bomb and shell craters. It was our first view of terrain that had been subjected to such naval devastation and then wrested from the enemy in tough, close combat. Later, when I had an opportunity to go ashore on one of the islands ringing the spacious blue lagoon, I observed more.

Under the palms had sprung up a small city of tents and Quonset huts, all with little slit trenches or sand-bagged dugouts nearby in case of an air raid. One tent was functioning as a cobbler's shop complete with machinery for repairing shoes. Somewhere else I saw an ingenious little wind-driven washing machine consisting of short vanes rotating an offset axle to which was fixed a vertical plunger. At the lower end of this plunger was an inverted mess cup sloshing up and down, up and down, ceaselessly (so long as the wind blew) in a bucket of laundry. There were basketball courts, a post office, a barbershop. Two Quonset huts had been joined at right angles and surmounted by a wooden steeple—the island's chapel.

In the meantime, the pre-invasion strikes against the Marianas had begun. On 12 June carrier planes blasted targets on Saipan, Tinian, Guam, and two less important islands. The following day ships of the fleet commenced their own systematic pounding of Saipan. Then, on 15 June the Second and Fourth Marine Divisions landed in waves on Saipan's western shore to begin the conquest. During the next few days several of the *Elden*'s former consorts were damaged near Saipan by Japanese aircraft. The escort carrier *Fanshaw Bay*, with whom we had performed hunter-killer duty, was hit by a bomb; the fleet oilers *Neshanic, Saranac,* and *Saugatuck* were attacked and hit while fueling destroyers and DEs. Fortunately, all four survived.

Our group of troop transports was ordered to leave Eniwetok and head for Saipan on the morning of 18 June. The *Deede* having been detached for other duty, the screen of escorts was reconstituted and strengthened, consisting now of the *Benson* class destroyer *Bancroft* (DD 598), the *Wileman* (DE 22), and the *Elden.* We felt elated about the recent landing on Saipan, the beginning of the conquest of the Marianas, and realized that for the first time the *Elden* was to become involved not merely at the fringes of activity but at a scene of immediate and critical combat. All through that day and into the night we pushed westward, every thrust of the propellers taking us closer to Japan itself than we had ever been. Then, to our surprise and dismay, came a radio message ordering our group to reverse course and return to Eniwetok. It was all too easy now to imagine the worst—a serious setback at Saipan, a reversal of American fortunes in the war, a jarring halt to our drive across the Central Pacific. The real cause of our unexpected return to Eniwetok was probably the menace of a powerful Japanese fleet detected approaching the Marianas from the direction of the Philippines. Should that fleet manage to slash through the American fleet and drive on to the Marianas, it *would* be a disaster, and the only ships needed at Saipan would be those capable of evacuating our troops and fleeing back to the Marshalls.

That night I had the midwatch, during which our formation complied with the unexpected orders by making a series of course changes that brought us around to a course for Eniwetok. Not until about 0600 that morning did I finally crawl into my bunk, tired and discouraged. It was late that afternoon when we regained the security of the great lagoon. There the *Elden* topped up her tanks from the U.S.S. *Sepulga* (AO 20), and settled down to await developments. The calm was suddenly broken at 2055 on 20 June by Air Flash Red, sending us to Battle Stations. But no enemy planes appeared. In the meantime, American carrier planes operating southwest of Saipan were so successful in shooting down large numbers of Japanese aircraft that the enemy fleet eventually had to abandon its attempt to interfere in the Marianas. The Battle of the Philippine Sea, 19-20 June, was decisive, enabling our forces at Saipan to continue the conquest.

On the afternoon of 21 June the *Elden* and her consorts again sortied from Eniwetok and headed for Saipan, relieved to know that the offensive was proceeding as before. The next morning the troop transports practiced scattering fanwise, as they might be required to do should enemy surface raiders appear. Two days later our screen was reinforced by a brace of *Fletcher* class destroyers—the *Philip* (DD 498) and *McNair* (DD 679), whose 5-inch and 40-millimeter guns added significantly to the group's firepower. That evening when I was standing the second dog watch we received Air Flash Red from Saipan and went to Battle Stations. The reason for the alert (not known to us at the time) probably was an attack by enemy torpedo planes from Guam upon American shipping off Saipan, less than 150 miles west of our position.

At 0430 on 25 June, a week after our first departure from Eniwetok, the *Elden*'s radar detected the beleaguered island of Saipan bearing 248 degrees, distant fifty miles. It was Mt. Tapotchau, rising to a height of 1,554 feet above sea level, that enabled us to pick up land at such a distance. Long before any land became visible, however, our watch on the flying bridge began seeing little blobs of eerie greenish-yellow light suddenly appearing in the predawn sky far off beyond the southwestern horizon, star shells being lobbed above Saipan by American fire-support ships to keep the battleground well illuminated for our troops. Beneath that sickish unnatural illumination crouched thousands of Japanese soldiers in foxholes, trenches, gun emplacements, and caves—young men who also loved their homes, their families, their country. Ardent patriots, imbued with the conviction that they were serving a divine emperor, they were fanatical warriors who seemed almost eager to expend their lives in combat. To defeat them invariably required the infliction of wholesale death and destruction—the terrible condition of warfare in the Pacific.

At 0622 we sighted the island itself at a distance of twenty-nine miles. Later, in passing by its northern end and proceeding toward the anchorage area off the western beaches, we saw numerous fire-support ships along the coast shelling enemy positions ashore. Saipan, at first glance, was reminiscent of Oahu on a much smaller scale. Marpi Point, the northernmost extremity, was simply a wall of sheer rock cliffs at whose base the restless sea constantly smashed in bursts of white spray. Beyond rose a complex of steep rock faces and irregular green hills, the latter thick with vegetation, forming a sort of pedestal for the dominating profile of Tapotchau. Here and there on the steep hillsides were grim outcroppings of rough, dark gray volcanic rock. Over this menacing terrain our troops were painfully advancing northward against desperately defended Japanese positions. As the *Elden* proceeded down the western side of the island, I could see how the high central ridge gradually subsided toward the lower and flatter southern end, where the former Aslito airfield, already in American hands, was located. On Saipan's western shore were the three principal towns—Tanapag and Garapan, whose harbor was formed by a long offshore reef, and Charan Kanoa, on either side of which our troops had landed ten days earlier. Through my binoculars I could make out the gaunt remains of a Japanese sugar refinery standing forlornly amidst the rubble of Charan Kanoa. Leaving the troop transports at the anchorage area among a swarm of other vessels, the *Elden* took up its station in the patrol line protecting the beach-head against interference from seaward.

At the time of our arrival on 25 June troops of the Second Marine Division were taking control of Mt. Tapotchau's summit, while the remainder of that division together with the Fourth Marine Division and the Twenty-seventh Infantry Division were deployed along an irregular front line stretching from the southern outskirts of Garapan on the west over the crest of Tapotchau and on to the east coast. With the exception of some Japanese holdouts on Nafutan Point at the extreme southern end of the island, the southern half of Saipan was ours; the northern half, including most of Garapan, remained in the hands of a very determined enemy. Clusters of dirty gray smoke crawling along the rugged hillsides roughly defined the zone of heaviest combat, and the sporadic CRUMP-CRUMP of artillery surmounted all other sounds.

Several miles south of the anchorage area lay the somewhat smaller and less hilly island of Tinian, held by nearly 9,000 Japanese troops (roughly 175 men per square mile). From our patrol station, as we methodically cruised back and forth, we could observe American 155-millimeter artillery near the southern end of Saipan firing across the strait onto enemy positions in the northern part of Tinian. The blast of a gun on our left would be followed by a shellburst on the green slopes of Tinian off to our right, over and over again, as the artillery methodically probed and pounded. In peacetime Tinian must have been quite attractive. Edged mostly with low cliffs of dark volcanic rock against which the white surf smashed and smashed again, the island rose gradually to a long central plateau green with scrubby growth, low trees, and palms. Ushi Field at the northern end and Kahe Field near Guarguan Point on the western side were the principal Japanese airstrips, now virtually useless under the close observation of American ships and planes. The only settlement of any size was known as Tinian Town, a village on the western shore a short distance below Guarguan Point.

The *Elden* and the destroyer *Bancroft* received orders to proceed that evening to the far side of Tinian, where the two ships were to spend the night maintaining a close watch along the western shore. If enemy planes approached and attempted to land on the island, we were to shell the airstrips. What was considered more likely, however, was that enemy troops would try to cross from Tinian to Saipan in barges or other small craft under cover of darkness and land behind American lines. Our task, in short, was to patrol up and down the western coast of Tinian, illuminating with star shells and delivering harassing fire on any targets of opportunity, especially in the vicinity of Tinian Town. The mission was under the immediate command of the *Bancroft*'s captain. For the first time since commissioning, the *Elden*'s gun crews, after all those many days of practice firing at artificial targets, were to direct their fire at the actual enemy. So the 3-inch guns were uncovered, the ready-ammunition lockers opened, and all made ready for action.

In a column of two, with the *Bancroft* about 1,500 yards in the lead, we began our systematic patrol roughly parallel to and approximately three miles off the hostile shore. The first jarring blast from one of the *Elden*'s 3-inch guns signalled our initiation into actual combat. From my battle station on the flying bridge I could see everything that transpired. We fired again and again as we cruised along the dark hulk of the island, illuminating the terrain with star shells and dropping high explosive shells on suspected targets. This was not like firing from a camouflaged gun pit. Our little ship and its sole companion were out in the open as though on a flat stage exposed to the eyes of every Japanese gunner on the western half of Tinian. Passing Tinian Town about every half hour, we hung star shells above the settlement and poured in a number of explosive shells, starting some fires. The helmeted gun crews worked in near darkness with almost perfect coordination, a pay-off from those many drills. Yet there came no answering fire. The enemy was shrewd and well disciplined. He knew that our nocturnal intrusion was a mere harassment, not an invasion, and so preferred to save his shots and not reveal his defenses. Our shots were little more than flies on a horse's flank. Thus patrolling and firing, the two ships carried on their mission in routine fashion until suddenly, about 0335, we detected a cluster of what appeared to be barges outside Tinian harbor, moving slowly along the shore. Both ships headed for those barges and opened fire. Soon, however, the destroyer exhausted her supply of illuminating ammunition, and ours was badly depleted as well, so it was decided to postpone further action until daybreak. In the meantime, the two ships would separate, one to patrol northward and the other southward, so as to prevent the barges from slipping around Tinian in either direction.

At about 0530, when it was becoming light enough to see objects at a distance, the *Bancroft* and the *Elden* approached Tinian harbor together. There we saw about a dozen small craft riding at moorings within the protection of a breakwater. Moving close, so close that I could see clearly the dwellings and even a distinctive red *torii*—a temple gate—in the little town, we opened fire. The small craft proved to be difficult targets, merely bobbing up and down at near misses, but we may have destroyed one or two and damaged others. While still engaged in this intensive firing, we saw on the nearby shore a sudden series of rapid flashes and then, a short distance off our bow, an equally sudden and rapid eruption of splashes. One or more Japanese 25-millimeter guns had opened fire with short bursts. Immediately the *Bancroft* warned us to withdraw, and the two ships moved off to a safer distance. That concluded the night's action. Altogether during the patrol the *Elden* had fired 111 star shells and 241 explosive shells from the 3-inch guns, and 965 shells from the 1.1-inch gun. We had started some fires, probably destroyed one or more small craft, and prevented a possible movement of enemy troops to Saipan. Not once during any of the *Elden*'s patrolling at Tinian, either then or subsequently, did I ever see a human figure on shore. All, civilians and soldiers alike, remained effectively concealed.

At 1815 on 26 June the *Elden* received orders by voice radio to join the screen of a task group forming up for a return voyage to Eniwetok. Clearly, the American high command at Saipan was convinced that they could carry on without us. So off we went, still excited by our brief brush with the enemy. Our convoy consisted of nine large vessels—the attack transports *Harry Lee* (APA 10), *J. Franklin Bell* (APA 16), *Cavalier* (APA 37), *Custer* (APA 40), *Fremont* (APA 44), *John Land* (APA 167), and *Herald of the Morning* (APA 173); and the cargo ships *Electra* (AKA 4) and *Jupiter* (AK 43). Escorting these were the *Dewey* (DD 349), *Hull* (DD 350), *MacDonough* (DD 351), *Bancroft* (DD 598), *Hopkins* (DMS 13), *Perry* (DMS 17), *Dent* (APD 9), *Steele* (DE 8), *Wileman* (DE 22), and *Elden,* deployed in a circular screen. Two of these ten escorts, incidentally, later came to unhappy ends: the *Perry* was sunk by a mine off Palau in September, and the *Hull* went down in a typhoon off Luzon in December, taking with her about two hundred officers and men.

As our group was pulling away from Saipan on the evening of 26 June we received Air Flash Red, causing the ten-ship screen to tighten the circle for anti-aircraft defense, but no attack materialized in our vicinity. Later the *Elden* was sent about seven miles ahead of the formation as an advance picket, resuming a regular station in the screen the next morning. That day our group was joined by three attack cargo ships from Saipan—the *Almaack* (AKA 10), *Centaurus* (AKA 17), and *Virgo* (AKA 20). A few hours later, at noon, three of our destroyers—the *Dewey,* the *Hull,* and the *MacDonough*—were detached, whereupon the seven remaining escorts formed a bent-line screen forward of and flanking the twelve-ship convoy.

We sighted Eniwetok at 1030 on 30 June. Once the large ships were all safely inside the lagoon, the escorts also filed in, and the *Elden* went alongside the U.S.S. *Lackawanna* (AO 40) to refuel. The following day we replenished our supply of ammunition, so as to be fully prepared for further action.

On the Fourth of July, without any special celebration, we went out on temporary patrol duty off Wide Passage, relieving the U.S.S. *Sederstrom* (DE 31). That evening while on station we passed a lighted hospital ship close aboard to starboard, a most unusual sight. No ordinary vessel, whether warship or merchant ship, dared show any lights while underway after dark. Hospital ships, in contrast, were deliberately kept well illuminated, with large red crosses clearly displayed in accordance with international law. The one we passed may have been loaded with wounded soldiers and marines from Saipan. The next day, after being relieved by the *Dionne,* the *Elden* re-entered the lagoon and anchored to await further orders.

Late on the afternoon of 6 July the *Elden* got under way as sole escort for a single merchant vessel, the SS *Cape Cod,* taking garrison troops to Saipan. Two days later, when we were about midway, a radio dispatch diverted us north of our intended track to avoid encountering a Japanese submarine that reportedly had been attacked the previous day. With a troop ship involved and only one escort to protect her, evasion was considered preferable to action.

Approaching Saipan, at 0637 on 10 July we had a sonar contact, causing the *Cape Cod* to make an emergency turn, but we quickly decided that it was not a submarine and resumed our normal progress. By this time the island was clearly visible on the port hand. Only the day before our troops had finally driven all the way to Marpi Point, the northern tip of Saipan, thereby ending organized Japanese resistance. In rounding Marpi Point and heading for the anchorage area we passed the floating corpse of a Japanese soldier face down on the surface of the gentle sea—a pathetic sight. Hundreds of frightened or defiant Japanese—men, women, and children, indeed, whole families—had cast them-selves over the edge of the sheer cliffs at the northern end of the island rather than be taken by the victorious Americans.

After depositing the *Cape Cod* safely, the *Elden* refueled from LST 218. Gone from the green hills were the smoke and sounds of battle, except at the southern end of the island where American artillery was continuing its methodical bombardment of Tinian. As night drew near, the *Elden* and her sister ship the *William C. Miller* were dispatched to Tinian's western coast, as before, to illuminate and harass. At 1850 the two DEs assumed station and commenced their watchful night patrol. Since our last visit, Tinian Town had been subjected to heavy bombardment and was now badly gutted. Once again we patrolled back and forth, periodically lighting up the shoreline with star shells and pouring 3-inch projectiles into the town. This time, however, we failed to start any fires which could be used as aiming points. From the Japanese garrison came little or no response. Then at 0255, as the *William C. Miller* was firing, we saw a sudden flash from a battery north of Tinian Town. In the faint moonlight the puff of smoke remained momentarily visible, giving our gunners an aiming point, and the *Elden* seized the opportunity to lay 14 rounds into that area. From the battery came no answering fire. On our final run past Tinian Town the *Elden* ceased firing at 0518, having expended altogether during the night 43 rounds of illuminating and 128 of AA service ammunition.

As we drew away from Tinian Town for the last time, we had little or no grasp of the enormous danger to which we had been exposed, and I can speak of it now only with deep gratitude for our escape. Ignorance, they say, is bliss, and if so, we were happy indeed. Just a little over a mile south of Tinian Town, well concealed in caves, were three 6-inch naval guns. More than once on 25-26 June and again on 10-11 July the *Elden* must have passed within 6,000 yards of those guns, and once on the former occasion she lay less than a mere 4,000 yards from their muzzles. The import of this is made only too clear by what happened there on 24 July, two weeks after the *Elden*'s last visit. Until that date the Japanese gunners all around Tinian Town had suffered under the frequent American bombardments with only minimal response, so as not to reveal their positions. But on 24 July, as the actual invasion of Tinian began, all such restraint was thrown off, with the result that the three 6-inch naval guns south of Tinian Town quickly scored twenty-two hits on the battleship *Colorado* and six on the destroyer *Norman Scott* (DD 690), inflicting heavy casualties. One of those who died, an ensign on the destroyer, was John Allen, a cousin of Tom Buffum. The *Elden* could have been devastated by those same guns; it was just our luck that the Japanese wanted bigger prey, at a more critical moment.

At 0750 on 11 July the *William C. Miller* and the *Elden* were ordered back into the transport area screen, where we spent much of the day on patrol. That evening the *Elden* joined a group of ships ordered back to Eniwetok. Our consort, the *William C. Miller,* on the other hand, remained in the vicinity of

Saipan, and three days later destroyed the submarine I-55, which had been ordered to attempt the evacuation of Japanese airmen stranded on Tinian. The group to which the *Elden* had been assigned included a number of merchant vessels and their escorts, the *Selfridge* (DD 357), *Shaw* (DD 373), *Porterfield* (DD 682), and *Baron* (DE 166). Yes, the old *Selfridge* was back in action, fitted with a new bow, so that Aut Aker and I could enjoy a cruise together! After considerable confusion while getting formed up in the dark, we set course for Eniwetok.

Shepherding merchant vessels was not always easy. Early in the morning of 12 July the SS *Cape Newenham* straggled far astern, forcing the screen commander to send back the *Baron* for her protection. Not until that afternoon did the two ships regain their stations. The *Porterfield* was detached at 0030 on 13 July, presumably for further duty in the Marianas. Two days later our convoy entered the lagoon at Eniwetok, followed by the escorts. The *Elden* refueled from the *Platte* (AO 24) and then anchored near the destroyer tender *Piedmont* (AD 17) to facilitate provisioning.

I had not heard from Tom Buffum for many weeks, and ever since D-Day in Europe I had been wondering about the *Partridge*'s involvement. On the morning of 15 July, the day we returned to Eniwetok, I came to the breakfast table just in time to hear someone reading from our daily news bulletin the just-released list of American ships that had been lost during the invasion of Europe. Among them was the *Partridge!* That name hit me like a blow to the stomach, for I knew that when a small ship goes down the survivors may be few. I spent a most unhappy morning thinking about Tom, our close friendship, our many good times together, Tom's brother Tim (also in the navy), and his parents in Providence. Gloomy thoughts. That same afternoon a fresh batch of mail arrived on board. Included was a V-mail for me *from Tom himself,* assuring me that he was one of the survivors!

As I was able to piece it together later, Tom's story began on the night of 10 June, when the *Partridge* departed from England and set course for Omaha Beach, towing a large pontoon runway. Very early the next morning the ship was at General Quarters because of action nearby, her men in life jackets. Tom's battle station was in a messing compartment with an ammunition party of thirteen other men. Suddenly at 0215 there was a tremendous explosion amidships—a torpedo from a German E-boat. Tom, dazed, was spun around toward the door. Instinctively he started toward it, and almost immediately found himself swimming through it and out into open water. In less than a minute the *Partridge* was gone, taking with her twelve of the fourteen men in the messing compartment. Although injured by the explosion, Tom managed to cling to some debris floating in the oily water. As soon as he could, he began collecting other survivors until there was a small group together hanging on for dear life to a large timber, with Tom doing his best to keep up their spirits. In about forty-five minutes a Canadian corvette appeared and pulled Tom and his companions out of the water. For his courageous exertion on behalf of his fellow survivors, my good friend subsequently was decorated.

The *Elden,* after three days of resupplying and rest at Eniwetok, got under way on the afternoon of 18 July as part of Task Group 53.19 bound for the invasion of Guam. The convoy consisted of a dozen large vessels carrying elements of the Seventy-seventh Division and their supplies—the *Doyen* (APA 1), *Feland* (APA 11), *Monrovia* (APA 31), *Bolivar* (APA 34), *Sheridan* (APA 51), *Frederick Funston* (APA 89), *Comet* (AP 166), *War Hawk* (AP 168), *Alcyone* (AKA 7), *Almaack* (AKA 10), the *China Victory,* and the *Claremont Victory.* Also with us were two escort carriers—the *Midway* (later renamed the *St. Lo*) (CVE 63) and *Nehenta Bay* (CVE 74). The screening vessels included the *Selfridge* (DD 357), *Conyngham* (DD 371), *Shaw* (DD 373), *Longshaw* (DD 559), *Aulick* (DD 569), *Melvin* (DD 680), *Mertz* (DD 691), *Callaghan* (DD 792), *Palmer* (DMS 5), *Zane* (DMS 14), *Baron* (DE 166), and the *Elden.* In formation, with Eniwetok dropping below the horizon astern, these twenty-six ships were spread over a considerable expanse of ocean, their wakes a series of parallel lines marking their westerly progress. The twelve vessels under convoy were grouped in three columns screened by eight escorts of which the *Elden* was one. Some distance astern were the two carriers with their own screen of four destroyers. Later in the war four of those ships were to go under—the *St. Lo* at Leyte Gulf in October, the *Palmer* at Lingayen Gulf in January, the *Longshaw* and *Callaghan* at Okinawa in May.

On the morning of 19 July our formation practiced emergency turns. The *Elden,* however, soon had to deal with a real emergency of a quite different kind. One of our men began displaying the symptoms of acute appendicitis, readily recognized as such by our pharmacist's mate, who was wise enough to know when a surgeon's skill was needed. Accordingly, Captain Hartman apprised the task group commander of the problem, and was ordered to bring the *Elden* alongside the attack transport *Frederick Funston* on the morning of 20 July for an under way transfer of the patient. Had we not been experienced in the technique of transferring supplies at sea, the procedure might have been a daunting prospect, but we handled it almost as a routine matter. The *Elden* pulled out of her station in the screen, maneuvered into position astern of the transport, and then eased up along her port side, very close, until she towered above us. What a show for the curious troops lining the transport's rails! The *Frederick Funston*'s deck gang was ready with a square platform suspended from a crane, carrying two sailors in lifejackets. When the *Elden* was in position, the platform was swung outboard and then carefully lowered until it came to rest on our main deck. Quickly the patient, securely strapped into a medical litter, was placed on the platform and, guarded by the two sailors, immediately hoisted up and away through the air to where a surgeon was waiting to perform the necessary operation. Then the *Elden* headed off to resume her station in the screen.

D-Day at Guam had been set for 21 July. The initial landings were made that morning by the Third Marine Division, the First Provisional Marine Brigade, and advance elements of the Seventy-seventh Division on beaches both north and south of rugged Orote Peninsula on the western coast. At that time our task group still was some 250 miles east of Guam but heading directly for the scene of action. Shortly after midnight on 22 July we began to see star shells over the horizon to the west. About half an hour later our radar picked up Guam bearing 304 degrees, distant 42 miles. Passing around the southern end of the island, we arrived in the transport area off the Agat beaches at 0750. With the convoy safely deposited, the *Elden* soon was assigned a patrol station off the beachhead.

From the sea the terrain of Guam seemed quite similar to what we remembered of Saipan. On the left as we faced the beach was Orote Peninsula—long, steep-sided and flat-topped, with a rather abrupt seaward end. In the opposite direction, to our right, was blunt, stubby Facpi Point, with a small, rocky islet offshore. Ahead of us the low beach was obscured by the mass of transports and supply ships lying at anchor and serving the troops. Beyond the beach we could see a long, irregular ridge thrust up by numerous steep-sided, green-brown hills covered with dense growth and cut by deep ravines. That ridge was a natural rampart across which our troops would have to fight their way.

The *Elden* remained in the vicinity for eight days, under way nearly all the time. Daytimes we usually were on patrol off the transport area where, from our vantage point, we could see the smoke of battle and hear the CRUMP-CRUMP of explosions. Battleships, cruisers, and destroyers loitered offshore delivering fire as requested by the troops. Once we watched a destroyer, her bow almost nosing into a cove south of the beaches, pouring rapid fire into Japanese positions. Our planes were busy dive-bombing and strafing just beyond the first ridge. Fortunately, our forces had gained complete control of the air—not a single enemy plane made an appearance. Each evening until 28 July we formed up with our task group and retired about seventy-five miles to the northwest, presumably to avoid having the vulnerable transports clustered off the beachhead during darkness when Japanese aircraft or submarines might attempt a desperate attack. Each morning we returned, deposited our charges, and resumed our usual patrolling.

On the morning of 23 July, while on patrol, the *Elden* suddenly had a sonar contact—a rather uncertain one. Rather than take a chance, we made a run for it and fired off a pattern of Hedgehog missiles. As the flight of twenty-four missiles receded through the air they spread, began dropping, and then slapped down into the water in a large oval pattern. For the next few seconds we watched intently, listening for an underwater explosion that would indicate a hit, but all was calm, nothing happened. Apparently, as so many times before, we had been echo ranging on a school of fish.

That same morning, the twenty-third being a Sunday, we held a service of worship on the fantail. It was a new experience for us to worship within sight and sound of combat ashore. Under the circumstances, we had reason for thanksgiving, compassion, and contrition, never doubting that our simple worship was acceptable. So, as the depth charge watch stood by, we sang hymns, offered prayer, and listened to the Word, conscious that ashore only a short distance away men of two nations were dying.

On 24 July the Second and Fourth Marine divisions stormed ashore near the northern end of Tinian, and began driving southward. Effective fire from the battleship *Tennessee* (BB 43) finally put out of action those Japanese naval guns that had so seriously mauled the *Colorado* and *Norman Scott*. On 30 July the marines occupied the ruins of Tinian Town, and two days later the entire island

Hedgehog pattern ahead of an escort ship. U.S. Navy.

was declared secured, although some isolated pockets of fanatical resistance remained to be cleared out.

The *Elden,* after returning from one of our regular nocturnal voyages on the morning of 25 July, refueled from the *Enoree* (AO 69) and then resumed patrol duty off the transport area. Two days later we were assigned, along with the *Palmer* (DMS 5) and the *Aylwin* (DD 355), the task of screening the *Enoree* while she fueled other ships of the fleet. Among the ships so serviced that day were the cruisers *San Francisco* (CA 38) and *St. Louis* (CL 49), and the destroyers *MacDonough* (DD 351) and *Halford* (DD 480). Again the next day we screened the *Enoree,* and topped off our own tanks that afternoon. At 1727 the *Elden* was detached and ordered to patrol a station off the anchorage. As Captain Hartman noted in the log with an uncharacteristic tone of exasperation: "Spent entire night dodging battleships, cruisers, and destroyers, even after station was modified because of interference with *Shaw.*" It was like trying to drive through Times Square in a blackout.

On the evening of 29 July, with much of Guam still in enemy hands, the *Elden* formed up with other ships for a return voyage to Eniwetok. Our convoy included some old companions and some not previously known—the *Wharton* (AP 7), *Monrovia* (APA 31), *Bolivar* (APA 34), *Comet* (AP 166), *War Hawk* (AP 168), *Golden City* (AP 169), *Starlight* (AP 175), *Rixey* (APH 3) carrying wounded troops, *Alcyone* (AKA 7), *Almaack* (AKA 10), and the depleted *Enoree* (AO 69). These large ships were screened by six DEs—the *Levy* (DE 162), *McConnell* (DE 163), *Osterhaus* (DE 164), *Parks* (DE 165), *Baron* (DE 166), and the *Elden.* It was strange how seldom the *Elden* operated with more than one or two DEs of her own Escort Division 16.

On the whole the voyage was uneventful. At 0725 on 2 August we sighted Eniwetok bearing 017 degrees, distant 15 miles. Not until that afternoon, however, did we enter the broad lagoon and drop anchor in the clear blue water. It seemed good to have the engines go silent, the rumble and vibration cease, to be at rest.

Eight days later Guam was declared secured. The American conquest of the Marianas proved extremely costly to the Japanese. Not only did they lose nearly 60,000 troops, the vast majority of them dead, but soon the home islands themselves, to say nothing of other Japanese bases in the western Pacific, would lie exposed to heavy air attack by bombers operating out of American airfields on the three captured islands of Guam, Saipan, and Tinian. With the loss of the Marianas, Japan lost the war.

In early August, a long, long way from Notre Dame, I completed my second year of active duty. And the *Elden* celebrated her first birthday, having steamed a total of more than 75,000 miles. To mark the occasion, Chief Steward

Manzala baked a huge rectangular layer cake complete with a frosted representation of the ship and appropriate lettering. Writing home at about this time, I remarked that "we have been very busy lately, and I have had time for practically nothing but work, eat, and sleep. With few exceptions the crew hasn't set foot on land in almost two months." But, I continued, "I would rather spend the rest of my life doing what I am doing now than leave this job unfinished. It would only grow up all over again. Somehow we must arrange it so that all the people of the world will live under international law and order." I still believe that.

7

THE ROAD TO
THE PHILIPPINES

The *Elden*'s stay at Eniwetok lasted until 20 August. By this time the former Japanese atoll had become so completely American-ized as to have its own armed forces radio station whose regular sign-on went something like: "This is *not* WEEI in Boston; this is WXLE, the American Expeditionary Station at Eniwetok, on the road to Tokyo." Then came music and news far superior to the fare we had been served by Tokyo Rose. Speaking of the female sex, it was in the broad lagoon at Eniwetok that the *Elden*'s men now sighted their first all-American girl in two long months. Her identity we never knew, for she was a nurse on a hospital ship some distance off, but suddenly there she was, clearly visible at the rail of her ship, crisply and delightfully feminine. This quite unexpected discovery on our part immediately created an almost frantic competition for the very limited supply of binoculars available. At a distinct advantage were the signalmen, who had in their control an actual telescope normally used for reading distant signals; alas, from the nurse they received none. Perhaps her attention was directed toward the larger ships.

Indeed, there were many ships, both large and small, in the lagoon. One day I discovered that among them was the new heavy cruiser *Canberra* (CA 70), in which Roger Hard now was serving as a gunnery officer. The two of us were able to exchange blinker messages across the intervening water, agreeing to effect a reunion at the earliest convenient moment. As the *Elden*'s motor whaleboat was not available, I stationed myself on the fantail and tried to thumb a ride to the *Canberra* in one of the many small craft that always seemed to be busy on errands here and there in the lagoon. Either I had lost the technique that had been so effective in college days, or else a different one was needed in the Pacific, for nobody pulled in to offer me a ride. Roger was more fortunate; he came over to the *Elden* in one of the *Canberra*'s several boats. We greeted each other warmly, and I was delighted to see that after more than two years of active service my old friend seemed much the same as ever.

On another occasion soon afterwards I did manage to get over to where the *Canberra* rode at anchor. After climbing the accommodation ladder to the main deck, I saluted aft, saluted the officer on watch, and requested permission to come aboard (anxious to demonstrate that an officer from a mere DE was familiar with the amenities). Thereafter I spent an interesting day with Roger, swapping yarns in his stateroom, touring a magnificent fighting ship whose nine 8-inch and twelve 5-inch guns made the *Elden*'s armament seem puny, and lunching with the other officers in the spacious and pleasant wardroom. Before I finally took my leave, Roger and I composed a joint letter to "Uncle George," telling about our visit together at a location we could not disclose. "Uncle George," in turn, saw that our message was speedily transmitted to Calvary's many service people around the world.

The commodore of Escort Division 16 seemed to have "battleship ideas" about uniforms, and had begun issuing orders specifying his requirements in the matter. These we had to obey even though he might be on another ship of the division hundreds of miles distant, and despite the fact, or so we believed, that his requirements ran counter to the trend in small ships operating in forward areas. Consequently, the *Elden*'s officers now had to wear neckties at the dinner table (but still could keep their shirtsleeves rolled up). On board the *Canberra*, by way of contrast, the officers at lunch were required to have their shirtsleeves buttoned at the wrists, but could dispense with neckties. I was moved to comment, in a letter home, that "this sort of thing leads to a type of insanity which compels a man, once he has become a civilian again, to parade down Weybosset Street in red BVD's shouting 'What are you going to do about it!' "

While at Eniwetok the *Elden*'s men were able to get ashore for the first time in about ten weeks to stretch their legs, enjoy a swim, drink a little beer or Coca Cola, and loaf on the sand. This makes it sound as though our sojourn were a summer holiday, which indeed was not the case. At 0400 on 5 August, for example, we received Air Flash Red, bouncing all hands out of their bunks for nearly half an hour of sleepy grumbling at Battle Stations until the All Clear was received. A week later the *Elden* was sent outside for two days of patrol duty off

Deep Entrance. During that rather monotonous patrol we test-fired our guns, and also conducted engineering and steering casualty drills that were impractical when in formation with other ships. After being relieved by the *Baron* (DE 166) on 14 August, we again slipped into the peaceful lagoon, took on more fuel, and found our anchorage.

Yearning as we did for eventual victory and a joyful homecoming, the *Elden*'s officers followed with keen interest the daily developments in the worldwide struggle against the Axis powers. We had adorned one bulkhead in the wardroom with a large chart of the Pacific theater, which enabled us to keep track of the various advances in that vast arena, including those in which the *Elden* had some share. On the opposite bulkhead was a National Geographic map of Germany and its approaches, on which we could circle in red, day after day, the towns captured by the Allied armies. Thus on both maps we rejoiced in the steady shrinkage of the areas under Axis domination.

It will be recalled that the great Pacific offensive actually included two simultaneous advances. While Admiral Nimitz's forces—of which the *Elden* was a part—were driving northwestward across the Central Pacific, South Pacific forces under General MacArthur, with the very active support of the U.S. Seventh Fleet, were pushing westward along the coast of New Guinea toward the Japanese-held Philippine Islands. Now, following the capture of the Marianas, Admiral Halsey's Third Fleet was to shift its attention temporarily southward to assist in the seizure of the Palau Islands only 500 miles east of the Philippines; next would be the long-awaited liberation of the Philippines themselves. In this impending operation, the *Elden* was assigned a role.

On the morning of 20 August 1944 we got under way from Eniwetok as one of the escorts for a convoy of fleet oilers, which meant that we were back at our old task of helping refuel the fleet at sea prior to strikes against enemy positions. Our destination was Seeadler Harbor, a commodious haven on the north coast of Manus Island in the Admiralties, a short distance north of New Guinea. Manus had been taken from the Japanese in March, and Seeadler Harbor now was to serve as the principal naval base in the campaign to seize Palau 1,000 miles to the northwest, and 500 miles beyond that, the Philippines. This meant that the Third Fleet was bypassing the enemy-held Carolines, including the major Japanese base at Truk, by dropping far to the south and then coming around westward in order to get at Palau.

Included in our formation for the southward voyage were the destroyers *Capps* (DD 550), *David W. Taylor* (DD 551), *John D. Henley* (DD 553), *Hall* (DD 583), and *Paul Hamilton* (DD 590); the destroyer escorts *Levy* (DE 162), *McConnell* (DE 163), *Osterhaus* (DE 164), *Baron* (DE 166), and *Elden* (DE 264); the escort carrier *Nehenta Bay* (CVE 74); and the fleet oilers *Lackawanna*

(AO 40), *Monongahela* (AO 42), *Tappahannock* (AO 43), *Patuxent* (AO 44), *Neosho* (AO 48), *Marias* (AO 57), *Manatee* (AO 58), *Mississinewa* (AO 59), *Cache* (AO 67), *Saugatuck* (AO 75), *Pamanset* (AO 85), and *Sebec* (AO 87). One of these oilers, the *Mississinewa,* later was to be torpedoed and sunk at her anchorage in the lagoon at Ulithi by a daring enemy submarine.

At first our course took us about 300 miles to the southeast in order to skirt the easternmost of the Carolines, after which we headed more toward the southwest. On the first afternoon out we exercised all our guns by firing at a sleeve towed by a plane sent out from Eniwetok. That evening one destroyer was sent ten miles ahead and another seven miles astern of the formation to serve as pickets. On the afternoon of 21 August the *Baron* was detached to proceed to Pearl Harbor, reducing the escorts to nine. The *Nehenta Bay* conducted flight operations on 22 August, sending her planes out on patrol missions. At 1737 that afternoon one of the fighter planes coming in for a landing made an error or suffered some failure, and plunged into the sea. Neither the unfortunate pilot nor his plane could be retrieved, reminding us that death always could come in sudden, unexpected ways.

The *Elden* crossed the equator shortly after noon on 24 August, some 1,600 miles west of where we had made our first crossing seven months earlier. Now we were due south of the Japanese-held Carolines. The next afternoon Captain Hartman made a thorough inspection throughout the ship, finding it generally "shipshape and Bristol fashion." In the galley the cooks, dressed in spotless whites, were busy preparing supper as the captain passed on through. Any one of the crew's living spaces was clean enough to be used as a sick bay. It's a well-known saying in the navy that "a clean ship is a happy ship," and we on the *Elden* did take pride in the quality of our ship-keeping, from the sonar hut to the after steering compartment.

At 0554 on 26 August the radar watch picked up Manus Island bearing 210 degrees, distant 53 miles. Several hours later our formation arrived off the chain of low, palm-covered islands that fringed the seaward edge of Seeadler Harbor, named for the German raider that had resorted there during World War I. Our fleet oilers made their entry in stately procession through the passage between Ndrilo and Hauwei islands, followed by the string of escort vessels. After taking on fuel, the *Elden* sought her assigned anchorage.

Each navy ship was supposed to be in an assigned, numbered anchorage shown as a circle on the official chart of the harbor. To find her assigned anchorage, a ship had to pay careful attention to at least two and preferably three clearly identifiable objects on shore from which bearings could be taken, and then follow a course leading to that anchorage. The approach had to be slow and careful, with constant checking of the bearings until, at precisely the correct location, the anchor was dropped. When all ships did this correctly, all might ride placidly at anchor for days on end, swinging slowly around together in the changing tides, without any collision. In such circumstances, one of the important duties of the OOD was to check the bearings periodically to make sure that the ship was not dragging the hook and drifting toward another ship's anchorage.

Manus is considerably larger than Guam. Rising gradually from the inland edge of the harbor are jungle-covered hills stretching off into the interior. We noticed at once the strong, pervasive odor of rank vegetation. Inland along the jungle trails American troops still occasionally flushed out fugitive Japanese soldiers reluctant to surrender. One story going the rounds at Seeadler Harbor told of two starving Japanese found standing unobtrusively in an American chow line.

The natives, we discovered, were very black. Both men and women wore a simple costume consisting for the most part of a dull-colored cloth skirt extending down to the calves. Of particular interest were the native sailing craft—long, low, outrigger canoes equipped with masts and sails, partially decked to carry more riders. Sometimes we saw several of these craft loaded with passengers of all ages, possibly a whole family on an afternoon outing, sailing happily past the great steel ships of the navy at anchor.

One of the islands at the seaward edge of the harbor had been designated a recreation area for navy personnel from the ships. Each ship could send a portion of her crew ashore as an organized group under the supervision of one or more officers to make use of the recreational facilities provided. These included a beach for swimming, open areas where sports could be played, and, demurely nestled under the gently rustling palms, a large pavilion called "Duffy's Tavern" where a strictly limited quantity of beer was rationed out to each *bona fide* group—two cans of beer per man. On three successive days the *Elden* made good use of all these facilities, each time sending one-third of the crew and several officers. There under the palms we had a boisterous good time while a few curious natives stood by and watched. I only had to break up one fight!

Alcohol was strictly prohibited aboard ship, but inevitably some of the more thirsty men would find or devise some form of relief, usually involving raw alcohol. Officers got ashore more often than enlisted men, which helped solve the problem for them, not always with salubrious results. Late one evening when I was OOD in Seeadler Harbor, the captain and his "exec" returned aboard together, the former perfectly in control of himself, the latter drunk and belligerent. When Sneed refused to subside, the disgusted captain finally ordered me to summon the master-at-arms and have him bring his nightstick!

So out blared the unusual command on the PA system: "Now hear this! The chief master-at-arms, lay up to the quarterdeck on the double, with a nightstick!" Before you could blink twice, the hatches began spewing up sailors curious to know what was happening, even as the stalwart master-at-arms, billy club in hand, made his official appearance. Thus there was a sizable audience to see the spectacle of the ship's executive officer hoisted over the master-at-arms' shoulder and lugged away to his bunk to sleep it off.

If alcohol could be a problem, food, at least, was never in short supply and, making due allowance for the complexities of a far-flung system, arrived on the mess tables in reasonably edible form. We had some good cooks and bakers. Whenever the *Elden* arrived at any base our supply officer, Ray Hartung, would leave the ship, hasten ashore, and start ferreting out any meat, fresh vegetables, and fruit that might be obtainable. A few crates of tomatoes were something to cheer about. Sometimes we actually acquired an oversupply of some item, which then had to be crammed down endlessly until the supply was exhausted. Asparagus was a good case in point—for weeks we seemed to have it at least once a day, sometimes in the form of soup. After awhile its dreaded green presence came to seem almost intolerable. As for dehydrated potatoes, of which we consumed our share—they tasted like paste. Actually, though, as any marine or soldier will testify without hesitation, navy personnel had no cause for complaint.

On 30 August the *Elden,* in company with the *Osterhaus* (DE 164) and the submarine S-45, went out for a day of antisubmarine exercises, our first opportunity in three months to hear some real echoes. That afternoon, after we had made our last simulated attack and the S-45 had surfaced, she went off to a distance and made a radar run on the *Elden.* At 1540 we completed our exercises and returned to Seeadler Harbor, where the *Elden* moored starboard side to the *McConnell* (DE 163).

Admiral Mitscher's fast carrier force was preparing to begin a series of strikes against enemy positions on Yap, Ulithi, and Palau in the western Carolines, which meant that the services of our Task Group 30.8 were urgently needed for refueling at sea. Accordingly, we sortied from Seeadler Harbor on the morning of 1 September, and set a northeasterly course for our first rendezvous. Shortly after noon the *Elden* made a sonar contact but refrained from attacking because of the possible presence of friendly submarines. In all probability we were echo ranging on a school of fish, so no real opportunity was lost. That same evening the destroyer *Paul Hamilton* (DD 590), in advance picket station ten miles ahead of the formation, did attack a contact which, no doubt, was every bit as fishy as ours.

Early the next morning our group made its rendezvous, which meant that when I ascended the ladders to take the morning watch I expected a busy four hours. In the dim light of early morning we could see carriers and other combat ships spread all over the surface of the ocean for miles, under the alert protection of the combat air patrol high overhead. That portion of Task Group 30.8 participating in the rendezvous was subdivided into task units each consisting of several oilers and their escorts, which now separated from each other preparatory to fueling the various units of the attack force. Task Unit 30.8.4, consisting of the *Lackawanna* (AO 40), *Cache* (AO 67), *Saugatuck* (AO 75), *David W. Taylor* (DD 551), and the *Elden,* reported to Task Group 38.2 and took course 110 degrees for fueling. After hours of slow cruising, with one ship after another coming alongside one of the oilers, generally two ships at a time fueling from each oiler, we ceased the operation and formed a cruising disposition for the night. The next morning we engaged in more fueling, after which the fast carrier force went on its way. During that afternoon the several task units reunited and set course for Seeadler Harbor.

We enjoyed nearly a week of relative quiet, swinging slowly at anchor in the clear blue water of the harbor, with only the endless routine of the ship to keep us busy. During nights in port far fewer of our officers and men had to be on watch at any one time, which meant that everyone had a good chance to catch up on sleep. As usual, we enjoyed the evening movies on the fantail, and would even sit through a light shower if the film was particularly interesting.

Then, on 12 September at the unusually early hour of 0423, it was "anchor's aweigh" for another rendezvous with the fleet, this time preparatory to the invasion of Peleliu in the Palau Islands. Instead of proceeding northeastward, as on the previous occasion, we headed northwestward toward an area about 150 miles southwest of Peleliu. Our course took us through waters plentifully sprinkled with coconut logs and even an occasional oil barrel, source unknown. To eyes constantly scouring the surface for a periscope or conning tower, a section of pole riding vertically in the water could be understandably disconcerting.

During the morning of 15 September, the day when the First Marine Division went ashore on Peleliu, all our escorts refueled, the *Elden* taking hers from the *Kaskaskia* (AO 27). That afternoon as our group was cruising in normal formation, the *Mitchell* (DE 43) on the starboard side of the screen reported a possible periscope. Immediately all ships turned 60 degrees to port. Five minutes later we were informed that the periscope was only a bit of floating debris. At 1800 an *Elden* lookout reported a suspicious object on the horizon. Hoping to avoid a false alarm, the officers on the flying bridge studied the object with their binoculars. It still looked suspect, and we had oilers to protect, so at 1810 it was "All hands to General Quarters!" and off the *Elden* went to investi-

A tense watch on the flying bridge. Jack Rickard is conning the ship, his hand on the voice tube as he communicates with the helmsman in the wheelhouse below.

gate. What she came upon fifteen minutes later was a large floating log or stump with numerous branches. So much for that "conning tower."

Sometimes we were entertained by a school of porpoises leaping out of the water as though for the sheer joy of it—graceful, glistening arches in motion. One morning we spotted a huge V of large birds cruising purposefully high up in the clear blue sky. It was reassuring to know that the creatures of sea and air still were pursuing their normal courses in spite of man's terrible violence.

At 0615 on 16 September, not far from little Merir Island, we sighted our friends of the fast carrier force, and soon were engaged in the familiar procedure of fueling the fleet at sea. The next day we made an early rendezvous with yet another task group of the fast carrier force, and spent the rest of that morning screening our oilers as they supplied the carriers and their consorts with essential fuel. Then the attack group went off on its next mission, while we headed back for Manus with some of the oilers, the escort carrier *Barnes* (CVE 20), and one or more escort vessels including the *Swearer* (DE 186).

That night was a black one. Even the carrier could be seen only as an indistinct mass slightly darker than the night itself. At 1925 the radar watch in the *Elden*'s Combat Information Center suddenly announced a single surface contact 7,700 yards—less than four miles—ahead. Immediately we notified the group commander, who ordered us to investigate while the formation began a series of evasive turns. The *Elden* went to General Quarters, the gun crews readied their weapons, and the engineers cut in our two idle engines so that we might gradually increase our speed as needed. It would be some minutes, however, before we could build up to our top speed of about 21 knots.

Cutting out of the screen and heading along the bearing indicated by radar, we needed to know what the contact was doing, for its behavior would dictate our response. On the radar scope down in Combat the contact appeared as a small blob of light whose changing bearing and range from the *Elden* could be constantly measured. Our radar watch called out the bearing and range at regular intervals, and those points were continuously plotted, giving us very quickly the stranger's course and speed. It soon became obvious that he had changed his course and was trying to escape at a speed of about 23 knots, at least 2 knots above the *Elden*'s maximum. Apparently, then, we had stumbled upon a Japanese submarine running on the surface, possibly carrying personnel or supplies to or from a bypassed enemy base. Since he could run faster than we could follow, it was imperative that we act quickly to stop him, if possible.

At 1950, to make certain that the stranger was not one of our own, the *Elden* challenged by blinker light. No response. Now Captain Hartman ordered illumination with star shells, even though the range already was more than 7,000 yards. Waiting tensely for illumination, we could feel the *Elden* vibrating as she surged forward at flank speed, her white wake boiling astern. How desperately we needed to penetrate that blackness, how infuriating the delay!

BLAM! The flash from the elevated muzzle of one of the forward 3-inch guns lighted up our superstructure for a split second as the first star shell began its high flight into the dark sky. It burst far off in the air ahead of us, a sudden bright ball of light that began a slow descent, all the while casting brilliance over the face of the ocean below, with a thin ribbon of glittering water stretching directly to the *Elden*'s own hull. To our straining eyes no object appeared; already the fugitive was beyond that glare. At intervals we fired more star shells as far ahead as we could make them reach, but still no craft of any kind was revealed. Yet the target remained on our radar scope, drawing steadily away from us, until finally, at a range of 6½ miles, it disappeared altogether. The *Elden* had been outrun. Drenched with frustration, we secured from General Quarters and rejoined the formation, as ordered by voice radio. Had the *Elden* been a destroyer, or even been able to make only three or four extra knots of speed, she might have overtaken the fugitive, forced him to submerge, and then attacked him systematically with the Hedgehog. Perhaps, though, we had only been chasing a phantom.

Our group arrived off the entrance to Seeadler Harbor on the morning of 21 September, and entered in the usual way, escorts last. After taking in a fresh supply of fuel, the *Elden* moored alongside the *David W. Taylor* (DD 551) in Berth 358. For a few days we rested undisturbed in the commodious harbor while awaiting our next mission, which could not be long in coming, since our fleet was continuing its offensive activity to the northwest and the marines were still struggling to overwhelm the Japanese at Palau. The *Elden*'s men enjoyed more beach parties at Duffy's Tavern, received a fresh supply of pocket money from a navy paymaster, and stood another formal inspection by the captain. On the morning of 28 September, together with the *Swearer,* we began exercising off Manus with the submarine S-47, but hastily broke off this activity and escorted the tame sub back to harbor when a destroyer, the *McCalla* (DD 488), reported that she had detected an unidentified submarine in the vicinity. Later the *McCalla* concluded that she had been echo ranging on a submerged reef. What next!

On 1 October we gained a new shipmate in the wardroom when Ens. Richard L. Cavagnero reported aboard. That same afternoon the *Elden* got under way for her next major mission in support of the fast carrier force of the Third Fleet, a voyage that was to take us closer to Japan than we had ever been. During the night of 5 October our group of heavily laden oilers together with the escort carrier *Rudyerd Bay* (CVE 81), heading northward well beyond Palau, passed about seventy-five miles west of the enemy base at Yap. Moving ahead of us now at a distance of 400 miles was a typhoon that left in its wake a violently disturbed ocean of heaving, surging, battering waves. The *Elden* battened down for heavy weather, as did all the other ships in our group, and by the sixth we were laboring northward through endlessly surging seas that swept through our formation, alternately cresting into hissing white foam and then sloughing down into dark valleys.

As I stood my watch on the flying bridge, with the *Elden* rolling from one side to the other while the tip of her mast traced an arc of 80 degrees or more across the leaden sky, I clung to the binnacle with my legs braced against the unceasing motion and watched the heavy, deep-set oilers doggedly butting their way through those seas. At one moment a nearby oiler would rise up to full view, white water streaming from her bows and weather decks; seconds later she would all but disappear behind an intervening roller, with only her masts and cranes and perhaps the top of her stack visible. The destroyers and DEs, striving to maintain their stations in the screen, were in constant violent motion, pitching and rolling. Any man moving about topside had to gauge the motion carefully, watch for sweeping seas, and always look ahead for the next hand-hold.

Below, in the *Elden*'s wardroom, the fiddleboards were on the table to prevent dishes and cups from sliding off onto the deck, and the chairs were roped in place. Eating a meal could be a test of balance and dexterity; on one occasion while I was seated there a sudden roll of the ship threw me over altogether. Yet despite the ceaseless motion of a watery world that seemed to have no element of stability whatsoever, those several days of rough going were for me a real personal triumph. I never was sick and never missed a meal.

Russ Morrow had the forenoon watch on 7 October when suddenly our lookouts sighted a floating mine close aboard. Had the *Elden* so much as brushed against it she would have been blown wide open, but we passed safely by and quickly warned the formation, which made an evasive turn to starboard. The *Levy* (DE 162) was detached to dispose of the drifting menace, a task she accomplished with gunfire.

At 0230 on the morning of 8 October, with the sea now moderating, our formation began subdividing into separate fueling units, each consisting of two or three oilers and a screen of two or more escorts. Our rendezvous with the fleet was in an area of restless ocean approximately 480 miles northwest of Saipan, 870 miles east of Luzon in the Philippines, and 960 miles due south of Japan. Soon the broad, heaving surface of the Philippine Sea was dotted with carriers, battleships, cruisers, destroyers, destroyer escorts, and fleet oilers, all slowly promenading on a westward course while engaged in the vital process of refueling. In the skies, mostly beyond our vision, roamed the combat air patrol, protecting the far-spread fleet in its vulnerable array. The *Elden* was teamed with the *Mitchell* (DE 43) as screen for the *Rudyerd Bay* (CVE 81) and the fleet oilers *Sabine* (AO 25), *Cache* (AO 64), and *Saugatuck* (AO 75). Our clients were units of Adm. Frederick C. Sherman's Task Group 38.3. Not until 2000 that evening was the operation completed, after which our group began its withdrawal toward the south. Other fueling units joined us, and before midnight the large ships had formed three columns screened by the escorts.

On the morning of 9 October the oilers began consolidating the residue of their cargoes and refueling the *Rudyerd Bay* as well as the escorts, an operation made somewhat tricky by the heavy swells. Shortly before noon the *Elden* came alongside the *Sabine* to begin taking on diesel oil. In the midst of the process, we were ordered to relinquish the hose and pull away, which we did. A little later we tried again, easing gingerly into position alongside and then hurriedly receiving the hose and coupling it to our valve. Both ships were wallowing in the running sea. Suddenly the *Sabine*'s bow dropped down into a trough and then surged upwards, creating a strong bow wave that pushed the *Elden*'s bow sharply outward just as our ship rolled heavily to port. This in turn caused the *Elden*'s port quarter to brush against the steep, unyielding side of the oiler with a sharp crunching sound. Quickly surveying the damage, we discovered that one of our depth charges in ready position on the port quarter had been punctured, exposing the explosive charge. As there was no imminent danger of a detonation, however, we continued taking fuel until we had all we needed, and then pulled away from the *Sabine*. The damaged depth charge later was jettisoned and replaced. At 1738 our group was detached, with orders to proceed to Kossol Passage, Palau, where the oilers were to discharge whatever excess cargo remained.

Arriving in Kossol Passage on the morning of 11 October, we found it to be a spacious haven well north of the island of Peleliu where the marines still were digging out the last remnants of organized Japanese resistance. The *Elden* remained at anchor only a few hours, our men amusing themselves by watching the exotic fish swimming deep below us in the clear water, while the oilers discharged their cargoes into station vessels. Then we were off again, to complete our return voyage to Seeadler Harbor. The next day Admiral Halsey's Third Fleet carriers began a series of strikes against northern Luzon and Formosa (Taiwan). On 13 October Peleliu was declared secured, which meant that American forces had gained another stepping stone along the ocean route to the Philippines.

That same day at dusk, about 100 miles east of Formosa, the heavy cruiser *Canberra* (CA 70), Roger Hard's ship, was crippled by a Japanese plane's torpedo, which left her lying dead in the water with both engine rooms flooded. Twenty-three of the *Canberra*'s men died in the blast. Because the stricken cruiser lay helpless so close to enemy territory, it might have been thought prudent to evacuate her personnel and send her to the bottom. Instead, Admiral Halsey ordered an attempt to tow the *Canberra* out of danger. The following day the light cruiser *Houston* (CL 81) was even more heavily damaged and nearly abandoned. But she, too, was taken under tow, and the forlorn procession of two cripples, heavily guarded by other units of the fleet, began a painfully slow withdrawal toward the southeast, hour after hour creeping out from under the constant threat of destruction by enemy aircraft or submarines. We on the *Elden,* hundreds of miles closer to Manus, learned of all this by deciphered radio dispatches, and I was able to follow that perilous retreat day by day, with deep personal concern. Finally, on 27 October the two cripples were towed into the relative security of the lagoon at Ulithi. Roger, I later learned, had come through the ordeal uninjured.

Our group, in the meantime, had continued on toward Seeadler Harbor, the *Elden* holding another one of its gunnery practices en route, with all guns firing at 3-inch anti-aircraft bursts. We arrived at our destination on the morning of 15 October, and entered the harbor for a short period of rest and repair before our next long voyage. Two new officers reported aboard for duty—Lt. (j.g.) David Habel and Ens. Dee L. Weaver, both of whom readily settled in among us and began learning the ship's routine. New faces made for new conversation, as well as a readjustment of duties and responsibilities.

The *Elden*'s sonar transmitter, located just below the keel near the bow, was not operating properly and needed urgent attention. Several of the officers decided that we should have a preliminary look at it ourselves, while at anchor, which meant swimming down underneath the hull. Unfortunately, we had no diving equipment, but Ned Lee and Russ Morrow put their heads together, and before long had rigged up just what was required—an air pump connected by a long rubber hose to an ordinary service gas mask. In order to help the diver descend, weights were inserted in the pockets of an ordinary cartridge belt. Finally, to serve as a guide down and back, a hogging line was rigged extending from the starboard rail all the way under the bottom and up to the port rail directly opposite. Several of us took turns going down, and with the water as beautifully clear as it was, there was no difficulty in examining the faulty unit. As it turned out, however, our external examination revealed nothing significant, and the trouble remained until the *Elden* went into a floating drydock for expert repair.

One day we received a batch of fresh mail from home, and Charlie Smart was standing on the main deck with a letter in hand when he accidentally dropped it into the water below. Charlie's eyes grew frantically wider as he saw that precious missive drifting slowly away from the *Elden*'s side. Determined not to lose it, he immediately called up to the flying bridge for permission to go overboard. The next thing we knew Charlie, having stripped off his outer clothing, was running along the deck with a look of wild determination on his face. Pausing briefly at the rail to take a bearing on the slowly receding letter, he dove neatly into the water. A few steady strokes and he had it in his grasp; a few more and he was back at the *Elden*'s side, ready to climb aboard and resume reading the now soggy missive. Mail from home *was* important.

At 1455 on 17 October the *Elden* got under way to screen the sortie of Task Unit 30.8.4 which again included a group of fleet oilers. As before, our course took us northward across the equator in the general direction of Palau. It was clear that some major new advance in the Pacific was imminent, with powerful forces assembling to effect it. Nor could it be expected that the Japanese fleet, still dangerous and becoming more desperate with every new American conquest, would fail to challenge this latest American advance.

On 19 October and again on the twentieth the *Elden* had a sonar contact, causing the formation to execute emergency turns, but in each case nothing developed. During the morning of 20 October, as our group of oilers was about 150 miles east of Palau and still heading northwestward, General MacArthur's forces began landing on Leyte in the Philippines. To Americans and Filipinos alike, the symbolic as well as strategic importance of this landing—the start of liberation for the Philippines—could hardly be overstated. News of this long-awaited invasion, together with enemy propaganda wildly exaggerating American losses, came quickly to the American public at home. Dad began a letter to me on 20 October: "As you can well imagine, we have been a little worried with the first news (Jap stories) of what was going on out your way. We did not believe our Navy would be there unless they had the strength to take it. However, it is possible to take a loss and still win." About the same time, I was writing home that the Pacific Fleet "is a pretty healthy outfit, considering that it has been sunk, wiped out of existence, and chased across the Pacific in disordered retreat. The Jap claims seem to grow more fantastic all the time."

Actually, the Imperial Japanese Navy, having been sent reeling back to the shelter of the Philippines and the home islands during the invasion of Saipan the previous June, now was determined to venture forth once again in a last desperate attempt to wreck our invasion of Leyte. What occurred as a result, from 23 to 26 October 1944, is known as the Battle for Leyte Gulf, one of the greatest, most decisive sea battles of modern times. It was a wide-ranging and complicated brawl consisting of several distinct engagements many miles apart, the climactic encounters occurring on 25 October. By receiving and deciphering radio dispatches, the *Elden* was able to gain some concept of what was going on, but I doubt that even Captain Hartman had anything resembling a full picture of these developments. We were off on the edge of it all, guarding the fleet oilers in a designated area of ocean roughly 400 miles east of Luzon, to which various carrier attack groups came for periodic refueling. Fortunately, Japanese air power was by now badly depleted and, so far as I am aware, our activity was not discovered. Had a powerful enemy naval force burst upon us in our fueling area, the result could have been disastrous.

The one Japanese fleet that might have come our way was the so-called Northern Force commanded by Admiral Ozawa. Consisting of the large carrier *Zuikaku* (the last surviving carrier of the Pearl Harbor attack force), three other carriers, a pair of battleships, three light cruisers, and eight destroyers, this group was proceeding southward from Japan toward Luzon. Ozawa's purpose was to lure Admiral Halsey's Third Fleet northward away from the invasion area at Leyte Gulf, leaving the transports, the beach-head, and units of Admiral Kinkaid's Seventh Fleet wide open to attack by two other powerful Japanese naval forces sneaking through from the South China Sea. Those two forces included six battleships, twelve cruisers, and twenty destroyers. Obviously, the threat was real and immediate.

In our fueling area off Luzon were cruising a number of distinct task units, each consisting of several oilers with their escorts of destroyers and DEs. In addition, we had with us a small number of escort carriers whose function was to provide Halsey's attack carriers with replacement planes as needed, while also furnishing air cover for the fueling operations. For two days, 22 and 23 October, the *Elden* helped screen the oilers while they pumped fuel into various ships of Admiral Mitscher's fast carrier force. On the morning of the second day we ourselves fueled from the *Marias* (AO 57). Late that afternoon three of our service units, including the one to which the *Elden* belonged, had completed the refueling of Task Group 38 and set course for Ulithi, while the attack forces resumed their hunt for the approaching enemy fleets.

Sometime on 24 October our group received an order to reverse course. Halsey had discovered Ozawa's Northern Force approaching, and knew that with major action impending, his attack groups would require yet more fuel. Accordingly, we were directed to make rendezvous with Admiral McCain's Task Group 38.1. That evening, as our group was returning northwestward toward the designated area, the U.S.S. *Weaver* (DE 741) was sent off to conduct a sonar search in the vicinity of a previous radar contact. For more than two hours our formation continued on its way in darkness, leaving the lone *Weaver* farther and farther behind pinging away in solitary diligence, well beyond the range of voice radio. Apparently, no time limit had been imposed upon her search. Finally, at 2150 the group commander decided that enough was enough, and dispatched the *Elden* to fetch the lone DE. Off we went along the indicated bearing, picked up the *Weaver* on our radar, established voice contact, and delivered the message. Not until 0113 the next morning were the two of us able to regain our stations in the screen.

It was on 25 October, as the Battle for Leyte Gulf was reaching its climax, that the Japanese launched their first successful kamikaze suicide attack on ships of the United States Navy, damaging the escort carriers *Santee* and *Suwannee.* That same morning we made our rendezvous with Task Group 38.1, whose ships began taking on the fuel they so urgently needed. While this was taking place, a radio dispatch from Halsey directed McCain to proceed as soon as possible to the vicinity of Samar, where elements of the Seventh Fleet were being hard pressed by the Japanese force that had managed to break through from the South China Sea. Fueling was completed at 0920, permitting Task Group 38.1 to begin that urgent mission.

On 26 October we fueled Admiral Sherman's Task Group 38.3 and Admiral Davison's Task Group 38.4, both of which had been heavily involved in the Battle of Cape Engaño the previous day. By this time the great Battle for Leyte Gulf was subsiding, with the surviving Japanese ships making their escape. Their losses had been disastrous—three battleships, four carriers, ten cruisers, and nine destroyers. Our beach-head at Leyte Gulf was secure. Never again was the Japanese fleet able to pose a serious menace to American domination of the western Pacific.

At home, the folks were ecstatic. According to my mother, "The news of the big naval victory is on everyone's lips. We have thought of you many times and wondered how near you personally were to all the excitement." The correct answer to that was not very—in fact, several hundred miles distant—for Ozawa's Northern Force had stayed well clear of our secret fueling area east of Luzon. Had it been otherwise, our fueling group might have been shredded. Would the *Elden*'s luck continue to hold? Our group expected to make another rendezvous for fueling on 27 October, but prior to that our orders were changed and we were directed to set course for Ulithi once again. This time we continued on our way. It seems ironic that the *Elden,* having played at least a small role in making possible the liberation of the Philippines, did not gain so much as a glimpse of that land until after the war had ended.

I had the forenoon watch on 28 October when a plane from the *Nehenta Bay* reported that a radar contact had disappeared from the scope. That sounded like a surfaced submarine suddenly diving, and so the *Nicholson* (DD 442) and the *Elden* were sent off to investigate. The two ships conducted a systematic sonar search until 1407, without result, and then hastened to overtake the formation.

At 1735 the next morning we sighted Ulithi Atoll eight miles to the south. As usual, the oilers preceded the escorts into the lagoon, which proved to be an extensive one with numerous vessels of various types riding at anchor. The *Elden* moored alongside the *Kennebago* (AO 81) to refuel and rejoice in the cessation of motion. It was also good to enjoy a quiet night's sleep in relative security. For two days we rode peacefully at anchor, baking contentedly in the sun.

Early on the morning of 1 November the *Elden* got under way, along with the *McCalla* (DD 488) and *LeHardy* (DE 20), to escort five merchant tankers as far as Eniwetok. By 0735 the tankers had completed their sortie and we were on our way. Jack Rickard had the deck on the evening of 3 November when our radar picked up a formation of ships twenty-three miles to the northeast and approaching. It proved to be Carrier Division 29 accompanied by four escorts. As the minutes passed and the distance between the two groups continued to shrink, it began to appear as though the other formation was determined to run us down. By 1935 an emergency turn to starboard was urgently required, but only one of the five merchant tankers noted our signal and executed the turn promptly. The others did so as they individually awoke to what was happening. Fortunately, there was no collision, and at 1950 we were able to make a compensating turn to port and continue on our way. Ships that pass in the night. . . .

At noon on 5 November, when we were close to Eniwetok, our convoy dispersed, the tankers being left to proceed independently to the Canal Zone, while the *McCalla,* the *LeHardy,* and the *Elden* entered the familiar lagoon. There the *Elden* moored port side to the U.S.S. *Beagle* (IX 112). A look at a chart of the Pacific will show that between 20 August and 5 November the *Elden* had completely circled the Japanese-held Carolines, including the principal enemy base at Truk. In doing so, we had seen a vast extent of ocean, but not a single Japanese ship or plane.

Where to next? Pearl, we hoped—and then the States. Yes, we all had a fond expectation that after a year of extensive service in the Pacific, the *Elden* would be sent to the West Coast for a yard overhaul, which would mean home leave for all hands. During the forenoon watch on 6 November we hauled up the anchor and got under way, with orders to proceed alone to Makin Atoll in the Gilberts, where we were to pick up a troop transport awaiting escort to the Hawaiian Islands. Because of a burned-out transformer in the driver of the sonar gear, the *Elden* was unable to echo range, but at least could use her equipment as a listening device to detect any suspicious sounds beneath the surface. We hoped that at Makin, where there now was a small American base, we would be able to acquire the needed part.

The *Elden*'s lone voyage from Eniwetok to Makin across 800 miles of empty ocean was for us an unusual and pleasant cruise. Not since leaving the Atlantic more than a year earlier had we been so delightfully alone on the broad blue platter of sea. It meant that for two whole days the *Elden* was her own boss, not subject to frequent commands from some other ship; the successive OODs on the flying bridge had only to remain alert, see that the correct course was being followed, and observe the daily routine. Best of all, we were freed from the care of constant station-keeping in formation. So, hour after hour, the *Elden* cut through the blue water at a speed of 18 knots, following a generally south-easterly course, her progress marked only by the long white wake trailing far astern. With perfect self-assurance, we approached the bypassed and long-isolated enemy base at Jaluit, where a disgruntled garrison still kept watch. During the evening of 7 November the *Elden* passed Jaluit on our port side at a distance of forty miles and, of course, saw nothing of the enemy.

The next morning at 0934 Makin came into view. It proved to be another fairly typical atoll, with palms gracing its low islands, for nearly a year now under American control. As the *Elden* proceeded to enter the sun-drenched lagoon, a fighter plane from the local airstrip came tearing by at low altitude, a salute suggesting the rarity of visiting ships where once invasion guns had thundered. All looked peaceful now. Waiting for us in the lagoon was the SS *Cushman K. Davis,* her troops already on board and eager to get going for the

Hawaiian Islands. Our first duty was to report to the assistant port director on the island of Butaritari, our second to seek a replacement for the burned-out transformer. Back came the word that no such part was available in whatever passed for a warehouse on Butaritari, which meant that the *Elden* would have to escort the troop ship without benefit of echo ranging.

We remained at Makin less than four hours, during which time we ate lunch. Then the *Elden* got under way once more and proceeded out onto the open sea, followed by the *Cushman K. Davis.* Ahead of us to the northeast lay 2,000 miles of ocean and then Oahu. During the long and largely uneventful voyage, the *Elden* simply patrolled ahead of the transport with very little chance of detecting and successfully attacking any hostile submarine that might approach. Fortunately, the Japanese were very much occupied far to the west, so our cruise proved to be a peaceful one, with the passing half hours, hours, and watches marked only by the traditional strokes of the ship's bell. By 15 November the *Elden* and her faithfully following troop ship were within 250 miles of our destination, and we began having contacts, both radar and visual, with friendly ships.

At 1758 on 15 November, in accordance with a new directive, the *Elden* switched on her red and green running lights, and kept them on for the remainder of the night, as did the *Cushman K. Davis.* How strange and wonderful it seemed, after more than a year of night-time steaming in total darkness, to be cruising through the Pacific night with running lights deliberately displayed. It was a slight foretaste of peace! The new rule applied, of course, only in areas east of a specified longitude, where enemy vessels were no longer likely to venture and the danger of night-time collision seemed greater than the danger of night-time attack.

During the midwatch that night our radar picked up Maui bearing 060 degrees, distant 95 miles. A few hours later our lookouts sighted the green hills of Oahu twenty-three miles to the north. For all hands it was a most refreshing sight. I had the forenoon watch as we made our approach, the island's shoreline becoming ever more distinct. As always, the signal post at Fort Kamehameha blinked a demand for identification, which we dutifully provided. Then the transport made her own way into Honolulu Harbor, while the *Elden* slid through the narrow entrance of Pearl Harbor and came to her assigned mooring. During the month since we had taken our last departure from Seeadler Harbor, the *Elden* had spent only two full days in port.

Without delay Captain Hartman hurried ashore to report our arrival and receive new orders—orders that we fondly hoped would direct us to the West Coast for a yard overhaul. When he returned to the ship, however, he brought disappointing news. The *Elden* was to have an overhaul, yes, but the job would be done at a tender in Pearl. Home leave—goodbye! All over the ship, faces were long, but soon all hands were busy with the routine of preparation—for repairs, modification of equipment, errands ashore, more training—and liberty, if not in San Francisco, then Honolulu.

8
HAWAIIAN INTERMISSION

The *Elden*'s safe return to the great naval base at Pearl Harbor brought many welcome changes. For one thing, we could again feel secure, free from the possibility of imminent attack by enemy aircraft or surface vessels or, especially, submarines. Night-time watches now were less frequent for everyone, which meant that a full night's sleep became the norm, sleep in a ship that was motionless and, except for the rush of forced air belowdecks, relatively quiet. We slept easy for a change. Our meals improved dramatically, with fresh vegetables and fruit and real milk appearing daily on the table. Again there was mail from home, our first in four weeks. The dates on the letters were fairly recent, indicating that some postal sacks of earlier date still were chasing the *Elden* around the ocean. When the missing mail finally did arrive, it included some letters from as far back as early September.

Despite minor wartime deprivations, my family at home seemed to be thriving. Tom Buffum, now fully recovered from his dunking in the English Channel the previous June, had been assigned to new construction as executive officer of the fleet tug ATR 79, destined for the Pacific. The October issue of *The Odyssey* (expertly mimeographed at the church office by Trudy Kraus) carried on its cover a rollicking Halloween photograph of a radiant Clara Miller and George Turner biting at an apple suspended by a string. Clara, I learned, would soon be leaving for training as a WAVE—another one of the old gang gone from home. The same issue published a cheery letter from Yeoman Second Class Mary Noyes, who took pride in being a member of the first all-WAVE band in the entire navy. Trudy reported on a recent Y.P.F. outing on the shore of East Greenwich Bay. Also published was a letter from a Y.P.F.'er on LST 917 in the Pacific, commenting on my previously reported reunion with Roger Hard. From "Uncle George" a little later came a typically sensitive message to all of Calvary's men and women in the service at a time when American casualties were mounting: "Dear friends, even if we do not talk in 'Thee' and 'Thou' we do have your eternal souls, even more than your beautiful bodies, on our heart and mind every day. We pray that you may through the very dark days ahead feel God's presence and care over you. As you talk with Him each day, may He bring you cheer enough to share with the men around you." It was "Uncle George" and Trudy, together with a corps of faithfuls such as Dottie Burdon, Patsy Farrow, Dick Johnson, Isabelle Kean, Carol and Hazel Lindquist, Bud Tucker, Elberta Waterman, and Grace Whitney, who kept the greetings coming, binding us all together in a warm web of mutual concern and remembrance. What a help that was in staving off the loneliness of operating far away in an all-male world of routine, discipline, and danger!

Soon after arriving back at Pearl we began seeing some of our shipmates depart for other assignments, their places being taken by newcomers. Among those who left the *Elden* at this time were our engineering officer Ned Lee and our chief steward Manzala, the latter being transferred to a heavy cruiser. Ned Lee's departure meant the loss of one of our tried and true originals, whose level-headed common sense and general good nature had been valuable assets. A welcome newcomer was Ens. Frank H. Krayer. The most significant change, however, occurred on the morning of 28 November when all hands mustered on the fantail for the *Elden*'s second transfer-of-command ceremony since commissioning. Our own able and congenial captain, Fred Hartman, relinquished his command to Ed Sneed, and proceeded to the command of the *Silverstein* (DE 534), a newer, slightly faster, more heavily armed ship. There went one more of the *Elden*'s original "plankowners." With this change, Jack Rickard became Captain Sneed's executive officer, moving across the wardroom passageway to the privacy of the single stateroom, while Leo Miller moved in with me. Frankly, few if any of the ship's company, officers especially, were pleased with the change of command, for Sneed was known to be problematical. He certainly had good intentions but seemed to lack both self-confidence and operational competence. In addition to these major deficiencies, he was known to be heavy on the bottle (how could any of us forget that night in Seeadler Harbor when he came aboard so drunk that he had to be carried off to his bunk by the master-at-arms, with many of the crew, wide-eyed, watching?).

On a more happy note, I enjoyed my first real liberty in more than five months. The greenness of fresh grass and spreading foliage, long shady avenues, rugged hills looming steeply in the background, the bustle of a friendly multi-ethnic community, all contributed to my delight. I ventured into a photographer's studio to have my picture taken. The proprietor, a bulbous little Chinese gentleman, chuckled amiably as we conversed; when he crouched down behind his camera, held up a pudgy finger, and made a coaxing face, it was all I could do to keep from laughing with him.

Such brief and all-too-infrequent excursions ashore were memorable breaks in the long weeks of hard work as the *Elden* was made ready for further missions at sea. Usually we were hard at it from eight o'clock quarters for muster, when the various divisions of the ship's company formed up at their assigned places on the main deck, to suppertime, when the officers gathered around the wardroom table for the evening meal. There was mail to be censored and much other paperwork to be done, work parties to be supervised, long and sometimes complicated errands to be accomplished on the base, usually involving personnel, or some form of additional training, or repairs to equipment. Offices and warehouses on the huge base could be hectic arenas where personnel from the various ships contended for attention. One day I stood in such an office for an hour and twenty minutes without being served. Finally, I broke the impasse only by confronting one of the harried minions who worked there and exclaiming in a tone of mixed exasperation and desperation, "Look, I've been waiting here since two o'clock. Can you do something for me?" He did take notice, and I think it was the look in my eyes that finally got him.

What was happening to the tired old *Elden* during these days was a general sprucing up. Needed repairs were effected by yard personnel; old equipment was modified and new equipment added for increased efficiency. On the third anniversary of the Japanese attack on Pearl Harbor the ship entered Marine Railway Number 2, high and dry, to have her hull scraped and painted. When this was completed she looked almost as good as new.

By 13 December, after nearly four weeks in port, the *Elden* was again ready for sea. On that date we commenced the first of a series of short training cruises testing our combat effectiveness. Among our consorts during this period were the submarine *Pollack* (SS 180), the destroyer *Colhoun* (later to be sunk off Okinawa by kamikazes), the destroyer escort *Silverstein* (DE 534), and the amphibious command ships *Eldorado* (AGC 11) and *Estes* (AGC 12). With student officers and their instructors aboard, the *Elden* practiced shore bombardment and anti-aircraft gunnery, expending nearly 400 rounds of 3-inch ammunition as well as large quantities of 1.1-inch and 20-millimeter. Early in the morning of 21 December, when I had the watch, our formation underwent a simulated predawn attack by friendly aircraft, always an impressive and exciting experience which made us doubly aware of the importance of good air cover, sharp evasive action, and rapid-fire gunnery. The next day, with the training completed, the *Elden* returned to Pearl and moored alongside the destroyer tender *Yosemite* (AD 19).

On 23 December our communication officer, Roy Werges, was sent to Base Hospital Number 8 with a case of pleurisy. He had been a most willing and helpful assistant to me, and I hated to see him go. At first we believed that he would return to duty on the ship, but that was not to be, and I was stretched to cover his duties as well as my own until a replacement could be obtained. On Christmas Day we opened packages from home and enjoyed the best feast our cooks could provide, which was very good indeed.

Starting the day after Christmas, the *Elden* began a series of submarine exercises under the direction of ComSubTrainPac that lasted until New Year's Day. Serving as both attacker and target, we worked out with the submarines *Devilfish* (SS 292), *Burrfish* (SS 312), *Sterlet* (SS 392), *Sennet* (SS 408), and *Piper* (SS 409). Other ships involved were the two vintage destroyers *Allen* (DD 66) and *Chew* (DD 106), the submarine tender *Pelias* (AS 14), the light minelayer *Sicard* (DM 21), and the destroyer escorts *Doherty* (DE 14), *Austin* (DE 15), *Deede* (DE 263), and *Finnegan* (DE 307). These exercises completed, the *Elden* entered Pearl Harbor and moored port side to the U.S.S. *McClelland* (DE 750). Again on 8 and 9 January we exercised with the *Deede* and *Pollack* southwest of Oahu.

During these weeks of renovation and training, Captain Sneed was trying to improve his own confidence and competence, without much real success. One time after the *Elden* had come in from sea, the captain brought her to the wrong mooring. Many of the officers, including our susceptible skipper, then went ashore, leaving Russ Morrow in charge of the ship. Scarcely had the captain disappeared from view when a marine officer, sent by the base commander, arrived at our gangplank with a written order requiring the captain to move the ship to its assigned mooring immediately—or else! With no possibility of recalling the captain, Russ took the initiative and moved the *Elden* as required, thereby saving the skipper's hide. Later that night Russ spotted Captain Sneed weaving along the dock, obviously drunk and greatly agitated, looking for a ship that was not where he had left it. At last, finding her in the new and correct berth, he staggered aboard and yelled at Russ, "You stole my ship! I'm going to have you court martialed!" Without stirring a hair, the object of this angry threat summoned a couple of petty officers and had them deposit the captain in his bunk.

On the evening of 10 January Captain Sneed again was ashore. About midnight, when most of us aboard were already asleep, he returned—sodden drunk—with the curious (and ironic) notion in his head that some of the crew were concealing liquor somewhere on the ship. Confronting the executive officer, Jack Rickard, he demanded that all hands be routed out of bed immediately to stand a captain's inspection for the purpose of discovering the imagined contraband. I was among the group of hastily clothed, sleepy-eyed officers who now assembled in the wardroom to be told of the captain's order. Of course we were outraged at this nonsense, and there was some discussion as to whether or not we should obey; fortunately, the cool heads of Jack Rickard and Russ Morrow prevailed and a decision was made to go through with the charade. Accordingly, the crew were required to crawl out of their bunks and stand to in their quarters while a drunken captain, trailed by his angry and embarrassed officers, stumbled through their midst on a futile hunt for imagined booze. It was a bad experience all round. A further touch of irony was added when, at about the same time, a barge came alongside and pumped into the *Elden*'s tanks 12,000 gallons of fresh water!

Obviously, all of us on the *Elden* were confronted with a serious problem involving morale as well as the very safety of the ship and her crew. Not only was our commanding officer a heavy drinker, but he also remained insecure in the knowledge and skill necessary for safe and effective handling of the ship under way. Quite understandably, then, with the *Elden* likely to be involved soon in the next major operation against the Japanese, Jack Rickard faced an agonizing dilemma. What to do, without running onto the rocks of insubordination? A captain's authority and power he well knew; a really vindictive captain could make life hell for any individual under his command. Jack Rickard was by profession an attorney. So was Russ Morrow. That much, at least, was to our advantage, for neither would act precipitately or foolishly. As it happened, Jack's brother-in-law, a captain in the regular navy, was stationed at Pearl Harbor. As soon as possible on the day after the midnight inspection Jack shared the problem with him, and was advised to consider the safety of the ship first and foremost, regardless of any possible consequences. So Jack whistled up his courage, went to the commodore of CortDiv 16, and told him about the midnight inspection. After that, things began to happen. It wasn't long before Jack and Russ together found themselves nervously reporting to DesPac (Headquarters, Pacific Fleet Destroyers) for an interview during which they freely and frankly stated the case. All this was accomplished, of course, without being revealed to the rest of the ship's company. Certainly I knew nothing of it. And there the matter appeared to rest.

Our next assignment was to help screen a formation of transports carrying marines for amphibious landing exercises at Maalaea Bay, Maui, as training for the next major assault. The *Elden* got under way at 0450 on 12 January, preceding the loaded transports. En route to Maui, with the Officer in Tactical Command aboard the U.S.S. *Auburn* (AGC 10), we conducted tactical and gunnery exercises. Then, at Maalaea Bay, the *Elden* easily settled into the old familiar routine of figure-eight barrier patrol to protect the transports lying just off the beach. Except for the beauty of land and sea, the successive watches were tedious and largely uneventful, with our sonar pinging incessantly across the assigned arcs of search as we patrolled back and forth, back and forth.

Finally on 17 January, having completed the amphibious exercises, the ships reformed for the return voyage to Oahu, with the screen commander in the U.S.S. *Fullam* (DD 474). We entered Pearl Harbor the next afternoon, and began approaching our assigned mooring. As we did so, our signal watch began receiving a blinker message from ComDesPac ashore, a message whose import quickly became obvious, spreading like wildfire the whole length of the ship. Captain Sneed was being relieved of his command and transferred! Those of us stationed on the flying bridge, in the captain's presence, struggled to conceal our elation, but elsewhere the rejoicing was considerably less restrained. By suppertime the officer designated to serve as the *Elden*'s next captain was on board, although the actual transfer-of-command ceremony did not take place until the next day. Quietly, in bitter disappointment, the displaced skipper left the ship forever. I felt sorry for him, a sad example of a man out of his depth, but I also was deeply grateful that the *Elden* would not have to sail under his command against the Japanese. The problem of command at sea is a critical one. It's a truism to say that authority and responsibility are inseparable—but how readily that can be forgotten. The relative isolation of a navy ship at sea, even when in the company of other ships, places upon the skipper's shoulders an awesome responsibility to match his awesome authority. Upon his quick judgment may depend the lives of the entire ship's company. A mutual bond of confidence and trust is essential. In this regard, the contrast between the *Elden*'s first two captains on the one hand, and the third one on the other, is especially striking. The latter, for all his earnest trying, had simply failed to create that bond, and so he had to go. I give the navy high marks for a decision showing that the brass did have regard for the safety and dignity of lesser ranks.

Lt. Comdr. J. F. Doubleday, our new skipper, came in like a breath of fresh sea air. He was a large man, jovial and hearty, with almost unbounded self-confidence, a fertile mind, and a taste for friendly kidding. Having already commanded another destroyer escort, he knew what he was about, which meant that on the scale of competence, too, we had come out of the exchange well ahead. Conversation at the wardroom table became more stimulating, while throughout the ship one could sense a revitalized spirit. In short, Captain

Doubleday seemed to be exactly what the *Elden* needed. About this time, too, I gained some much-needed assistance in the person of Ens. Marvin W. Ziesmer, who reported aboard as Werges's replacement.

Early in the afternoon of 22 January the *Elden* got under way as sole escort for the *Anne Arundel* (AP 76) and the *Gen. M. L. Hersey* (AP 148), a pair of troop transports ordered to Eniwetok. As we slowly proceeded toward the Pearl Harbor exit, the *Elden*'s motor whaleboat was being hoisted to the davits on the port side amidships and secured for sea. A coxswain, Henry Duncan, Jr., was standing on the bow of the motor whaleboat when suddenly, without warning, a rat-tail stopper parted, causing the forward falls to drop about six inches. This sudden drop was enough to throw Duncan off balance. Falling, he struck his head and plunged into the water. "Man overboard!" Quickly all engines were stopped and the ship went to General Quarters as the "man overboard" signal was run up to advise nearby ships of the emergency. Now the drill we had practiced so often became a grim reality, with a shipmate's life at stake. Topside all eyes were on the harbor water astern, but no head bobbed to the surface. Duncan had simply disappeared. Within less than three minutes of the accident our boat was in the water and beginning a search, with other boats in the vicinity assisting. After about twenty minutes of searching without success, we had to give up, recall the motor whaleboat, and continue sadly on our way out to the open sea. Later we were to learn that Duncan's body had been recovered in the harbor. The *Elden* had suffered her first fatality, and a young wife had to be notified.

Once at sea the two transports formed in column, with the *Elden* 2,000 yards ahead, and the three ships commenced zig-zagging in accordance with Plan 11. Two days later, as Leo Miller was standing the second dog watch, our sonar picked up an echo. Quickly we notified the convoy, which made an emergency 45-degree turn to port away from danger, while the *Elden* continued her run toward the target, took an appropriate lead angle, and laid a 12-charge pattern set shallow. After the twelve hammer-blows were over and the explosive gouts of white water had settled back into the sea, we concluded that the results were negative. Further probing with our sonar turned up nothing new, so the *Elden* set course to rejoin our consorts while reporting the incident to the base at Pearl Harbor.

Hour after hour, watch after watch, the ships followed the erratic course prescribed by our zig-zag plan, advancing farther and farther westward. About noon on 26 January, just after Leo Miller had relieved the previous OOD, the sonar hut again shouted "Contact!" This one was broad on the starboard bow of the formation at a range of 2,000 yards from the *Elden*. Again the two transports were notified by voice radio, causing them to spin their wheels and turn sharply to port. With a possible submarine so close, the *Elden*'s response was quick—a 13-charge pattern set shallow. Again negative. At 1215 our sonar regained contact and we made a second run, this time dropping an 11-charge pattern set medium on the assumption that the submarine, if that's what it was, had started to dive. Again no result. By this time the transports were well out of harm's way, and we could take our time. Sonar regained contact at 1232, with doubtful echoes. The captain still wanted to take no chances. Accordingly, we made a standard approach directly toward the target at a deliberate speed. I alerted the Hedgehog crew forward, and crouched over the range recorder, aligning the echo traces as they accumulated on the steadily moving paper. "Stand by—Fire!" There was a rippling rumble as the flight of twenty-four missiles took off. Immediately I rushed out of the sonar hut to watch them go. With a flurry of quick *splats* the projectiles hit the surface in the prescribed oval pattern. Then silence as the *Elden* pushed on toward the spot. Still silence, as all hands forward watched and waited. No explosion at all. Either we had missed, or else there was no submarine. Realistically, on the basis of the quality of the echoes, the character of the recorder traces, the discoloration of the water, and the action of sharks in the vicinity, we concluded that what we had been attacking, regrettably, was a school of fish or whales. At 1245 the *Elden* broke off the search and proceeded to rejoin the convoy.

Every week one of the crew came to my stateroom to clean my Colt .45 semi-automatic pistol. On the morning before we reached Eniwetok he came while I was elsewhere, extracted the weapon from its holster, and began examining it. WHAM!! It fired, driving a lead slug right through the palm of his left hand and on into my desk. In a state of shock he at once headed aft for the sick bay, leaving a trail of blood along the main deck. Our pharmacist's mate examined the wound, poured on antiseptic and sympathy, applied a bandage, rigged an arm sling, and sent the victim off to his bunk. We later recovered the misshapen slug from my desk and gave it to him as a souvenir.

At 0610 on 30 January the *Elden*'s radar picked up Eniwetok at a range of 15 miles, bearing 260 degrees. Eighteen minutes later we could see it. As usual, the convoy entered first while the *Elden* patrolled offshore. Then, when the two transports were safe in the lagoon, we followed. After taking on fuel from the U.S.S. *Beagle* (IX 122), the ship proceeded to a designated location and dropped the hook. It was a little like returning to an old familiar neighborhood.

At about this time Allied troops in western Europe were beginning their drive into Germany, inaugurating what we all hoped would be the last phase of the long, terrible war in that part of the world. It was our fond assumption that, once the war in Europe had been won, enormous military and naval power would be shifted quickly from that area to the Pacific for the final crushing drive against the Japanese home islands. Then we could all go home. In my letters to Mother and Dad I conveyed my optimism: "Don't worry about me in any way. You would be amazed at how methodical and routine this business is, and how tremendous are the forces involved. Barring unforeseen circumstances it is just a question of time and space before we occupy Tokyo itself." As yet, we had little awareness of the deadly kamikazes and, of course, no knowledge whatever of the atomic bomb.

And now it was back to Pearl again, another routine mission far removed from the zone of active combat. The *Elden* sortied from Eniwetok on the afternoon of 31 January, in company with the *Cabana* and *Dionne,* as escort for the U.S.S. *Gen. S. D. Sturgis* (AP 137). At 1815 the formation commenced zig-zag Plan 6. A few minutes later we were joined by the destroyer *David W. Taylor* (DD 551), the forward part of whose hull had been blasted open by an underwater explosion off the Japanese base at Chichi Jima. Now she was limping toward Pearl Harbor for repairs, and remained with us less than twenty-four hours before continuing independently. I had the watch on the morning of 6 February when we made our landfall at Oahu, distant thirty-six miles. At 1010 we commenced our barrier patrol covering the transport's entrance, and then entered Pearl ourselves, mooring as assigned in Middle Loch.

About this time I shifted my own berth once again, moving into the communication officer's stateroom on the starboard side forward, with Dave Habel, the *Elden*'s engineering officer, as my new roommate. This arrangement, like the preceding ones with Russ, Jack, and Leo, worked out well. In such small spaces congeniality and consideration were important.

It was during our stay in Pearl that the ship experienced the trauma of a visiting dignitary—a buff tomcat that had been picked up ashore by one of the crew. Somehow, once on board, this independent-minded feline made his way into officers' country, where he promptly established residence. Being naturally fond of cats, I accepted the newcomer with a degree of equanimity not shared by all my companions. The tom spent his first day snoozing in unaccustomed luxury. Then, answering the call of some deeply rooted instinct, he spent the night prowling and yowling mournfully. During his second night as our guest he ungraciously left an aromatic souvenir in an obscure corner of Leo Miller's stateroom, and another, not so obscurely, on the wardroom divan. That did it! As quickly as possible the cat was carried down into the motor whaleboat for a last trip ashore where he belonged. This apparently suited him not at all, for he promptly scrambled over the boat's side and into the water, whence he was hauled, dripping and despondent, by one of the crew. And so ashore he did go, willy-nilly—drummed out of the navy, so to speak.

9

OPERATION DETACHMENT:
Iwo Jima

A ll the key islands in the Marianas now were under American control, with extensive runways and other base facilities being rushed to completion. Back at Pearl Harbor, by early February we on the *Elden* felt pretty certain that our little ship was in for the next big go, officially known as Operation Detachment—the attempt to capture Iwo Jima. Extending southward from the vicinity of Tokyo Bay toward the Marianas is a long chain of small volcanic islands known as the Bonins. The southernmost of these except one is Iwo Jima, 660 miles south of Tokyo itself and some 625 miles north of Saipan, the nearest American base. Shaped much like a pork chop with its narrow end pointing toward Saipan, it is less than five miles long and a little over two miles wide at its broadest part. Mount Suribachi, an inactive volcano at the southern end of this barren little tract, rises steeply to a height of 556 feet above the sea, commanding the entire island.

Nearly everyone had heard about Iwo, and knew that if the Japanese had fought fiercely against the Americans at Saipan, Tinian, and Guam, they would fight even more desperately to prevent American air power from gaining a base so close to their homeland. In fact, onto this grim eight square miles of rugged volcanic terrain the Japanese high command had poured more than 20,000 courageous, determined warriors who had busied themselves digging in like moles. As a result, Iwo Jima was ingeniously fortified with elaborate networks of concrete bunkers, gun emplacements, caves, and interconnecting tunnels virtually immune to ordinary bombardment. That volcanic island, over which brooded the grim gray turret of Suribachi, would be a very nasty little package to untie, the worst ever encountered by American fighting men. Why try? Why not bypass Iwo Jima as we had done so many Japanese-held islands from the Gilberts to the Marianas? The answer was that it lay very close to the direct air route between the Marianas and the Japanese home islands. Radar on Iwo gave advance warning of B-29s headed for Japan; enemy fighter planes on Iwo could scramble to attack our bombers both coming and going. Too, we needed a good landing field in that area, a haven for any badly damaged B-29s unable to make it all the way back to the Marianas. So the decision had been made to launch a fullscale amphibious attack and wrest Iwo Jima from the enemy's hands.

Admiral Spruance was given overall command of Operation Detachment, employing the Fifth Fleet, with Vice Adm. R. K. Turner as commander of the Joint Expeditionary Force, and Lt. Gen. H. M. Smith leading the landing force, which was to consist of the Third, Fourth, and Fifth Marine Divisions. The *Elden*'s modest role, at the outset, was to help escort a convoy of transports carrying army troops who would garrison Iwo Jima after its capture. So, for the first time we were to venture into Japan's own back yard. Would our luck continue to hold?

Unfortunately, that wasn't the *Elden*'s only concern. Amos Curland, the commodore of CortDiv 16, responsible for six destroyer escorts which often were operating hundreds of miles apart on varied assignments, followed the practice of periodically shifting his pennant from one of his DEs to another, which meant that he and his staff would move in, bag and baggage. That, in turn, meant serious overcrowding, as berths had to be found for additional personnel. Even the captain would be displaced, yielding his own comfortable stateroom to the commodore and betaking himself to the tiny, cell-like sea cabin adjacent to the Combat Information Center. As yet, the *Elden*'s turn to play host in this way had not yet come, but we all knew that the time was drawing near, and we dreaded it, not only for the overcrowding but even more because we knew Curland's reputation. An exacting and imperious officer, difficult to please, he seemed to relish his power over those beneath him. He was capable, it was said, of reducing grown men to tears, and we had the distinct impression that every ship on which he flew his pennant became tense, worn down, and generally miserable until the blessed day when he finally moved on.

By early February we on the *Elden* were sure that the commodore's arrival was imminent; we braced ourselves and began making the best preparations we could. Captain Doubleday was, perhaps, the only one not daunted by the prospect. Being our resident expert on winning friends and influencing people—actually, a walking example of the Dale Carnegie philosophy—he was fairly bubbling with ideas for impressing the commodore and making him content. In performing our many duties, he reasoned, all hands would rise to an unprecedented level of diligence and efficiency. Our good crew would be inspired to present an even smarter appearance than usual and keep the *Elden* more shipshape then ever. We would anticipate Curland's every wish. A seaman orderly in immaculate whites, cap squared above his eyebrows, would be stationed in the passageway just outside the commodore's cabin, ready to perform his bidding. In short, by our obvious eagerness to please we would win Curland's approval in spite of himself, and all would be well.

Der Tag turned out to be 10 February. The ship's company made the necessary adjustments in living arrangements, while Captain Doubleday threw into gear our program to please. Now we had new guests at the wardroom table—the division medical doctor, the division ASW officer, and of course the commodore himself, a middle-aged, somewhat paunchy Southerner with a disdainful heavy-lidded stare.

One evening at supper our steward's mates served, among other edibles, a large bowl of boiled green beans, well drained and lightly seasoned. Tasting these critically, Curland was moved to inquire if we ever had had the great pleasure of dining on green beans *cooked Southern style.* Instantly Captain Doubleday was fascinated by the thought, listening with rapt attention as our guest from the Southland favored us with a culinary description. Later, in private, the skipper had a brief conference with the head steward. Thereafter, so long as the commodore remained on board the *Elden,* whenever we had green beans they *invariably* were cooked *Southern style,* laced with scraps of fat meat.

Already the massive movement of fighting ships toward Iwo Jima had begun. Advance formations were sporadically pounding the heavily fortified bastion with bombs and shells. The date set for the *Elden*'s departure from Pearl Harbor was 11 February when we were to begin serving as one of the escorts for a convoy consisting of the attack transport *Samuel Chase* (APA 26), the army transport *Yarmouth,* and a brace of merchant vessels, the *Santa Monica* and the *Cape Bon.* Included in the screen were the *Bache* (DD 470), the *Cabana,* the *Dionne,* and the *Elden.* The commodore, being the highest-ranking officer aboard the escorts, was screen commander, which entitled the *Elden* to station number one.

Every officer was straining to avoid any mistake, no matter how trivial, that might arouse the anger of our imperious guest. Under especial tension were the captain, the "exec," and each successive officer of the deck, a tension surpassing anything I had known since Midshipmen's School. At any moment during any watch, but especially during the daytime, Curland might appear on the flying bridge and ease himself up into the captain's chair on the port side, narrowed eyes peering from under the visor of his cap, probing everywhere. "Leach! What's the range and bearing to the guide?" I grab the voice tube. "Combat! What's the range and bearing to the guide?" Slight delay while the radarman studies his scope. In the meantime, I take a visual bearing. "Combat to Bridge! Range to the guide is two-oh-five-oh. Bearing zero eight four, Sir!" "Commodore, the guide bears zero eight four, range two-oh-five-oh." "Are you on station?" "I'm adjusting now, Sir." "Very well." A few minutes later—"Leach! What time is sunset?" Oh, thank goodness I had remembered to tuck that one away in the back of my mind. "Sir, sunset tonight is at—1842." What question would come sizzling out of his brain next? Once, in a letter home, I went to day-dreaming. "When I am feeling particularly far-sighted," I wrote, "I can cause myself to be instantly wafted into the future to that scene where I am actually released from the Navy. Inevitably there is a desk in an office, with an officer seated behind it. He signs the paper; I sign the paper. Then comes the warm handclasp, the walk out of the office, the long white corridor, an immediate view of my present Division Commander bending over the drinking fountain—" Well, I needn't go on. I could dream, but I also had to cope with reality, which was navy routine for a ship at sea advancing ever closer to the enemy.

The daily dawn alerts came before 0600, with all hands at Battle Stations swaying sleepily with the rhythmic motion of the ship. By 17 February we were west of the international date line, and plowing on. For awhile our formation was joined by the escort carrier *Roi* (CVE 103), until she again went her own way. One fine day, with a following sea imparting just a comfortable motion to the ship, I caught some much-needed rest. Taking a blanket and pillow forward to the forecastle, I spread the blanket on a small but clear area of deck near the anchor chains. There, almost free from the ceaseless vibration of the engines and rumbling of the propellers, I was lulled by the sssshh—sssshh—sssshh of the bow as it surged through the waves, sounding much like surf at a beach. Arriving in the huge lagoon at Eniwetok on 20 February, the *Elden* refueled and then enjoyed one night of rest.

During our voyage from Pearl Harbor important developments had been occurring elsewhere in the Pacific. American troops landed near the southern tip of Bataan Peninsula and on the island of Corregidor, places fraught with evil memories of previous Japanese triumphs. On 16 February ships and aircraft of the fleet commenced the final intensive pre-invasion bombardment of Iwo Jima. Three days later successive waves of landing craft churned toward the two-mile-long eastern beach, and the desperate fight for the "steaming island of ashes" was under way.

On the morning of 21 February the *Elden*'s anchor chain came rumbling up through the hawsepipe, the dripping anchor rose out of the clear green water, and we were on our way for the place of battle. The screen was the same as before, a destroyer and three DEs, but this time our convoy was Task Group 51.7 including the U.S.S. *Canotia* (AN 47), the U.S.S. *Silverleaf* (AN 68), the U.S.S. *Zebra* (AKN 5), and the merchant ships *Britain Victory, China Victory, Cape Fear,* and *Sea Sturgeon,* transporting Garrison Group One to Iwo. That afternoon Leo Miller was standing the first dog watch when, at 1715, our radar picked up a bogey—an unidentified aircraft. The alarm for General Quarters sounded, the ships maneuvered into air defense formation, and we all stood ready, watching and waiting. Some time later the bogey was identified as friendly, so we relaxed once again and resumed normal cruising order. The same thing happened again the next afternoon.

Twelve hundred miles to the northwest of our position, in the vicinity of Iwo Jima, Japanese kamikazes had started boring in on the fleet. On 21 February, the day we pulled out of Eniwetok, they managed to sink the escort carrier *Bismarck Sea* (CVE 95), and damaged both the Saratoga (CV 3) and the *Lunga Point* (CVE 94). Whether for this or some other reason, the next day our formation received a secret diversion order from the commander of Task Force 51 which caused us to change our course from northwest to west, making Saipan instead of Iwo Jima our immediate destination. Shortly after midnight on 25 February the *Bache, Canotia, Silverleaf,* and *Zebra* were detached to proceed independently on other duty, while the remainder of the formation steamed on. That morning at 0828 we sighted Saipan at a distance of forty-three miles, and by early afternoon were in the anchorage area on the western side of the island. After taking in 11,000 gallons of diesel oil from the U.S.S. *Wabash* (AO 64), the *Elden* came to her assigned anchorage. In that vicinity we remained for about a week, drinking in the daily news reports from Iwo Jima and awaiting orders to move on up.

All around us were many ships of many types, swinging lazily at anchor against the backdrop of Saipan's rugged hills. After dark, voice radio watches on these vessels kept up an almost ceaseless exchange of unofficial chatter about life and the war, despite occasional stern rebukes from some more official voice threatening dire penalties if radio discipline were not restored. This irresponsible behavior was new to my experience. It reflected, I suppose, a mounting confidence in approaching victory and a feisty defiance of normal caution. With the enormous strength now mustered in the Western Pacific, including more and more ships of the Royal Navy, we had gained a clear but dangerous sense of invincibility, even though most of us realized that the war could go on for much longer.

We received welcome mail from home. Among the Y.P.F.'ers on leave who had managed to appear at Calvary in recent days were Aut Aker, Charlie Boutilier, Bob Greene, and Lambert Lindquist. Also home at last, as my mother reported, was Roger Hard, whom I had last seen in Seeadler Harbor. Ties to Calvary and the Y.P.F. were proving to be amazingly durable, thanks in part to "Uncle George" Jones and the faithful staff of *The Odyssey.*

No one then at Saipan could fail to be aware of the important activity of the large fleet of B-29 bombers based there and on nearby Tinian, using greatly extended runways. These large planes were carrying out raids on the Japanese home islands with increasing frequency and success. One day I stood on deck and watched them returning from such a raid. For what seemed a very long period of time they droned in from the north, singly, widely separated, to make their individual approaches and landings—an awesome sight.

At the end of February, as the *Elden* still rode at anchor off Saipan, my first roommate and fellow sufferer in rough seas during the early days, Russ Morrow, was detached and sent back to the States for reassignment. Never had I been more reluctant to see a shipmate leave, but I knew that Russ deserved and needed the change. Besides, he had a wife at home. Of the *Elden*'s original complement of officers only Jack Rickard, Leo Miller, Jack Leggett, and I now remained.

Up at Iwo Jima, after the original landing on 19 February, the marines had managed to push directly across the narrow waist of the island to the opposite shore, and then had begun expanding their lines northward toward the two airfields and southward up the steep, dirt-gray slopes of Mount Suribachi. Upwards of 80,000 men all told, Americans and Japanese, were at deadly grips in an area of only eight square miles, a tiny fighting ring roped off by the cold sea. American advances were slow and costly, against extremely stubborn Japanese resistance, with heavy losses on both sides. It was going to be a longer struggle than originally expected. Nevertheless, by the end of the month the hard-fighting marines had managed to occupy the lower two-thirds of the island, overrunning both airfields, and had raised the American flag on the crusty summit of Mount Suribachi. Still, the battle was far from over, with large numbers of Japanese well dug in on the northern third, determined to make the invaders pay dearly for every yard.

At last our group at Saipan was ordered to sail for the embattled island. On 5 March we got under way, the four merchant vessels with their garrison troops being screened by the *Cabana,* the *Dionne,* and the *Elden.* At 1100 the entire formation, with the *Elden* at the forward point of the screen followed by the transports in two columns, began zig-zagging in accordance with Plan 11. As watch succeeded watch and we pushed ever farther northward, we noticed that the wind blowing over the top of the sonar hut was becoming considerably cooler, an invigorating change after so many months in a warm clime. I dug out a woolen sweater, and made more frequent use of my watch jacket.

All during this short voyage we were very much on the alert for possible enemy interference. At 0145 on the second day out the *Cabana* made a sonar contact, causing the formation to veer off to starboard while she investigated the suspicious echo. It proved to be no submarine, and the *Cabana* rejoined. At 0725 our radar detected an unidentified aircraft, so we went to General Quarters and the escorts shifted to anti-aircraft stations, but again it was a false alarm. A few hours later the *Elden's* sonar watch picked up an echo, investigated, and reported nonsub. Then at 1802, about the time I was relieving Leo Miller on the flying bridge, another sonar contact was announced. Again the other ships took evasive action while the *Elden* investigated, with the same negative result. At 1838 we went to General Quarters for the routine evening alert.

It was on the morning of 7 March that our lookouts sighted Suribachi thrusting up out of the restless ocean ahead of us. We were at Iwo Jima. Astern stretched 3,000 miles of reconquered ocean all the way back to the remote Gilberts and Marshalls, where the *Elden* had first joined the great drive across the Central Pacific more than fifteen months earlier. The three DEs delivered their convoy to the anchorage area just off the landing beach on the eastern side of the island, and reported to the commander of Task Group 51.2 for duty.

Peering intently through binoculars, we gained our first detailed impression of the volcanic battleground that was making headlines in newspapers around the world. There at the southern extremity was grim old Suribachi, its sides scarred by shellfire. Along the landing beach, beyond the miscellaneous throng of ships lying at anchor in the open seaway, was strewn the wreckage of a contested landing. On the slightly higher ground inland we could discern the vast clutter of hastily established marine camps and supply dumps, with vehicles moving here and there, each raising a cloud of dust. Farther north, on somewhat higher, more irregular ground, the contending forces were locked in combat marked by the smoke of bursting shells. Offshore around the northern half of the island prowled the fire-support ships, mostly destroyers, laying in shellfire as requested by the fire-control parties ashore, beating down concentrations of enemy resistance. At the near edge of one of the airfields we could see discarded segments of aircraft displaying the bright red rising sun. Also within view, well behind the American line, was an area marked by rows and rows of white wooden crosses. As the days passed, that area was to continue expanding.

Iwo Jima was completely surrounded by a ring of antisubmarine ships constantly patrolling about five miles offshore, while still farther out were yet other vessels on the alert for approaching enemy aircraft or submarines. Never before had we seen such a complete defensive barrier—not at Saipan, not at Guam. Each barrier patrol station in the ring was typically some 8,000 yards in length, its limits defined by range and bearing from Mount Suribachi (code-named "Hotrocks"). We were, of course, thoroughly familiar with the barrier-type patrol, the ship echo-ranging constantly as it follows over and over again a course shaped like a greatly elongated figure-eight, turning outward at each end of the patrol. The officer of the deck takes frequent visual bearings on Hotrocks to make sure of his position, while radar measures the distance. What was especially impressive was the fact that this patrolling was coordinated by the clock, with each ship in the enormous ring moving at a set speed, so that they all reached the end of their stations at the same time and made their outward turns simultaneously. This system kept the patrolling vessels always about the same distance apart, leaving no gaps through which an enemy submarine might slip undetected and attack the large ships in the anchorage area. It was like a great circle of dancers all moving in perfect coordination, twenty-four hours of each day. Whenever one of the ships had to leave her station to refuel or go on some other mission, a replacement would arrive to relieve her, or, in some instances, the adjacent ships would extend their patrols to cover the vacated station.

The *Elden*'s first assignment was to an outer patrol station about six miles southeast of Hotrocks. Later we were shifted into the main ring, to patrol an area southwest of the island. In subsequent days the *Elden* was assigned to various stations elsewhere—north of Iwo, west of Iwo, east of Iwo. We saw every side of that dry, ugly, cruel lump of land. Hour after hour, watch after watch, day after day we traced out our long, narrow figure-eights, sonar pinging relentlessly, radar antennas sweeping sea and sky. Occasionally the *Elden* was permitted to drop out of the ring and proceed to the anchorage area for fuel and mail. Such brief visits brought us fairly close to the landing beach amidst troop transports, supply vessels, hospital ships, landing craft. An LST was serving as a floating post office, and I made one rough trip over to her in our motor whaleboat, the sea off Iwo being always rather choppy. Back on patrol station, at night, we occasionally saw the remarkable spectacle of a large white hospital ship, coming to or departing from Iwo, illuminated to show the large red cross on her side. All other ships, without exception, maintained a condition of total darkness.

As 9 March began the *Elden* was on station six miles southwest of Hotrocks, and I had the midwatch from midnight to four. About 0330, just as I was pampering my weary self with thoughts of bed, we received a warning by radio that Japanese aircraft were approaching from the north. I notified the captain and commodore, and had the General Alarm sounded. Feet pounded on decks and ladders as the men ran to their Battle Stations. Gun crews whipped the canvas jackets off their pieces, and undogged the ready-ammunition lockers. We were primed for imminent action. By voice radio we could follow the progress of the developing air raid, as reported by the navy control station. Approaching were at least four groups of possibly eight to ten planes each. Friendly aircraft were being directed to meet the attackers. Long minutes went by, with every ship on the alert. The enemy planes came to within fifteen to twenty miles of Iwo, and then for some reason turned away and withdrew. We never saw them. At 0510 the "All Clear" was given and we secured from General Quarters. About forty minutes later the ship went to General Quarters again, this time for the routine dawn alert, which meant for me nearly another hour of conning. When that was over I was more than ready for breakfast and some real shut-eye. Again on 11 and 12 March came warnings of impending air attacks that somehow never materialized.

Our various stations and missions gave us almost a grandstand view of the action ashore from a reasonably safe distance. I can describe what we saw during those cool March days only as a sequence of distinct impressions locked in my memory—a bulldozer laboriously carving a crude road on the steep side of Suribachi, American aircraft busy over the island, American armored vehicles firing, the malignant orange-red spurt of a flame-thrower reaching out to incinerate some enemy hideout. I watched a dive bomber roaring down toward a Japanese position near Kitano Point, strafing as he came. Near the bottom of his dive he released the bomb, which fell, hit, bounced end over end, and then exploded. After dark the landscape was fitfully illuminated almost constantly by the yellow-green brilliance of star shells. Here and there I could see a machine gun firing across the lines—a stream of tracers, some bouncing high as they ricocheted off the rocks.

Our most complete break from the monotony of barrier patrol began on 16 March, the day when the American command officially proclaimed the end of organized Japanese resistance. (In fact, however, sporadic fighting continued for some days thereafter.) At 1050 we were ordered to proceed to an area twenty miles north of Hotrocks to help American antisubmarine aircraft investigate a contact made by sonobuoy. Cleaving the waves en route, the *Elden* established voice communication with the circling planes, and at 1224 arrived to find the place already marked with a broad pool of dye. Our sonar picked up no echo, so we commenced a systematic search of the area. About two hours later the planes again reported a contact in the same vicinity. Approaching the indicated spot, we occasionally stopped all engines for two minutes at a time so that the planes could listen better. Again nothing. So the *Elden* commenced a new expanding search.

At 1757 we cut off all power for two minutes, maintaining total silence. One of the pilots now reported hearing suspicious underwater sounds and asked the *Elden* to get out of the way, as he intended to drop a secret antisubmarine weapon. We were quick to comply, retreating at flank speed. At a safe distance we again stopped all engines, and watched to see what would happen. The result was negative.

Again the *Elden* resumed her search. At 1910 the sonar watch reported a contact bearing 345 degrees, range 1,900 yards. Boring in, we fired the Hedgehog over the bow, without result. Soon, however, we regained contact, this time at a range of only 1,000 yards. Once more the *Elden* headed directly for the contact, and at precisely the right moment sent a flock of twenty-four projectiles over the bow to splash down in a large oval pattern ahead. Intently we watched and listened. No detonation. Our sonar failed to regain contact. At 2100 we commenced yet another systematic search which we continued, with some modification, through a foggy, drizzly night. One ASW aircraft remained with us, flying a fairly extensive patrol around our search area, with more or less effective voice communication being maintained. Occasionally, too, we could hear his droning in the murk overhead. But no Japanese submarine did we find.

About 0600 the next morning our friendly pilot announced that he had just been fired upon by a target which then submerged, near Kita Iwo Jima, a small island lying forty miles north of Iwo. Naturally, we hightailed it toward the indicated area. Next the aircraft reported a target fifteen miles from Kita Iwo Jima, at the same time confessing that he was "mixed up in his navigation" and could not be certain of his exact position. Having ourselves some notion of the location, we proceeded there only to find one of our destroyers on radar-picket duty. Had the destroyer actually fired on the ASW plane (and then submerged)? Or had the pilot simply imagined it all? It seemed best not to inquire. In all probability there was at that time no Japanese submarine between Iwo Jima and Kita Iwo Jima. Or, if there was, we never found her and she remained ineffective.

While in that vicinity the *Elden* was ordered to carry out a close visual observation of Kita Iwo Jima to see if we could discern any evidence of Japanese military use. A navy fighter plane was assigned to escort the ship during this mission. Approaching the island, we went to Battle Stations, not knowing what kind of reception we might get. Just offshore were dangerous shoals, requiring constant caution. With the fighter on the alert overhead, we commenced circling the island in a counterclockwise direction at a range of 1,800 to 2,300 yards from the beach, with all possible guns bearing. The island was steepsided, its top mysteriously sheathed in clouds. With our binoculars we searched the shoreline and slopes, alert to discover any concealed guns that might suddenly open fire. We did see a few small habitations, a windmill, and some wrecked craft along the shore, but not a single human being or even a dog. Nothing stirred. All was peaceful and, apparently, deserted. We completed the circuit, always closely attended by the navy fighter, and then at 1102 set course for Iwo Jima. Somehow it was a relief to get back with the crowd, as the *Elden* slid into a patrol station in the screen.

Throughout our stay at Iwo, Commodore Curland seemed determined to be a tough boss. Try as we would, and did, we simply could not defuse that imperious man. Consequently, everyone was constantly on edge, most of all the captain, in spite of his high hopes before the commodore's arrival. On at least one occasion Curland actually rebuked and humiliated the skipper on his own bridge before his own officers and crew, in a display of self-important authoritarianism. I dreaded every watch, every General Quarters, when the commodore might be on the flying bridge. Our good-natured and well-intentioned captain, who only a few weeks earlier had been entertaining such rosy visions of our ability to placate the commodore, was by now reduced to quivering jello. Perhaps we needed that kind of discipline, but all in all I felt that the *Elden* had been doing her job conscientiously and well. Anyway, all we could do was grit our teeth and hang on in hope of the day when some other ship of CortDiv 16 would have to take in that unwelcome guest.

During most of their service in the Pacific since late 1943, the six DEs of CortDiv 16 often had been widely scattered, operating on different missions with other ships of all types. But now all six were together at Iwo functioning in a single major operation. As seemed fitting, we also departed together. CortDiv 16 and the high-speed minesweeper *Howard* (DMS 7) were designated to escort a group of transports carrying one of the battle-torn marine divisions back to the Hawaiian Islands. Once again our eager noses sniffed the air and sensed the possibility of Stateside leave. The commodore, as screen commander, had officer messenger mail for the U.S.S. *Rockbridge* (APA 228), one of the transports then lying at anchor off the western beach, so early on the morning of 20 March the *Elden* headed that way. Drawing close to the *Rockbridge,* we lowered the motor whaleboat and I climbed down with the official mail. The coxswain clanged the bell and off we roared, bouncing over the waves, to reach the transport's high side. After climbing to the main deck, I found myself looking into the haunted faces of men just paroled from hell— marines in fatigue dress, lounging idly, waiting for the voyage to begin. I quickly delivered the mail to the proper ship's officer, and returned to the *Elden.*

Soon the seven-ship screen formed ahead of the transports, all bows pushing southward. Gradually the rough cone of Mount Suribachi became smaller and smaller, lower and lower, eventually dropping out of sight astern. The marines were not the only ones glad to see it disappear. Adding to the celebration was a fairly boisterous sea, and the *Elden* rolled happily on through that first night away from Iwo. Our group passed about eighty miles west of Tinian, later picked up Rota Island on radar at a range of fifty-two miles, and then sighted our immediate destination, Guam. We entered Apra Harbor during the afternoon of 22 March.

Resuming our voyage the next morning, we now set an easterly course for Eniwetok, with every passing hour taking us farther and farther away from the war. The escorts did make some sonar contacts, none of which proved to be the real thing. On the morning of 27 March the palms of Eniwetok came into view and we processed, with the dignity of veterans, into the spacious lagoon.

After one night's rest at Eniwetok the group reformed and headed for the Hawaiian Islands—blessed destination. Easter Sunday fell on the first day of April. As that was the day our formation crossed the international date line, we had two Easters, on one of which Captain Doubleday conducted a service of worship on the fantail. Certainly we had ample reason to give thanks for our safe withdrawal. Some of our compatriots were not so fortunate; the first of April also was the date when powerful American forces began the invasion of Okinawa, the critical operation in which so many Allied ships were sunk or seriously damaged by kamikazes.

At 0515 on 4 April our radar picked up the hills of Oahu due north at a distance of fifty-eight miles—a most welcome landfall. As the ship entered Pearl Harbor early that afternoon the same question was in everybody's mind: will the *Elden* now be sent to the West Coast for overhaul? Scarcely had we reached our mooring when a boat from DesPac came alongside with an officer bearing instructions. The news was good! Everywhere topside our men were grinning and laughing in jubilation. We were homeward bound at last— away from the war! The next day brought still more rejoicing as the commodore shifted his pennant to the unfortunate *William C. Miller.* Because of censorship I was not able to tell my family about our imminent return to the States, but I did get off an unusually brief message with the cryptic statement, "I am fine and happy." That, I figured, should do the trick. Mail from home brought the interesting news that Tom and the ATR 79 were at San Francisco.

It was the glorious morning of 6 April when the *Elden,* in company with the *William C. Miller,* the *Cabana,* and the *Canfield,* steamed out of Pearl Harbor and set course for Frisco, home of ice-cold cracked crab and many other delights. All hands were anticipating the joys of Stateside liberty and home leave, while making preparations for arrival. On each of the ships a traditional "homeward-bound pennant" was being fabricated—a foot in length for every man aboard, with a star for every officer. During the voyage the four DEs cruised in scouting formation, line abreast, at intervals of 4,000 yards in the daytime expanding to 16,000 yards at night. Again, as on the voyage up to Iwo Jima, we noticed the air becoming more cool and the sea more rough. In mid-voyage came a coded radio dispatch which, when deciphered, ordered me transferred from the *Elden* for assignment to a postgraduate course in Applied Communications to begin later that year on the East Coast. My cup ran over!

On the morning of 12 April—Landfall!— the golden gate to our dreams. Dress blues were specified as the uniform of the day; it was the first opportunity we had had to wear them since November 1943. The four DEs had formed a column, the *William C. Miller* (with the commodore) leading, followed by the *Elden, Canfield,* and *Cabana.* Up went the homeward-bound pennants, each about 200 feet long, to trail proudly aft, whipping in the wind like enormous kite-tails. The formation paraded under the soaring arch of the Golden Gate Bridge, slowly rounded the metropolitan waterfront and, on signal, simultaneously dropped anchor almost directly under the Bay Bridge. Soon we received instructions sending us up the bay to the Mare Island Navy Yard where, upon docking, I had my first chance to step ashore—*Stateside.* Our euphoric sense of elation, however, was now tempered with the unexpected and sobering news that President Roosevelt, our commander in chief, had died.

At Mare Island we unloaded all the *Elden*'s ammunition, a necessary precaution for a ship about to undergo a major overhaul. That task accomplished, we steamed back down the bay to Oakland, where we docked in a large and very busy commercial shipyard. Tom, I discovered, had sailed for Pearl Harbor some days earlier, which meant that our two ships probably had passed each other en route.

Soon thereafter, with my typed orders carefully pocketed and my wooden sea chest directed to Rhode Island, I emerged from the old familiar wardroom, paused on the quarterdeck to salute the officer of the deck and then the flag at the stern, and strode down the gangplank to the dock. I left the *Elden* in the care of my shipmates and a swarm of yard workmen in T-shirts, dungarees, and heavy-soled work shoes. Electric cables, water hoses, and compressed air lines sprawled like snakes across her salted decks. That was the way she looked the last time I saw her—lean, gray, and a bit grimy from prolonged service. Many long years have gone by since that day, and the *Elden* is no more. I know now that I would leap at the opportunity to walk back up that gangplank once again, make my way along the main deck to find here and there about the ship—in the wardroom, on the flying bridge, in the crew's quarters below—my shipmates of 1943–45 with whom I shared so many adventures across so many thousands of miles.

But in April of 1945, having been detached from the *Elden,* I was feeling the

U.S.S. *Elden* at the dock, May 1945. The circles indicate alterations made during overhaul. U.S. Navy.

exultation of new, unaccustomed freedom ashore and the prospect of an early visit home. I reported immediately to Headquarters, Twelfth Naval District, San Francisco, and was assigned a comfortable room in a downtown hotel pending the arrival of further orders. For the next few days I bore no responsibility, which in itself was a delight. My room was splendidly furnished, and I took great pleasure in making good use of two items in particular—the bathtub and the bed. I soaked myself luxuriously in steaming hot water, and slept many hours in a real bed that stood foursquare on a carpeted floor. My voyaging, at least for the immediate future, was over.

EPILOGUE

om Buffum's younger brother Tim, also in the navy, happened to be stationed in San Francisco when I arrived there in 1945. He and I had some good times together while I was awaiting orders for home leave, and it was Tim who eventually accompanied me to the railway station in Oakland for the start of my long-anticipated transcontinental journey. When the wheels underneath the Pullman actually started turning and the rumble began, I knew that I was on my way home. Reaching New York after several days of relaxed riding, I boarded a train for Providence, having notified Mother and Dad of my imminent arrival. Rapidly the train clicked and clattered along the same track I had traveled in December 1942 as a shiny new ensign. Stamford, New Haven, New London, Westerly, Kingston—each an old familiar stop along the way, closer and closer to Providence. Mother and Dad, I knew, would be at the station to greet me, and so they were, bursting with the joy and relief of such a reunion. Providence looked much the same.

During the month of May I was home on leave, sleeping as late in the morning as I cared to (no dawn alerts) and relaxing in the old familiar surroundings (no watches to stand). Needless to say, Mother's home cooking was everything I had remembered and more. I visited the Brown campus, but encountered few familiar faces. On my first Sunday home I returned expectantly to Calvary, where I was warmly welcomed by a host of older friends.

Most of the Y.P.F. gang, however, especially the men, were still away, as I knew they would be, scattered all around the globe. Germany's surrender on 8 May was cause for joyful celebration and mounting confidence.

When my much-relished leave came to an end, I reported to Headquarters, First Naval District, Boston, and was given temporary· duty in the coding section until it was time for me to begin the course in Applied Communications at Harvard. I was in Cambridge when I first heard the news of a terrible new weapon, the atom bomb, having been detonated directly above a Japanese city. At the time, I confess, the full import and tragedy of that event escaped a mind partially desensitized by the awful inner logic of twentieth-century war. I saw this frightful weapon only as a practical means of hastening the end of such a prolonged and devastating conflict. Then, on 14 August 1945, came the final capitulation for which the world had so long been waiting. Japan surrendered. Again celebration—unrestrained, unforgettable—together with deep gratitude. For a time I disported with other ecstatic celebrants in the teeming streets of Boston. Then I jumped aboard a train for Providence, where I soon found friends also celebrating. Many people were taking the opportunity to kneel in the quiet dimness of Grace Episcopal Church, lifting up prayers of thanksgiving. Peace, and a new chance to build a better world for generations yet to come!

By the following February I had accumulated the requisite number of points for release from active duty. On the thirteenth of that month, with keen anticipation, I reported to the Separation Center, located in the very same office building where I had enlisted forty-nine months earlier. There I underwent a physical examination (without the need for any bananas and water), had a little chat with somebody called a "civil readjustment officer," and then finally clutched my official discharge papers. Walking out of the Separation Center onto Causeway Street, I entered a familiar old world that somehow was becoming a new world. Before me the future lay open, with a vision of graduate school, a career in higher education, perhaps marriage, and years of peace.

But I musn't forget the *Elden*—really I should call her the "lucky *Elden.*" By the time I left her at Oakland she had steamed more than one hundred thousand miles in two oceans, earning five battle stars on the Asiatic-Pacific Area service ribbon—Occupation of Kwajalein and Majuro Atolls, Marianas Operation, Western Caroline Islands Operation, Leyte Operation, Assault and Occupation of Iwo Jima. Yet—almost incredible fact—not once through all that did we ever sight an enemy ship or plane. Nor was the *Elden* ever damaged by enemy fire; her only casualties were the result of accidents. Lucky indeed!

After the *Elden*'s period of refitting at Oakland she went back to the Western Pacific and was operating with the Third Fleet at the time of the Japanese surrender. Later she stopped in at Okinawa, the Philippines, and Tokyo Bay where, ironically and tragically, she suffered her greatest loss—five men drowned in the capsizing of a liberty boat. Leo Miller eventually succeeded Frank Doubleday as captain and brought the ship safely back to the West Coast where, on 18 January 1946, the colors were hauled down for the last time. Later the *Elden* was sold for $22,200 and broken up for scrap. So there really is no way for me to walk back up that gangplank and rejoin my shipmates—except in memory.

Having read this far, you are aware that one important thread running throughout the story has been my relationship with Calvary Baptist Church. All during the period of the war when so many members were away, the Church had been wonderfully caring and supportive. Pastor Earl Hollier Tomlin, "Uncle George" Jones, and the faithful core who kept the choirs and the Y.P.F. alive, publishing *The Odyssey* as a means of keeping all of us in touch with each other, had been determined from the outset that the ties reaching out to individual members would be well tended, and that all the cherished links of fellowship would be ready for us to resume when eventually we returned. Calvary, as it happened, experienced relatively few fatal casualties; most of us did return. We came in one by one, quietly and gladly, oftentimes seeming to slip back into our old familiar places almost as though we had never been away. Clara Miller returned from the WAVES, as did Ann Dick, Mary Noyes, and Bonnie Tomlin. The men came also—Charlie Boutilier, Bob Greene, Lambert Lindquist, Bob Noyes, Herb Tucker, Herb Waterman, and many others. Tom Buffum was long delayed in the Pacific but finally showed up unexpectedly, grinning broadly, on the evening of Easter Sunday, 1946. So it was that the old gang gradually reassembled, happy in renewed friendship, delighting in a seemingly endless round of fun and fellowship. I formed a barbershop quartet with Bob Greene, Dick Johnson, and Bud Tucker; most of the gang listened to us patiently, and even evinced some real enthusiasm. For a few months, at least, enjoying church, home, friends, and old favorite activities, we could almost believe that the dark, heavy curtain of the war was little more than an illusion. Everything seemed much as before.

What really counted in the long run, however, was the four-year break entailed by the war. Each one of us was four years older, and that made all the difference. Gradually we did become aware that an irreversible change *had* occurred, a change that was both natural and inevitable. For one thing, there now was a younger element rising in our midst, youngsters who had not gone off to war and whose interests were somewhat different from ours. Even more important, perhaps, was the fact that we older ones, fellows and girls, now were showing an accelerating tendency to pair off, both within the Y.P.F. and beyond its circle. Indeed, what has been called the marrying game had begun already and was picking up speed. Roger Brown, before going overseas as an army dentist, had married a vivacious Boston brunette. Others who had found or were finding spouses beyond the circle of the old Y.P.F. included Clara and Ethel Miller, Mary Noyes, and Leland Jones. But Tom followed a different route. The girl with whom he finally joined hands and heart had been at Calvary all along, one of the faithful core to whom all of us were so indebted, Trudy Kraus. And lest you think that I was somehow immune, I hasten to add that in 1950 I married a lovely newcomer at Calvary named Brenda Mason. The wedding took place in the sanctuary where Mother and Dad had taken their vows in 1919, and my best man, of course, was Tom Buffum.

During the past forty years I have devoted much of my time to the study of history, reflecting now and then upon the Second World War and my small part in it. Although it seemed hard and dangerous at the time, I realize in retrospect that my wartime voyage was a relatively smooth one, with minimal hardship or loss. Beyond question, humanity did benefit greatly by the painful excision of the Fascist malignancy, a victory worthy of thankful celebration. There is no denying the awful brutality of the German and Japanese regimes. Our enemies were the perpetrators of the rape of Nanking, the blasting of Rotterdam and Coventry, the Bataan death march, and, incomparable atrocity, the Holocaust. Many individual Germans and Japanese, no doubt, acquiesced all too readily in these horrors, and for that may deserve much blame, but not everlasting hatred. The fact is that all of us involved in that devastating war must to some degree share the guilt; there is enough to go around. In the compelling quest for a much-needed victory, even with the best of intentions, we were inevitably caught up in the corruption of eternal values. Think, for a moment, of Dresden and Hiroshima, and remember the tens of thousands of human beings who suffered in such death traps. I can't speak for anyone else, of course, but as for myself, even though at the time such terrible blows seemed both justified and necessary, I now feel a deep sense of regret and remorse. All of us everywhere need to step back and ponder very carefully what we have done and are doing, even now, to God's earth and God's people. All of us have fallen short; all stand in need of cleansing and forgiveness. This I deeply believe. As for the future, the only true course is the way of universal justice and peace.

In April 1984, after much thought and planning, I returned to the Central Pacific, to the Marianas, taking Brenda with me. Forty years after the *Elden* threw shells into Tinian Town, we found ourselves occupying a room in the one small hotel there (today the village is known as San José). Gone, of course, were the whining dive bombers, the booming artillery, the roaring B-29s. Gone were the thousands of grimy, weary fighting men. Like the *Elden,* all the grim gray ships of war had long since sailed off to their ultimate destinations, some to the ocean bottom, some to the scrap yard. Across an open field behind our little hotel stood an American-style school serviced by a typical yellow school bus. Nearby was a graceful Roman Catholic church. Tinian in April was clothed in sun-drenched greenery, with brilliant flame trees in bloom, all contrasting with the shining blue of the sea. Down at the small harbor just below the village I stood at the water's edge and looked seaward to where the *Elden* once had prowled while firing into the very area where I now loitered. A Japanese vessel was busy loading tuna; I went aboard and stood on a Japanese deck in peace, at Tinian Town. Venturing on my own along the irregular coast, a short distance south of the village I came upon a secluded little cove with a small sandy beach, possibly a favorite swimming place of young Japanese soldiers long gone. I followed them into the clear, cleansing water. Brenda had a somewhat different experience—the thrill of sighting a rare bird, the Tinian monarch.

So it was that I came away from Tinian, from the Marianas, from the Central Pacific, with a satisfying sense of peace restored—in microcosm the world as it was meant to be—not perfect, but livable and potentially happy. Let us make this our new and even more important victory.

INDEX